Music as Mission

Nashville ✦ 2012

Music as Mission

A HISTORY
OF MUSIC IN ST. GEORGE'S
EPISCOPAL CHURCH

Nashville ♦ 2012

Copyright © 2012 by St. George's Episcopal Church

St. George's Episcopal Church
4715 Harding Road
Nashville, Tennessee 37205
http://www.stgeorgesnashville.org

ISBN 978-0-615-57250-5
Library of Congress Control Number 2012932245

PHOTO CREDITS:
Nashville Public Library, Special Collections: *Nashville Banner*,
November 25, 1966: Greg Colson and Trio, page 28; *Nashville Banner*,
December 16, 1966: John Fitzgerald, page 34; *Nashville Banner*, 28, 1966:
group photo, *Noye's Fludde*, page 35. Vanderbilt University Special Collections
and University Archives, Scott S. Withrow, page 50. *The Tennessean*,
January 23, 1966: Mr. and Mrs. Noah and animals from
the ark, *Noye's Fludde*, page 35. Gary Gore: page i.

This book was printed in the United States of America
by Lightning Source, Inc.

ROBERT CANDEE HILTON
*has underwritten this book
in memory of his parents*

CECELIA CANDEE HILTON
Vestry Member from 1970 to 1973

and

ROBERT CLARK HILTON
*Vestry Member from 1968 to 1971
Senior Warden, 1971*

Contents

Foreword	ix
Introduction	xi
1. Strength and Dignity: Music of the Anglican Tradition	1
2. Beginnings	11
3. Fulfillment	65
4. Anticipation	135
5. Organs and Bells	151
Afterword	159
Appendices	161
Acknowledgments	250
Index of Personal Names	253

Foreword

During my seven years as Rector of St. George's Episcopal Church, Nashville, I have stated many times my strong belief that worship is our highest priority as Christians. Therefore, I am very grateful to belong to a parish with a rich and well-known tradition of beautiful, dignified, and reverent worship. Critical to this reputation and our ongoing liturgical life is our church music ministry. St. George's is blessed by one of the very finest church music programs anywhere, and this book is inspired by that legacy that I trust will continue to enrich our shared life for many years to come.

Two very formative experiences give shape to my spirituality. One was listening to my mother lead worship every Sunday as a church Organist in the small Virginia town where I grew up. The second was my daily immersion in the *Book of Common Prayer* as a high school student at a boarding school where the Daily Office of Morning Prayer was mandatory. The intertwining of sacred music with prayer book liturgy is woven very intimately in my Christian life.

Church music generally, and St. George's choral and concert tradition particularly, function to affirm our basic beliefs about the faith. But even more than that, our music has the capacity to raise us out of a domesticated and worldly orientation toward an experience at once sacred and sublime, lofty and joyful. Music in the church is meant to lift our attention and our affections toward God. I agree with J. S. Bach, who said, "The aim and final reason, as of all music, . . . should be none else but the Glory of God and the recreation of the mind." St. George's is extremely fortunate to claim a music ministry that is more than up to this holy task.

We give thanks for the extraordinarily gifted and committed professional musicians who have led our music ministries at St. George's over the years. You will read about these committed and visionary ministers in these pages. We have incredibly talented Choir members, providing the most beautiful choir singing I have been exposed to in my ordained ministry. Our church is also known for hosting very impressive concerts and internationally respected guest musicians. When I hear the compliments about St. George's music ministry, I want to be able to give credit where it is due. And now, with this book in hand, I am able to relive the early years of our music programming, track the development of what we have today, and better appreciate our future musical directions. That same experience awaits every reader of this book.

It is most appropriate that the musical element of our church's history has been extracted and defined singularly in this history. The first chapter on the Anglican musical tradition is helpful in setting the stage on which we rest. The three chapters picturing the chronological passage of St. George's musicians and music are unique in that they are written by longtime Choir members, devoted to the church as well as the Choir. The final chapter tells the story of our organs and bells. In the Appendices, there are interesting financial considerations, detailed interviews with the current Music Directors, and descriptive words about future plans for our music. The helpful Index of Personal Names will make this book an excellent reference tool over the years to come.

As pointed out in the Acknowledgments, this book is the work of a devoted group of St. George's parishioners. They have worked on the book over a period of almost three years. Thanks to the generosity of Robert C. Hilton, the financing of the project has facilitated its realization.

Since the music of our church is a part of all of us, and all of us are a part of our church's music, I hope that all of us will read this history and enter into the worship in our church with ever greater appreciation and exuberance. With the increased appreciation of what has been our musical past, we all share a responsibility—and a joyful one—in not just preserving, but furthering our musical future.

THE REVEREND R. LEIGH SPRUILL
Rector, St. George's Church
Epiphany, 2012

Introduction

Qui cantat, bis orat. "He who sings, prays twice." These words of St. Augustine of Hippo (354–430) summarize the role of music in the Anglican tradition. *Anglican Church music tradition* refers to the music written for and performed in the Church of England and the related churches, such as the Protestant Episcopal Church in the United States of America, and others throughout the world. While its musical origins are primarily liturgical in nature (preces and responses, psalms and service settings) over the almost five centuries of its existence, it has expanded into choral elements (anthems and motets) and congregational song (hymns). This is the tradition of church music to which this written history of music in the worship of St. George's Episcopal Church over the past sixty years relates.

Liturgy and music are the cornerstones of the Anglican worship service. A general history of a church tends to record numerical figures—dollars and cents, membership rolls—as well as bricks and mortar. Oftentimes, liturgy is taken as a given and little mentioned. Such a history may record big-ticket musical items such as organs, but music as a particular aspect tends to be underrepresented. This book attempts to compensate for that by taking the music of St. George's over its six decades and recording it for both memories' sake and future awareness.

The first section of this book is an essay explaining the Anglican musical tradition. Most treatises on the subject are erudite, frequently heavily theological, and full of professorial terminology. This essay by Gerry Senechal is written in lay language in order to offer a more comfortable way to approach this topic. He leads us through that tradition and relates it to worship at St. George's. The hope is that both increased appreciation and participation in this important aspect of our worship will result.

This is followed by a chronological narrative history. It focuses on Music Staff persons and musical presentations, as well as the stories of our different choirs—adult and youth. Exceptional musical programs and tours are remembered. Just as each Rector has left an imprint on our church, each musical staff person—sometimes called Organist, sometimes Organist-Choirmaster, more recently Musical Director—has left his or her mark as well. That mark might be a particularly moving service, perhaps a special program, possibly even the playing and singing of a favorite hymn, the nurturing of a child's interest in music being turned into a love of music. It is important that these people are not forgotten. In the writing of this book, several instances of such forgetfulness have been encountered, and the discovery of those histories and the subsequent recording of them have contributed to making the preparation of this book worth every effort. Written by Jennifer Orth with Giny and Jeff Bailey, all Choir members of long-standing, this section provides a lively transit from our earliest days as a mission parish to our present position as a major presence in our community and region.

Next is a section telling the story of our organs and bells. While not necessarily living elements of our music history, these musical instruments are cornerstones of our musical program and worship. They call us to worship; they lead us in worship; they accompany our praise. They deserve, and are given, their due sense of place in our history by Kevin Carson's essay.

In the Appendices you will find some nuts and bolts. There is a layperson's analysis of financial considerations. Transcriptions of interviews with Mark Ring and Gerry Senechal offer insight into their hopes and dreams for music at St. George's. There is a key report by a committee that carefully studied music at St. George's several years ago and whose words will continue to serve as both a guiding light and a beacon for our musical journey over the years. There follows some information that explains four future projects for St. George's music: the Music Scholarship awarded several years ago as an initial step; the need for Choir stalls and/or risers in the Chancel; the rationale for a new organ; and the hopes for developing a secondary school for the arts, with music as its hallmark, at St. George's.

It has been a group of St. George's parishioners who have welded this book together. Each of the contributors has used his or her own strengths and interests to contribute to the whole. They are recorded in detail in the Acknowledgments section of the book. No single person is responsible for its coming into existence. What we all have had in common is a love for St. George's and a love of its music, an appreciation of how important that music is as a crucial ingredient in making our church a friendly, active and, most important, worshipful house of God.

1

Strength and Dignity: Music of the Anglican Tradition

GERRY SENECHAL

If one were to ask a parishioner of St. George's whether the Anglican musical tradition is an instrumental part of the church's identity and regular worship life, the answer would very likely be yes. However, the same parishioner may not be as readily able to define this Anglican tradition or point to ways in which our specifically Anglican worship differs from that of other traditions. What sets apart the musical worship of the Anglican tradition? Further, how does our worship at St. George's reflect our Anglican heritage?

The heart and soul of the Anglican tradition lie in Britain. Just as the spoken rites of the 1979 *Prayer Book* descend directly from the various iterations of the *Book of Common Prayer*, so artfully crafted by Archbishop Cranmer and others, so does our musical worship have its very foundation in England. This is evident when first-time American Episcopal visitors to English churches or cathedrals find themselves quite at home, as the order and content of the service, as well as much of the music, are familiar. While there are subtle differences between American Episcopal worship and that of the Church of England, the form and content of worship are largely identical. Many of the great hymns, anthems, and service music that are considered the core of the Anglican musical tradition are the heritage of five centuries of British sacred composition.

Much of our own *Hymnal 1982*, currently in use by the Episcopal Church, originates from England. When asked to name a great hymn of the Anglican tradition, one may offer "For All the Saints" (*Sine Nomine*), "The Church's One Foundation" (*Aurelia*), or "Guide Me, O Thou Great Jehovah" (*Cwm Rhondda*), all of which were written by British composers and are in regular use in England. Not surprisingly, these hymns and others of similar stature are also found in the hymnals of most American denominations due to their exceptional strength and dignity. However, hymn selection is where *The Hymnal 1982*, as an excellent representation of the Anglican musical tradition, differs most noticeably from the hymnals of other liturgical denominations. While many American hymnals include hymns from the revivalist movement, such as "In the Garden" or "Blessed Assurance," *The Hymnal 1982* instead includes lesser-known English or American Anglican hymns, such as "Dear Lord and Father of Mankind" (*Repton*), "I Bind unto Myself Today" (*St. Patrick's Breastplate*), and "I Heard the Voice of Jesus Say" (*The Third Tune*). The hymnal committee for *The Hymnal 1982* did bend enough to include the mainstream American hymns "Just as I Am" (*Woodworth*) and "Rock of Ages" (*Toplady*), but these are an unusual departure from the style of the remainder of the hymnal.

Among the Anglican tradition's most beautiful offerings are its choral anthems. For five centuries, Anglican composers have produced glorious anthems for use in the services of the church. Among the most well-known might be C. Hubert H. Parry's *I Was Glad* (used almost without exception at royal weddings and jubilees), John Ireland's *Greater Love*, and Thomas Tallis's *If Ye Love Me*. Many of Anglicanism's most treasured anthems were written during what are generally recognized as the two "golden eras" of Anglican music. The first such period is the Renaissance, during which the timeless and beautifully crafted music of Tallis, Byrd, Gibbons, Morely, and Tomkins was written.

Many consider the second period to be the late nineteenth century, when composers such as Stanford, Parry, Bairstow, Elgar, and Wood brought new levels of dignity and strength to the Anglican repertoire. In the twentieth century, composers such as Vaughan

Williams, Howells, and Rutter have made substantial contributions to the music of the tradition.

While English music makes up the lion's share of the Anglican musical tradition, a portion of our worship music comes from other nations. A substantial number of hymn tunes appearing in most every liturgical hymnal are German *chorales*, written during the Reformation to provide, for the first time, a vehicle for congregational singing. These chorales have earned an enduring place in the liturgical tradition thanks to their tuneful melodies and robust harmonic textures. Some hymn tunes from other nations are also included in the Anglican body of hymnody, though in much smaller numbers than the chorales.

The choral anthems of the Anglican tradition enjoy more diversity than the hymns, in part because hymns are generally in English, whereas anthems may be sung in other languages. While English anthems are among the most loved, choral works from Germany, France, Italy, and Russia have earned a place in the repertoire of Anglican choirs.

Unique to worship in the Episcopal Church is the volume of service music, hymns, and anthems written in America. Individual congregations incorporate varying degrees of American music in their choices of hymns and anthems. Spirituals, early American works, and shape-note hymns are made available through hymnal supplements or separate anthems. While some American music is in use in other corners of the worldwide communion, it is not used to the same degree as in our own nation.

Perhaps the highest treasure of the Anglican musical heritage, as well as its most distinctive expression, is the service of Choral Evensong. Created by Archbishop Thomas Cranmer by blending the Catholic daily offices of Vespers and Compline, Evensong is among the grandest examples of the music and liturgy of Anglicanism. Evensong, held in early evening, calls for several purpose-written pieces, such as choral settings of the Song of Mary (*Magnificat*) and Song of Simeon (*Nunc Dimittis*) as well as a set of intonations and responses between the Officiant and the Choir known as the Preces and Responses. This service has inspired a host of beautiful anthems suitable to the close of day. Among the most popular may be *Hail, Gladdening Light* of Charles Wood, *Evening Hymn* of Balfour Gardiner, and *Save Us, O Lord* of Edward Bairstow.

Evensong is a prime example of another uniquely Anglican practice: the choral office. The majority of singing during Evensong is performed by a trained and well-rehearsed Choir; the congregation sings very little, typically just one hymn. This may initially appear to be more of a spectated performance than an act of corporate worship; however, the Choir is serving as an extension of the congregation itself. Just as the body of Christ is made up of many different and vital parts, the Choir represents the most gifted voices the congregation has to offer. Thus, the congregation allows the Choir to lift the praise of the whole in the most beautiful and fitting manner possible. This is evidenced by the long-held Evensong practice of the congregation standing in silence as the Choir sings the *Magnificat* and *Nunc Dimittis*. During a Eucharistic service, the rubrics call for the congregation to stand only when it is actively participating in worship; for the congregation to stand in Evensong during these two canticles suggests that it is indeed actively worshipping through the Choir's voice.

Most every Christian worship tradition uses the wonderfully expressive book of Psalms in its worship. The Anglican tradition sets the Psalms to music in a unique and beautiful way known as Anglican chant, in which the text of the psalm is metered so that it may be sung by the Choir to the music of a four-part chant. Many psalters have been published pairing psalms with suitable chants of appropriate tone and character. As a result, psalms sung to Anglican chant are capable of a wide range of emotional expression. As the emotional focus of many psalms changes regularly, single psalms often call for the use of several contrasting chants to animate and express the text properly. While the lectionary typically calls for ten or fewer verses of a psalm for Eucharistic use, English cathedrals, in the course of singing daily Evensong, chant the entire psalter in one month's time; the Choir may sing four or more complete psalms during a daily Evensong. Given this great quantity of psalms, cathedral choirs chant with impressive regularity, precision, and unity.

Anglican chant is a blank canvas for the organ accompanist. The organ part may consist of simply doubling the choral parts, or the Organist may instead choose to express the text of the psalm richly using the written chant only as a base. While the harmonies the choir is singing must remain unchanged, a seemingly limitless amount of creativity may be applied to the melody, texture, color, and register of the organ accompaniment. This technique can make psalm chanting even more expressive by further suiting the music to the text.

The original and perhaps most authentic form of the Anglican choir is the traditional choir of men and boys. In many parts of Europe, choirs of men and boys were in existence by the middle of the fifteenth century with some beginning substantially earlier, such as the choir of St. Paul's in London, which was founded in 1127. A cathedral choir is typically composed of approximately twenty boy "trebles" and eight to twelve men, often known by their medieval titles as "lay clerkes." Somewhat of a curiosity in the cathedral tradition is the use of men to sing the alto line. While Continental choirs often use boys to sing both soprano and alto, English choirs use *countertenors*, which are typically basses, to sing this higher part in their *falsetto* voices.

The boys usually attend a Cathedral School, where they board and are subject to a time-sensitive and rigorous training regimen. Boys who are old enough to remain musically focused must be quickly taught how to properly sing the glorious but difficult music of the Anglican tradition because their treble voices are of finite duration and their ability to serve in the choir does indeed have a quickly approaching end. Many cathedral choirs sing Evensong nearly every day of the week, including Sunday, when services such as Holy Eucharist and Matins are sung as well. Several hours of training per day make possible the unceasing and unparalleled offerings of the cathedral choir.

This trademark "cathedral tradition" choral sound combines the pure, clear sound of trebles on the highest vocal parts with the rich, mature tones of the men below. This ensemble produces a striking and beautiful sound, particularly when it occurs in a generous acoustic. In the late twentieth century, several cathedrals founded girls' choirs to complement the offerings of the boys and men. While boys and girls do in fact have quite different vocal sounds, girls have proven themselves fit for the Anglican musical tradition and have become an active and vital part of many English choral foundations.

The Anglican tradition does not exist only in cathedrals; in fact, most churchgoing Britons are not exposed on a regular basis to the ethereal strains of a choir of men and boys, but rather to the largely volunteer efforts of the parish church. While many Anglican parishes strive toward the ideals of the cathedral tradition, few churches can boast the resources necessary for such a choral program. Instead, the majority of parish churches rely on a more modest choir as well as the hearty singing of the congregation to give voice to their praise. A substantial amount of music suitable to the parish service has been composed. While it is more accessible to choirs of lesser training and rehearsal time, it is still of sufficient strength and dignity to be offered during the Anglican liturgy.

The parish choir is usually composed of men and women, perhaps with the addition of some aspiring youth. The congregation is known to bear a more active role in the parish setting. Beginning in the nineteenth century, the churches of England became known for the strength and passion with which their congregations sang hymns and other service music.

Across the Atlantic, the Anglican tradition, though adapted, remains largely similar. America is fortunate to have several choirs of men and boys, the most notable being St. Thomas', New York; Washington National Cathedral; and Grace Cathedral, San Francisco. While other cathedrals and large parishes do have choirs of men and boys, they are more the exception than the rule; there are far more cathedrals and large parishes that maintain the cathedral tradition through adult choirs of men and women. Many other parishes of less extravagant musical resources still offer fine Anglican worship through the parish church tradition. Whatever the makeup of an Anglican choir, its purpose remains twofold: first, to act as the mouth of the body of Christ by offering the most beautiful and worthy praise to God in worship, and second, to inspire the congregation in order for them to become further elevated into the presence of God. The Anglican choir accomplishes these two priestly duties through the beautiful, timeless, and dignified music of the Anglican tradition.

It is difficult to overstate the centrality of the organ to the Anglican musical tradition; no other liturgical tradition calls for greater use of the instrument in worship. The task of the Anglican organ is a widely varied one. While the instrument must be able to render organ repertoire for opening and closing voluntaries beautifully and faithfully, its primary use is various types of accompanying. First, the organ must be able to accompany effectively the congregation during hymns, responses, and service music. In order to do so successfully, the instrument must be able to surround the congregation with a controlled, comforting strength without the distractions of harshness or loudness. The singers, whether for a small funeral of fifty or an Easter Day Eucharist of over one thousand, must be supported and encouraged in their praise. Second, the organ must be able to accompany the choirs as they sing psalms, anthems, and other service music. In doing this, the organ must never be dominant, but must provide a foundation on which the choir's sound is properly supported. In order to match and even enhance the textual and musical expression of the choirs adequately, the organ must possess a diverse palette of musical "colors" in order to render effectively a variety of differing emotions. The choir being accompanied may be a young children's choir of five or a massed, intergenerational group of two hundred or more; in these instances and all in between, the organ must be able to provide the proper volume and color of sound. Finally, the organ must simply be able to accompany liturgy itself. Several moments in the Anglican service call for the organ to sound alone; this is not solo performance, but rather an opportunity to express more deeply an ongoing liturgical act. Examples of this include gospel processions, necessary interludes between verses of hymns, censings of the altar, gospel, and people, and the ministration of Holy Communion among many others. During these moments, the organ should be capable of producing sound of exquisite beauty, dignity, and strength, doing so at volumes ranging from a mere whisper to reverent, majestic thunder. As always, the sound of the organ in these times should be a source of inspiration to all present, lifting their hearts and minds above the imperfections and griefs of this world and ever closer to the throne room of heaven.

These requirements are unique to the Anglican tradition and do not seem to be a naturally occurring phenomenon in the organ world. The incredible adaptability required of an organ suitable to accompanying the Anglican service is the result of the intentionality of those responsible for the organ's creation. Many well-meaning parishes have designed organs based on the historical legends of Germany or France in order to render most faithfully the incredibly stirring music of the Baroque or French Romantic masters; unfortunately, the organs these instruments are modeled upon were never intended to serve in any sort of accompanying role. A movement in the American organ community in the mid-twentieth century sought to create instruments that incorporated elements of several organ-building traditions in the hopes that the resulting hybrid instruments could successfully render a wide array of organ repertoire. However, the intentionally *Anglican* organ holds as its first priority the ability to accompany successfully rather than stand in its own right as a solo instrument. Without this focus, it is difficult for any organ to possess the subtlety and control necessary for effective Anglican liturgy. Happily, organs designed in the Anglican tradition also exhibit an outstanding ability to perform effectively almost any genre of organ literature. This is largely due to their versatility and expressive abilities.

How has this Anglican tradition survived in a world that seems to value only the new and improved? The answer lies in the fact that the Anglican musical tradition continues not because of some fusty obligation to safeguard the relics of the past, but because the tradition holds tremendous value in worship. The Anglican musical heritage has given us some of the most exquisitely beautiful music ever written, particularly for corporate worship. While we often prefer to take advantage of the latest advances in technology, we seem to find a great deal of comfort in the unchanging rhythm of the Anglican liturgy. Anglicanism is not solely a celebration of past triumphs. While much of the music most loved by choirs is one hundred, perhaps even five hundred years old, there is quality music being added to the repertoire even today. The music of the tradition is strong and dignified; these qualities are timeless. Well-written music, even from some of the least memorable periods of composition, does not strike the listener as sounding "dated," as does so much written in the early 1800s or 1970s, but instead as being beautiful, expressive, and inspiring. Indeed, inspiration lies at the heart of what drives the Anglican musical tradition. Without worship as its sole focus, Evensong becomes little more than a concert, and the most moving organ voluntary is little more than a celebration of human skill. Instead, the music of the tradition represents the very finest music that we are capable of offering to God in worship. The great Anglican composers such as Tallis, Wesley, Stanford, and Vaughan Williams stand round as our "great cloud of witnesses."

Today we worship in the Anglican tradition with the benefit of the tremendous musical heritage of those who have gone before, with the passion and creativity of those with us now, and with joyful expectation for what lies ahead.

2

Beginnings

JENNIFER ORTH

he Anglican understanding of sacred music, according to *The Anglican Musical Tradition* by Harold Chaney, Charles Don Keyes, and Arnold Klukas, is that "God is the audience.... Thus, the function of music is not to assuage the emotions of the hearers. In other words, its purpose is not to entertain the congregation, but to be a part of what the congregation offers to God in its liturgy.... [It is] to be 'an outward and visible sign' of the worth which the congregation gives to God in its public worship."

If that is indeed the case, then St. George's Episcopal Church has given God great worth through its music program. From the establishment of St. George's as a mission of Christ Church in 1949 to the present and looking into the future, St. George's has sought excellence in its musical offerings, both vocal and instrumental.

This effort has been aided over the years by Nashville's preeminence as a center for music and for higher learning. Many of the Organists, Choir Directors, and Choir members who have contributed to the music program at St. George's came to Nashville either to study or to teach at one of the music schools in the area. Up until the mid-1980s, in fact, the Music Directors at St. George's served on the faculty of various institutions at the same time. This arrangement allowed the church to have some of the best talent available to build its music program without having to employ them as full-time staff. These exceptional musicians built what has become a nationally recognized music program.

1949

When St. George's first came into being, however, volunteers were at the helm of the music program, with Miss Frances Patrick playing the electric Hammond organ. Maxwell Benson recorded his appreciation of their efforts:

How faithfully, how valuably (and how voluably) this early chapel choir worked. Miss Mildred Joy was the first volunteer choir director before she married another choir member and became Mrs. Donald Cowan.

Mildred Joy, 1951.

Easter Day, 2011.

Not much is known about Frances Patrick, but Mildred Cowan remained a lifelong supporter of the music program and member of the church.

For the very first service on September 11, 1949, though, F. Arthur Henkel, the Organist at Christ Church, played the organ. An account of the service is contained in the Christ Church Vestry Minutes of September 12, 1949:

> St. George's Chapel opening services were held on Sunday, September 11, with Holy Communion and Sermon at 11 a.m. with the Rt. Rev. E. P. Dandridge, Bishop of Tennessee, the Rev. Jonathan N. Mitchell, Vicar, and the Rev. James R. Sharp, Executive Secretary of the Diocese of Tennessee, conducting the service. It was a beautiful autumn day and the

F. Arthur Henkel.

church was filled to capacity with the overflow being seated in the Parish Hall. 418 were present. The newly organized Chapel choir rendered the musical program.... The Bishop stressed the point that another foothold had been established, another stride made in the progress of the Kingdom of God.

Evidently progress was being made in the development of the music program at St. George's as well.

1950–1956

The first professional Organist and Choirmaster at St. George's was Dr. Thomas Wynn Cowan, who was engaged for $900 per year. Thomas Cowan was born in a small town in Arkansas in 1916. He served in Europe in WWII, playing the trumpet in an official Army band. He used the GI Bill to come to Nashville and earn his master's

Dr. Thomas W. Cowan.

degree and Ph.D. in Music at Peabody College for Teachers in 1948. He then served as the music and band teacher at Peabody Demonstration School—now University School of Nashville. He was also a bass player in the Nashville Symphony Orchestra for more than thirty years.

Dr. Cowan did a great deal to build a firm foundation for the music program at St. George's during his tenure. Within a year of his arrival, there were thirty-one members in the Senior Choir and another thirty-seven members of the Junior Choir.

The Junior Choir was directed, at least initially, by a volunteer—Mrs. Robert (Madeline) Terry. A 1951 edition of the church newsletter, *The Chapel Bell*, suggests that Mrs. Terry had somehow resolved a problem that has faced many a youth choir director:

> Enlisting young women singers never has been too much of a problem, but until this Fall the male of the species has been

Junior Choir, 1951.

very shy about donning vestments and singing hymns. But not now. Something new has happened at St. George's. Boys consider Junior Choir membership a mark of distinction and a real opportunity to do something worthwhile for the Chapel.

It may very well be true that the boys found distinction in being members of the Junior Choir and satisfaction in serving the Chapel. However, it could also be that the ten cents Choir members received for every practice was an inducement. It could also be argued that Dr. Cowan stacked the deck since his twin boys, Tom and Dick, sang in the Junior Choir.

Another uncommon aspect of the music program at this time, at least from the perspective of anyone familiar with the typical church choir, is the apparent shortage of sopranos in the Senior Choir. The December 1952 newsletter has an appeal for volunteers to join the Choir—"particularly altos and sopranos." This edition of the newsletter also reports that new vestments were on order and that a library of anthems and church music was being assembled. Dr. Cowan was putting together the necessary ingredients to have an exceptional music

Adult Choir, 1951.

program. It was also in 1952 that St. George's ceased to be a Chapel and became a full-fledged congregation.

In 1953, a Moller organ was installed in the church, replacing the Hammond organ, which was given to St. Philip's Church in Donelson. The new organ was dedicated on Christmas Eve, 1953. The aforementioned F. Arthur Henkel gave an organ concert on January 17 to show off the instrument's capabilities.

It is possible, however, that the Moller organ taxed the capabilities of Dr. Cowan. While he was an accomplished pianist and bass player, the new organ was certainly more complex than the Hammond instrument that it replaced. Whatever the reason, complaints about the organ music surfaced in the Vestry Minutes on February 15, 1955:

> [Eugene] Holeman in reporting on his Music, Gifts and Interior Design Committee brought up the subject of the criticisms of St. George's current organ music. After discussions ranging from acoustics to the lack of zeal upon the part of parishioners to sing because of the music, it was suggested that our organist be asked not to attempt to sing and direct at the same time that he was playing the organ; and further,

that if such activities were necessary, that the possibility of erecting a screen between the organist and the communicants be explored.

Apparently the situation was resolved, at least temporarily, as the next month's Vestry Minutes reflect:

> Holeman ... reported on the conference held by him with Mr. [the Rev. Robert] Shaw with our organist. As a result of this conference, Holeman reported the committee did not believe it would be necessary to erect a screen between the organist and the communicants; the organist has agreed to hold his gestures and articulations to the minimum; the organist is taking organ lessons this summer.

The year 1955 was not without its accomplishments, however. By this point the children's music program had grown to the point that there was a Youth Choir in addition to the Junior Choir. Mrs. John (Winnie) Breast was assisting with the Youth Choir and occasionally playing the organ as well. The Senior Choir had shrunk to twelve regular members, but was doing good work.

Unfortunately, criticism of the organ music continued, and in 1956 Dr. Cowan left St. George's. His son, Dr. Richard Cowan, who was about eleven years old in 1956, recently recalled his impression of what happened:

> I remember Dad was terminated soon after we had the minister's family over for dinner, and the kids were too rowdy upstairs in the attic space and their daughter's dress got torn accidentally. We then switched to a new church, St. Bartholomew's, where Dad had a similar job.

Dr. Thomas Cowan went on to become the Chair of the Music Department at Austin Peay State University, where he built an impressive faculty. He also served as the Organist at Trinity Episcopal Church in Clarksville. Two of his choir members there, Bill and Nita Jacobs, shared their memories of him:

> Tom was a wonderful choir director. He was a very patient

man and treated all of us with great respect, regardless of our musical capabilities. He also had the capacity to get great music out of us. He had a wonderful ear for hearing what we were doing and a great capacity for telling us exactly what he wanted to hear and coaching us into better sounds. He actually, over time, transformed a few people who had very limited vocal skills into voices who performed solos—quite well.

His musical taste was very traditional—he chose mostly traditional Anglican music. He had a great knowledge of composers and music history, and also of the Anglican tradition. He believed in performing music that was within the capacity of the choir, rather than difficult music that we would struggle to perform well.

Thomas Cowan died in a car accident in 1993. He unquestionably established the sense of Anglican music for St. George's, forged the role of Organist-Choirmaster, and initiated a long sequence of highly qualified musicians who have led St. George's steadily toward its goal of worship through liturgy and music.

1957

The Vestry Minutes from October 1956 suggest that the church was seeking to hire Mr. Ralph Erickson, who was the Organist and Choirmaster at McKendree Methodist Church at the time, to replace Dr. Cowan. However, the Vestry must have turned instead to Second Presbyterian Church, hiring their organist, Gregory Colson, to be the new Organist and Choirmaster at St. George's. Originally from Middlesboro, Kentucky, Greg received his master's degree in piano from Peabody College. When he first started at St. George's, Greg was also working as an organ teacher and salesman with the Roy Warden Piano Company.

Small wonder, then, that the "Choir Mother" felt the need to spring into action when she realized that Mr. Colson was playing the organ without his shoes. She no doubt thought him to be a starving artist. In the March 1957 church newsletter, Greg addressed the issue:

> **GREGORY COLSON IS THE NEW ORGANIST AT ST. GEORGE'S**
>
>  Gregory Colson was born in Middlesboro, Kentucky. While attending high school there, he was organist at St. Mary's Episcopal Church. He received a B.A. degree in music from Western Kentucky State College in Bowling Green, during which time he was organist at Christ Episcopal Church. It is interesting that Al Kershaw (of $64,000 fame) was rector there at that time.
>
> Greg came to Nashville to continue study with Johana Harris and received a Master's degree in piano from Peabody College. He has appeared twice as piano soloist with the Nashville Symphony, and in the most recent concert, played the organ parts with the orchestra. Greg has made numerous appearances on radio, television, in concert, and for the past two years was organist at Second Presbyterian Church. He is employed by the Roy Warden Piano Company as organ teacher and salesman.
>
> Greg is married to the former Betty Nohe of New Orleans, whom he met at Peabody when she was also doing graduate work in music. Betty writes the program notes for the Nashville Symphony and is head of the department of music and films at the Nashville Public Library. The Colsons have a home on Stanford Drive.

Announcement of Greg Colson's hiring, *St. George's Church News Letter.*

Now about the bare feet—in order to insure the greatest ease and accuracy when playing my first services, I slipped off my shoes. The Choir Mother became so concerned about my welfare that several local firms were contacted in quest of "shoes for an organist." It will now be noted that in addition to a new cassock almost six feet long, and a new surplice with complete freedom for the arms, the organist is outfitted with soft black shoes which afford the utmost in comfort and flexibility.

She was probably justified in her concern. Although the Vestry Minutes immediately preceding Mr. Colson's hiring indicate that "salary requirements" necessitated the shifting of funds from other areas of the budget, the Organist and the Choir Director, Mrs. John (Winnie) Breast, combined earned all of $2,400. Perhaps some of the $393 that was spent on the catch-all budget line item labeled "tuning, laundry, music, and vestments" covered the cost of the shoes. In any event, the Junior Choir spent only ninety-three cents of its $1,500 budget, so

Greg Colson at the organ.

the music department was doing its part to keep the church's operating budget in the black.

On Sunday, March 24, Mr. Colson gave a program of organ music, which, according to a snippet in *The Dragon Watcher* (the new name for the monthly parish newsletter), had been "carefully chosen to demonstrate the varied possibilities of our organ." Apparently the rest of Greg's first year went well, as the Senior Warden reported to the congregation at the end of the year that

> 1957 has seen continued development in the quality of our music. We are deeply indebted to Mrs. John Breast, Choir Director, and Mr. Gregory Colson, Organist, and their devoted associates for the many inspiring programs they have presented.

1958–1959

The congregation embarked on a search for a new Rector in 1958. Perhaps the preoccupation with that endeavor explains why *The Dragon Watcher* and the Vestry Minutes are virtually silent about the music program during that year. In due course, the Rev. Arthur Fippinger was called. Greg was no doubt delighted by this, as he and the Rev. Fippinger were good friends. In fact, it was he who made the suggestion that Greg meet with the Rev. Robert Shaw back in 1956. Greg recalled in a recent interview that the Adult Choir was comprised of about twenty singers, with perhaps four paid soloists. The Choir was rehearsing in what was then Murray Hall, since relocated, with a small piano. In addition to his duties at St. George's, Greg had a small band that was in high demand for social events, duly noted in the society pages of *The Nashville Tennessean*, Nashville's morning newspaper at the time.

The Choir resurfaces in the May 1959 edition of *The Dragon Watcher*, in which an article appeared calling for more volunteer Choir members from the congregation. More interesting than the need for additional volunteers, however, is the fact that the article highlights a perception that has plagued the Choir ever since:

> Some have said, "Don't you have to be a professional to sing at St. George's?" This is a malicious rumor which hurts the music of the parish.

Choir procession, 1959.

Indeed, the fine reputation of the Choir has been a double-edged sword. While it has inspired the congregation in worship, it has also undoubtedly intimidated any number of would-be volunteers to the point that they have hesitated to join. Fortunately, enough hardy souls have answered the call over the years to keep the Choir in full voice.

1960–1961

At some point during 1960, Winnie Breast left as Choir Director, and her duties were turned over to Greg, giving him the title of Organist-Choirmaster. By 1960 the Adult Choir was filled to its capacity of twenty-four members. Mr. Colson noted in his Annual Report to the congregation:

> The limit is imposed by seating space [in the church], vestments, and music copies available at the present time. We have been able to employ a fine double quartet of professional singers to help us with high-quality musical efforts, and we have a majority number of parishioners who give their time and service. There is a small waiting list at present which will be accommodated soon.

The report goes on to outline another issue that has been an ongoing problem:

> We did a good program on Eastertide choral music on the Sunday after Easter which was well attended by visitors but not by our own parishioners. The other big program was done on the first Sunday of Advent and was very well received by a small congregation.

The Easter program in question was an Evensong given on April 24, 1960—the first such "in many years," according to *The Dragon Watcher*. While the appreciation of the music at Sunday services has been, for the most part, steadfast, the attendance at Evensongs, concerts, and music-related events at other times has been somewhat less so, even to the present.

Nevertheless, the recruiting success of the Adult Choir was

matched by the music program for the young people in 1960–1961. There were no fewer than three youth choirs: the St. Ambrose Choir for boys, which boasted eighteen members in 1961; the St. Dunstan Choir for girls; and the St. Gregory Choir for mixed voices, singing three-part harmony. The records suggest that the youth choirs were now singing at the 9:00 service every Sunday, occasionally switching with the Adult Choir and singing at 11:00 instead. In addition to these duties, the youth choirs regularly sang Christmas carols at Travellers Rest, a historic house, and Castner-Knott department store and made "pilgrimages" to Sewanee and to other churches in the Nashville area.

The swelling participation in all of the choirs created a need for more space. On March 10, 1960, Dr. R. S. Duke sent a letter to the Vestry:

> I am writing on behalf of the Choir to call your attention to a very pressing need for physical space in St. George's Church. At the present time the Choirs have no adequate space assigned to them for rehearsals, for vesting, or for the rapidly growing Choir library. The traffic problem from the present vesting rooms to the rehearsal room is very difficult. The Choir is always moving in the opposite direction from the congregation entering or leaving the Church proper.

Indeed, the Property Committee of the Vestry had already written a report to the Vestry as a whole about a number of space issues in the church—not the least of which was the Choir situation:

> The choir now meets in Murray Hall for its rehearsals on Wednesday and its pre-service rehearsals on Sunday mornings. The members of the choir vest in one of three places: men and women in the upstairs rooms over Hampton Hall [now Johnson Hall], and the children behind the stage of Murray Hall. The choir is forced to rehearse on Sunday morning with all of the confusion of Church School classes gathering in the same room.
>
> The choir needs a room of its own for filing cabinets, rehearsals, office for the director, and vesting. We recommend

that [Associate Rector Douglas J.] Berndt's office be given over as a choir room, and that the vesting rooms be moved from their present location to the second floor above Miss Frazer's office.

These landmarks mean little anymore because all of these spaces have since been demolished to make way for new church offices. However, the Choir was not given a room of its own at that point and continued to meet in Murray Hall.

1962

The music program took some major strides in 1962, not the least of which was that the position of Organist-Choirmaster was made into a full-time position. Mr. Colson was offered $7,000 for his services—roughly $52,000 today, adjusting for inflation. Although the Choir didn't get a dedicated rehearsal space, apparently some new arrangements were made for robing, along with a new office for the Organist-Choirmaster:

> I would like to thank the parish for its response and enthusiasm about our obvious musical growth. The senior choir has expanded to a full thirty members, and the combined youth choirs (seventy strong) make a thrilling sight in processional. The remodeling has provided new spaces for vestments and dressing; and has given me a spacious room, which I have enjoyed decorating (at my own expense) to be used for the many hours of teaching, practice, study, and planning that go into the music program.

The reference to paying for his office decoration may have been intended as a bit of a reprimand. Mr. Colson recalls that $1,000 had been donated for the refurbishing of his office and another $1,000 for the Youth Choir room, but that money was ultimately put into the general fund and was not given to the music program—at least not directly. In any event, that slight didn't impede the process of making music, as the Annual Report goes on to say:

Greg Colson, 1966.

The adult choir sang for the six Lenten midweek services, and for special Communion services on Maundy Thursday, Ascension Day, Easter, and Christmas Eve. On Good Friday, the youth choirs sang for a morning service, and the adult choir gave an evening program of Lenten music. A very special musical effort was the Memorial Choral Service in October which drew the largest crowds and best response of any program yet given. The youth choirs sang at Communion services on Thanksgiving, Christmas Eve, and Christmas Day.

We hit the road in 1962! The youth choirs gave a Lenten program at St. Peter's in Columbia, and followed with a visit to St. John's at Ashwood and a picnic supper. The adult choir traveled to St. Paul's in Chattanooga and St. John's in Memphis during Eastertide and won the hearts of those parishes by their singing.

Other excitement was caused by the visit of the Glee Club of Sewanee Military Academy which sang at the nine o'clock service on Passion Sunday, and by three choral weddings! ... Oh, yes, the boys and girls had their usual enjoyable evening of carol singing at Castner-Knott's Green Hills store.

One of the volunteers who joined the Choir in 1962, John Fitzgerald, seemed to take to it, as he has returned to the Choir again and again over the years since, crediting Greg Colson with his becoming an Episcopalian as well as his love of Anglican music:

> I remember coming to Vanderbilt as a freshman in 1962 with a firm recommendation from our local piano teacher, Ladelle Lloyd from Lewisburg, Tennessee, to look up her friend, Greg Colson, at St. George's Episcopal Church, and volunteer to sing with him. This was the beginning of a happy relationship that lasted me through undergraduate and law school, with confirmation into the Episcopal Church

and marriage to a cradle Episcopalian along the way!

I can remember the long Sunday morning worship services after my fraternity Saturday nights when Greg was always patient and upbeat, in spite of having been playing with his band on some of those Saturday nights for a society wedding or reception or even one of the many cocktail parties for which he was in such demand (it was often said that one called Greg before one called the caterer when a party was in the works). The old Moller organ, placed back on the side of the chancel where it would scarcely be heard but for Greg's coaxing, rumbled along behind us in the choir stalls between congregation and altar, keeping me awake—which was a good thing as we were definitely on display—none of this dozing off in the choir loft!

I remember singing in the bass section with our beloved Marsh Polk, who had a great sense of humor and entertained this college student with many wonderful stories. Ma [Edina] Cotton, of great esteem, and her sons, Dick and Larry, and daughter, Margie, were also fixtures of the choir. We also managed to snag several fine professional singers occasionally to swell the ranks and make us sound better. Another of my favorite tenors was Bob Latimer, a faithful soloist who worked for Vanderbilt University at the business office, I believe. We spent many happy rehearsals in friendly competition between the tenor and bass sections! Our Diva, Dottie Rumbaugh, was my favorite. She managed to combine a not insignificant operatic tessitura with a sense of humor that could be withering! Her work with the choir and in the community was significant, but she could always be seen in the choir stalls Sunday morning looking out directly into the congregation to see who was there (or who had slept in), what they were wearing and with whom they had come!

1963

The music program continued on an upward trajectory with an extremely successful Epiphany program:

Greg Colson and his trio, November 1966.

The four choirs, along with members of the Nashville Symphony, gave a service of music which included a cantata by Bach and the world premiere of a work written for the occasion. The program drew a crowd of nearly five hundred which, added to one hundred choristers and fifteen instrumentalists, created a standing-room-only kind of excitement.

This occasion was followed by a special "Choral Service of Thanksgiving and Praise" in which all four choirs performed. In his Annual Report, Mr. Colson noted that the choirs

> did some of the best combined singing they have ever done. As usual, the attendance at these services indicated a greater interest throughout the community than in the Parish itself—a fact which adds to the missionary value of the music program.

Despite the "missionary value" of the program, the monetary value assigned to it was to decrease in the coming year, as the report goes on to mention a churchwide budget cutback for 1964.

1964

If it was a lean year for the church financially, it was certainly not reflected in the accomplishments of the music program. Quite the contrary, it was an extremely busy and satisfying year for everyone involved, building on the idea of the music program serving a missionary purpose within the church and the community. In his detailed Annual Report, Greg drew particular attention to the young choristers:

> The Youth Choirs are responsible for the nine o'clock service each Sunday, and must be prepared to lead the congregation in hymns and responses as well as to perform special music. They must know the Christian year and understand the seasonal changes in the service in order to lead properly. In addition to their regular Sundays, they sang for . . . five Evensong services in Lent and nine in October and November, Good Friday Children's Service, Thanksgiving, and Christmas Day.

Clearly the Youth Choirs were deeply involved in the worship life of the parish. To sing every Sunday takes a great deal of preparation, not to mention the additional fourteen services of Evensong—a feat

Greg Colson with the boys of the St. Ambrose Choir, 1963.

not repeated by any choir at St. George's, youth or adult, in the more than forty-five years since! The dedication of the children involved is further demonstrated by the fact that they sang on Christmas morning, as they had done and continued to do for many more years, when they might have been expected to be opening their presents instead.

Greg goes on in his report to outline other services performed by the choirs during the year outside of regular Sunday services, including singing at three weddings and two funerals. Greg himself gave a lecture to the Women of the Church on the history of church music and played a recital of Lenten music at Christ Church, while the women of the Choir gave a program of French music during Holy Week. However, the "musical mountaintop" came during another special music program:

> The most significant single event of 1964, for music as well as Christian Education, was the performance of the great *Requiem* by Brahms. The overflow crowd of 800 was involved in a great worshipful moment which was denied those who were turned away because of lack of space. By a miracle of electronics, we have been able to preserve the performance in an album of two stereophonic records which are available at the Bookshop. Since the cost of such a stupendous offering to the community must be underwritten completely by personal efforts of the choir and private donations, rather than from any part of the music budget, we urge you to tell your friends of the records (which are tax deductible) so that the proceeds will aid St. George's Performance Fund to provide for expense of orchestra and music for further masterwork performances.

Indeed, Greg recalled recently just how massive the undertaking was:

> We raised $4,000 for the forty-piece orchestra, and we did a rehearsal and a performance. That was a lot of money back then. We literally, since I had coached the piece with Shaw, worked on it for a year. That's why it was so solid. Richard Rivers, who was the baritone soloist, was a nationally known person.

Copies of the recording are still in the collections of many Nashville families, as well as in the music office at the church. The significance of the achievement is thrown into greater perspective when one considers that it was the first of only three recordings ever done by the Choir as of this writing.

1965

The success of the Brahms *Requiem* was the catalyst for even more ambitious programming in subsequent years. Greg recalled,

> That was the beginning. Then we started a series on every fourth Sunday. We did fifty-four major works in my last four years. Thirty-one I think were the first Nashville performances.... I was the pianist with the Symphony, and so I worked with these people. They found that they could come to St. George's once a month and earn a little money and do a program that was worth doing. These hardened musicians would come in, and once they found out that the Choir wasn't going to embarrass them, they became very enthusiastic and loyal.

The list of the works performed in the series is impressive, among

Choir and orchestra rehearse for the Brahms *Requiem*.

them the *Requiems* of Fauré, Mozart, and Duruflé, Benjamin Britten's *A Ceremony of Carols,* and Leonard Bernstein's *Chichester Psalms* in Hebrew. The works that were Nashville premieres included several Bach cantatas and at least one piece that has become a Choir standard, C. Hubert H. Parry's *I Was Glad When They Said Unto Me.*

Although the series was well attended, it was not without its difficulties, according to Greg's report:

> First, out of the large attendance at these programs, only a small percentage have been members of St. George's; second, the people concerned are more than willing to work for the financial support of these programs outside the regular budget, but this work would be more rewarding if the Choir Fund did not have to raise a thousand dollars each year to spend on necessities which had to be cut from the Church budget because of non-pledging members.

Despite his obvious displeasure with the financial support of the music program and with unnamed members of the congregation, Greg apparently received a letter from a sixteen-year-old visitor to St. George's that made his travails worthwhile. He quoted it in his report:

> On Sunday, May 23, I attended one of my finest musical experiences at St. George's Church. The Youth Choirs' anthem at the offertory was very beautiful. It displayed the best youth choir I have ever heard. I was impressed by their professional yet pure sound.
>
> The concert was a novel experience for me. I have never heard a voice-orchestra concert before with such a variety of styles and such an impressive sound.
>
> I have constantly found myself doubting the doctrines of Christianity, but such a concert as this makes me forget its dogmas and paradoxes and gives me a definitely brighter outlook on man and on life in general.

Could any church music program really ask for higher (or better phrased) praise of its efforts than such a letter? High attendance at concerts and favorable reviews are all well and good, but this young man's letter is a lovely reminder that all such service is rendered to the glory of God or it is without merit.

1966

It seems likely that Greg Colson took the letter very much to heart as he entered his tenth year at St. George's—a decade that, he said, "has been a fantastic segment of a life which seems to have been forever filled with frenetic musical activity." He outlined his philosophy of church music in his Annual Report. As it has been shared by all of those who have led the music program at the church, it bears inclusion here:

> 1. Participation of congregation is of utmost importance in all services. (We can now sing the complete Merbecke and Willan Communion settings and about three different settings of each canticle with good response, and new hymns are introduced from time to time cushioned with sturdy favorites.) The best way to insure good participation is the training of the youth choirs who are the congregation of the future. This makes for a stronger Christian Education aspect because so many people in the program learn not only the mechanics but the meaning of liturgy.
> 2. All the music—prelude, hymns, offertory—should serve to emphasize the liturgical theme of the day as worked out by the priest and the choirmaster. Funerals should express Easter joy; weddings, a feeling festive yet reverent.
> 3. The music program of a parish should be an active means of reaching and affecting the people of the entire community through special programs.

The first two points of this philosophy were borne out in the services on Sunday mornings and at various feast days and special services throughout the year. The third point was most evident in the Sacred Masterworks Series, which included some special offerings, as Choir member John Fitzgerald remembers:

> Greg was forever thinking of ways to educate us and the rest of the community to the wonderful repertoire of the Anglican

John Fitzgerald, fez in place, 1966.

tradition and beyond, as lists of performances elsewhere in this volume can attest—from Beethoven's *Missa Solemnis* (we had to march around Hampton Hall during rehearsal to master the complicated and counterintuitive rhythms) [performed in 1967]—to *Amahl and the Night Visitors*, with yours truly as one heavily made-up page (by his favorite soprano, the aforementioned Dottie Rumbaugh) trying to remember his two lines and keep his fez from toppling.

Remarkably, *Amahl and the Night Visitors* wasn't the only staged performance at St. George's that year. Another offering during the Sacred Masterworks Series was Benjamin Britten's *Noye's Fludde*, which was performed during at least one subsequent season. As the picture on the next page shows, there was a cast of thousands in the front of the sanctuary. The sets and costumes were designed by Ann Hill, daughter of *Nashville Banner* publisher James Stahlman. The performance was extremely well received, as evidenced by a letter from an attendee:

> We went to see *Noye's Fludde* yesterday afternoon, the children and I.... We were all frustrated because we couldn't applaud long and loud and this letter is supposed to take care of that.
>
> Your *Fludde* was lovely—to see, hear and experience—and we thank you for letting us be a part of it. To me, the whole thing was unbelievably fine—the singers, you, the musicians, props, costumes, and the children's faces, the tension of the bell ringers, one small dove, the voice of God and the forever unexplainable magic. I believe helping children to be creative and understand and love art and music is probably the only positive contribution that anyone can make towards peace in this world.

These performances were presented by the St. George's Chorale—a group that Greg formed the year before to present larger works:

> After our Brahms, which was just the choir, I began to get calls from other community singers: "Can we come and sing?" So we formed the Chorale, which was bigger than the choir. The choir was the nucleus.

Clockwise from upper left: Dottie Rumbaugh as Mrs. Noah. Animals from the ark (left to right): Sherry Stewart, Carol Fippinger, Suzanne De Moss, and Chris Berry. The cast of *Noye's Fludde* in the sanctuary.

The Chorale performed yet another major work in 1966—Bach's *Mass in B Minor*. An article in Suburban News West (a local newspaper owned by James Charlet) on Thanksgiving Day, 1966, gives an overview of the Chorale and the Sacred Masterworks Series:

> The Chorale is a community chorus including singers from many churches and college choirs of the Middle Tennessee area which was organized in 1965 by Mr. Colson to perform major sacred choral works written for voices and orchestra and seldom heard in this community.... The Chorale members have taken the responsibility of raising the necessary funds to provide for the orchestra, music scores, and programs for this performance through the presentation of an evening of music from Broadway, by appearances at local functions and by donations from interested members of the community.

The article goes on to say that Greg had served as rehearsal accompanist for the *Mass in B Minor* with Robert Shaw the previous summer, which no doubt inspired him to put it in the series at St. George's. The performance was well received, according to a review in *The Nashville Banner* by Werner Zepernick:

> Gregory Colson conducted with authority and exhibited remarkable music spirit and insight at Sunday night's complete performance of Bach's *B Minor Mass* by the St. George's Chorale. Conducting the complete performance with a splendid choir and a full complement of soloists and orchestra must be a high point in the life of any choir director.
> Since his appointment at St. George's [Mr. Colson] has shown continued growth as a choral conductor, taking courses with Robert Shaw and studying great choral compositions.
> ... The success or failure of any great choral composition depends primarily upon the quality and preparation of the choir. Never have I heard the chorale sound better than Sunday night.

Clearly this "fantastic segment" of Greg Colson's life had also been a fantastic decade in the history of the St. George's music program.

1967–1968

In 1967, St. George's welcomed a new Rector, the Rev. Dr. Thomas A. Roberts. Greg recalled Dr. Roberts's thoughts on the Chorale:

> When Tom got there, he said, "Since you all raise all of your own funding, the church budget doesn't pay anything"—we raised our own money for the orchestra—he said, "You ought to do something that doesn't call it the St. George's." I did not name it. The singers did.

The name the singers chose was the Colson Chorale. Greg said at the time that "this vote of confidence has been a most meaningful thing for which I am truly and humbly grateful."

On September 3, 1968, Greg tendered his resignation in order to accept the position of Organist-Choirmaster at All Saints' Church in Atlanta, beginning January 1, 1969. In actuality, he took the month of December as vacation, effectively leaving St. George's at the end of November. The Vestry Minutes from the September meeting indicate that the Committee on Worship was to put together a search committee to replace Mr. Colson at "a maximum salary of $7,200 plus the expense of moving to Nashville." Apparently the success of the music program had not done much for the Organist-Choirmaster's salary prospects. However, Greg's tenure at St. George's had done a great deal to improve the prospects for the music program's continued success. John Fitzgerald had these thoughts to add about Greg:

> Greg was a consummate musician and understood the vagaries of performers like few others with whom I have worked. He could be expected to achieve more than the sum of the parts of those gathered for special or ordinary services. His best times were probably at Easter, when he would arise early on Sunday morning and call each of his regulars, announcing, "Jesus is risen! Have you?" Of course, those special occasions could not have flourished without the steady

support of such "choir mothers" as Mrs. Leslie [Laura] Reuther, Mrs. Marcus [Louise] Shannon, Mrs. Walter [Margaret Ann] Robinson, Ms. Elizabeth Watts, and Mrs. Bill [Julia] Stifler. They always could be depended upon to provide food and drink for thirsty Choir members and young choristers.

No history of that period of music at St. George's would be complete without including Greg's wife, Betty, who was a constant contributor to the Choir and musical offerings while carrying on her own teaching and committee responsibilities in the Nashville area. We owe the Colsons a huge debt of gratitude for the foundations that they laid here.

1969

In January, Dr. Sam Batt Owens came to St. George's as Organist-Choirmaster. Sam Batt was born on February 14, 1928, in Ashland, Alabama. A composer of sacred music, musician, and college professor, Sam Batt was a graduate of the Birmingham Conservatory of Music and received his M.Mus. in organ and music composition from Birmingham Southern College. He had served as Director of Music and Choral Activities at Fisk University, conducting the famous Fisk Jubilee Singers.

The salary cap indicated in the Vestry Minutes was a mere $200 above what had been paid seven years previously, so one might assume that the church had decided to make the Organist-Choirmaster position a part-time post once again prior to hiring Dr. Owens, though the volume of work was in no way diminished. In any event, Sam Batt was on the faculty at Vanderbilt University as Director of Choral Activities when he took the position, so he was indeed only part-time at St. George's. He was assisted by Karen Cooper Allen, who served as Associate Organist-Choirmaster and conducted the Youth Choir. The Sacred Masterworks Series ended with Greg Colson's departure, but the worship on Sundays and on other occasions continued apace, including some with orchestral accompaniment:

The Adult Choir prepared and sang fifty-five regularly scheduled services, Choral Evensong on two Sunday afternoons with choral masterpieces which used an orchestra, one funeral, and the Rev. Charles Fulton's Ordination to the priesthood. The Youth Choirs prepared and sang for forty regular Sunday services (during wintertime) plus the Family Eucharist on Thanksgiving Day and the Festival Eucharist on Christmas Day. This represents a great many hours of rehearsals and performances by many devoted people of our Parish.

Sam Batt Owens.

Choir member Jennifer Orth was one of those people, joining the Youth Choir in 1969 at the age of eight. With the exception of her college years, Jennifer has sung in the Choir ever since. She remembers that first year:

> I can picture sitting in Murray Hall with Mrs. Allen at the piano for rehearsals. The "test" for joining the Choir was that you had to be able to read and pronounce the words *cherubim* and *seraphim*, because they were the two most difficult words in the hymnal in Mrs. Allen's estimation.

For Sam Batt, who was referred to as an "Episcopalian musician" by his colleagues, his first year at St. George's was clearly a happy one:

> I cannot help but take this opportunity to express my deep and grateful feelings over being able to remain in "my" church and how wonderful it feels to be "home."

1970

The Annual Report for 1970 repeats a familiar theme: the need for more volunteer singers from the parish. There were only three parishioners in the Adult Choir that year, along with four volunteers from Peabody College and the community and sixteen paid singers—which is as many paid singers as the Choir has ever had. Sam Batt put out the call:

> We Episcopalians are accused of being great "watchers" of the action! The statistics of the personnel involved in St. George's music program may, unfortunately, confirm this accusation. And yet, we've never been busier than we are at present in preparing and singing the praises of God and His Son, our Saviour, than during this past year. . . . Musically, we are in excellent health but insofar as *involving* our own family in the music program of the parish, we're not doing so well. Will you help in some way, if you can at all, during 1971?

The Youth Choirs weren't faring much better. Mrs. Allen was no longer the Associate Organist-Choirmaster and therefore no longer directing the Youth Choirs, but the records don't indicate who took her place. In any event, whoever it was must not have been effective at recruiting. From the high under Greg Colson of three choirs for young people with a total participation of over seventy, including a boys-only choir with eighteen singers, the Youth Choirs now had just twenty-three members: twelve high school girls, seven junior girls, and four junior boys. Sam Batt was concerned enough about the downward trend to try something new:

> The Choirmaster and Organist has just mailed a letter to families in the parish who have children in grades four through twelve in the hopes of greatly enlarging our Youth Choirs which sing at the 9:00 a.m. Sunday services. I have provided an extra rehearsal time on Saturday mornings for our youth in the hopes of providing a more convenient time for you and your children to rehearse and be a part of the Youth Choirs at St. George's. The children we have are excellent—we simply need more.

1971

The twentieth year of St. George's becoming a full-fledged parish found the congregation once again searching for a new Rector. Dr. Roberts left for a new church, having told the congregation that he had completed his work at St. George's and it was time for him to move on. Nevertheless, the work of the music program continued. All of the efforts to bolster participation seem to have paid off, at least for the Youth Choir program. With his wife directing the children, Sam Batt's Annual Report for 1971 is decidedly more upbeat:

> Many wonderfully bright spots stand out in the music program of St. George's Church for the year just past and foremost among these is the superb progress made in the Youth Choir program in four short months. I have to write this first and before my lovely wife, Dr. Jeanne Owens, catches me and forbids my "bragging on her." It must be pointed out, however, that Jeanne could not develop these youngsters into a choral organization without their interest in being here and the effort it takes on many parents' part in seeing that they have a way to be here. . . . If some of us older parishioners haven't heard them, they are doing remarkable work and in a day when the youth choir is becoming passé in many urban parishes, coupled with the fact that practically no other denomination expects a choir of young people to prepare and sing a public service of worship every Sunday. Most youth choirs practice for months and sing at Easter, maybe Christmas.

The choirs were also given dedicated space for rehearsing and robing on the second floor of the Dandridge Building next to Akers Hall, which was known then as "the porch." The Organist-Choirmaster's office was a good deal smaller than the space previously occupied by Mr. Colson, but it must have been a great relief to have the music, robes, and rehearsal space consolidated into one spot.

Apparently the Adult Choir was no larger, but looked a good deal better:

> You may have noticed the women in St. George's Choir on Christmas Eve resplendent in their new vestments. For the first time in the history of St. George's Parish, the women of the choir now wear "proper" vestments and our most hearty thanks must go to Mrs. Robert H. (Frances) Polk and the Service Day Ladies who sewed for months in order to complete the vestments by Christmas. These ladies saved our parish one-half of the price of a set of twenty new vestments for the women.

Other members of the parish anonymously donated money for new vestments for the older members of the Youth Choir, which Betty Brown took care of as the Youth Choir mother. Louise Shannon, still in the volunteer post she had occupied for almost a decade, saw to the Adult Choir robes.

Another longtime supporter of the music program, Mrs. Samuel G. (Helen) Robertson, Jr., provided funds for the commissioning of a major choral work in celebration of the twentieth anniversary of St. George's as a full parish and in memory of her husband. The church's anniversary celebration was delayed in order to wait for the arrival of the new Rector, but the Choir was ready to welcome him and a new decade in the history of the church.

1972

St. George's did indeed call a new Rector in 1972. The Rev. James L. Johnson, his wife, Leslie, and their four children brought new life to the church and new members for the Youth Choir:

> Again all year the Youth Choir has done the impossible! Prepared and sung the 9:00 a.m. service every Sunday of the winter season and with less time for rehearsal than the Adult Choir uses. Twenty-seven young women and girls are enrolled in the Youth Choir which is an increase over the number from last year.

Apparently an attempt was made to reinstitute a boys-only choir late in the fall with less success:

We have been disappointed in the fact that the response to the Boy's Choir has brought forth only three young men, but both the Rector and I realize that beginning a program such as the proposed Boy Choir in the middle of the year after Winter activities have been set has taken its toll here. We shall begin recruiting late next summer before all boys are involved in other programs through their school in the hopes that this dream may become a reality.

The Adult Choir continued to be comprised primarily of non-parishioners who received a small salary:

> We could lament and bemoan the fact that we still don't have many volunteer parishioners as members of the choir, but the spirit has to come from within to give the extra time and effort in preparing the great amount of music for our corporate worship.... In the meantime our song shall remain—*Soli Deo Gloria*—"to God alone the glory!"

1973

The most lasting development of 1973 was the institution of a Christmas Eve afternoon service—a tradition that continues today. Less lasting seems to have been the staying power of the various assistants charged with conducting the Youth Choir. For the 1973–1974 school year, the job of Youth Choir Director fell to Denver Sherry.

Rather than give a recitation of the year's accomplishments, the Annual Report from the music department took on a more philosophical tone, as did an article that Sam Batt contributed to the December 1973 issue of *The Dragon Watcher*:

> How many times has this writer heard, "I never had a chance to study music and I am determined that Susie will get the chance I missed." Why "determined to give Susie a chance?" Is there a God-given instinct in us that knows we missed something? What about music in church—and why bother? I can't explain it any better than the non-musician in the pew. All I can feel sure of, after being an organist and church

musician since the age of twelve, is that when words can no longer satisfy our longing to feel closer to our Lord, we lift our voice in song in an attempt to glorify those same words on a higher and more personal level.... It is unfortunate that music and art are having to be justified in schools today, but this justifying the "frills" will pass and music—great music—will survive our current preoccupations along with her sisters in the humanities as they have survived from the beginnings of the history of man.

Sam Batt carried this theme into the Annual Report:

It appears there are places of "safety" for great music and art—the church—even though it is so easy to become sidetracked into getting on the "popular" bandwagon.

Thank God! Music in St. George's has not become "music-to-walk-by," and, trusting in God's guidance, it shall never become so. Great music is like a great sermon: it should disturb and wake the soul! There is nothing wrong with "fun" unless fun becomes our primary objective. But second-rate cheapness in music—used for immediate "fun"—has no place in the DEEPEST place in our lives—the church of God.... This is the case of the Rock Music of today and the "whatever-we-call-it" music of tomorrow.

God will be the first to laugh with us in fun when that fun stems from the happiness of serving each other in joy. God will be the first to object when our personal fun leads us away from seeking Truth in Him. May our music-making in St. George's always lead us a little step nearer God's Truth.

It is difficult to imagine that these thoughts were written almost forty years ago, as the issues seem as pertinent today as they did in 1973.

1974

The first musical event of 1974 was a concert of Lenten music, including works by Bach and Caldara, performed on Palm Sunday evening by the Adult Choir and accompanied by stringed orchestra and organ. Shortly thereafter, *The Dragon Watcher* reports, Sam Batt received a Doctor of Musical Arts degree from Peabody College with a double major in musicology and in organ performance—the first performance doctorate ever awarded by Peabody.

The fall was full of many positive developments, according to the Annual Report:

> Our "newest" activity is St. Cecilia's Choir for five, six, and seven-year-olds. Twenty-eight bright and happy faces singing, and learning to sing, in church! When the choirmaster made the decision to form this group, we placed a minimum number of fifteen little ones as a reasonable number to actually have a small choir. Much to our delight, the twenty-eight are enrolled, vested (thanks to the Rector) and we have heard them. Thanks be to God for bringing [the Rev. James Lloyd] Edwards and family to us and an extra hallelujah because Judy [Edwards], with a degree in music, is training St. Cecelia's Choir.

The position of Youth Choir Director was once again open in the fall of 1974. Sam Batt reported that he had had five assistants in six years, so he took over directing the Youth Choir himself, "so that a sense of permanency might take hold with these fine youngsters" who were "small in number, but superb in performance." There were, in fact, only twelve members in the Choir as the fall schedule started.

The Adult Choir continued much as it had for a number of years with a primarily paid membership. However, Sam Batt doubted that the salary was much of an inducement for this contingent of singers:

> A number of small salaries are paid, but I daresay our adults continue here because of loyalty to our church, to each other, and because of the musical experience they discover in our parish.

One paid member of the Adult Choir would take on a larger role in coming years. Kay Withrow Thomson (then Kay Wilkinson) became the Youth Choir Director in 1975. She remembers her early years at St. George's with Sam Batt:

> Sam asked me to sing with the choir, first for some of the special concerts they gave... that was in 1973. I first met Sam when he subbed for Scott [Withrow] for a number of symphony chorus rehearsals.... I don't know the reason why. Sam's style of conducting was very much like Scott's although he preferred music to be much "bigger" and less controlled than Scott. Sam was always a great tease and loved to poke fun of my accent [Kay is English] ... also had lots to say about my mini-skirts of the time! But kidding aside he was a very thoughtful soul and extremely supportive of his friends.

All of the choirs were given the opportunity for a new musical experience with the first Festival of Lessons and Carols. An article in the December issue of *The Dragon Watcher* offers a great sense of anticipation:

> We have a treat in store involving us all! With Father Johnson's permission, a Service of Lessons and Carols has been scheduled for the Fourth Sunday in Advent, December 22, at 5:00 in the afternoon. The Service being used is patterned after the one sung in King's College Chapel in Cambridge, England. Seven Lessons followed by carols sung by all three of St. George's Choirs—St. Cecelia's, The Youth Choir, and the Adult Choir from the rear gallery. Happiest of all, it gives the congregation an opportunity to sing many hymns and carols that always seem something of a let-down after Christmas Day. SEVEN carols with congregational participation. Save the date to be in St. George's!

One can only hope that the service itself inspired half the zeal of its anticipation! In any event, Sam Batt seemed pleased as he looked to the future in his Annual Report:

> We are far more active in using the church than we were six years ago insofar as music required is concerned. It seems a most healthy sign for the life of the parish. No need to be-

moan the fact that we have the worst organ in town while all around us are installing fine instruments. It will come in due time as we make the decision for our second quarter of a century.

1975

The January issue of *The Dragon Watcher* included the notice of a concert that foreshadowed the events of the new year:

> We shall have a concert of unusual interest in St. George's Church on Monday evening, January 27, at 8:00 p.m. The recital will be for music for two organs with Sam Batt Owens and Scott S. Withrow as the organists for the evening. The second organ will be supplied by Street's Piano and Organ Company and its new Allen Computer Organ.
>
> In addition to several compositions which Mr. Withrow and Dr. Owens have performed together before, a Mass for choir and two organs will feature St. George's Choir. The program is being presented by the Nashville Chapter of the American Guild of Organists and the public is cordially invited to attend.

On July 1, Scott Withrow took over the position of Organist-Choirmaster at St. George's. He had this to say about Dr. Owens in his Annual Report:

> The decision of Dr. Sam Batt Owens to leave St. George's and Nashville at the end of June was a severe loss to the parish. Organists of his background, ability, and dedication, capable of administering a demanding music program, are too often taken for granted, and the work of such people is not easily continued when they are gone.

It appears that salary considerations were a primary reason for Sam Batt's departure. Kay Withrow Thomson had this to say:

> Although St. George's considered the position to be a full-time one, the salary was simply insufficient to support an individual. I think that Sam was paid somewhere around

$9,000 and when he moved to Grace-St. Luke's his salary doubled and included a housing supplement.

Sam Batt Owens went to Grace-St. Luke's Episcopal Church and School in Memphis as their Organist-Choirmaster and Director of Music and Fine Arts. He also served at St. Mary's-on-the-Highlands Episcopal Church in Birmingham, Christ Church Cathedral in Louisville, and St. Andrew's-on-the-Sound in Wilmington, North Carolina. He was the president of the Association of Anglican Musicians from 1989 to 1991 and established its Placement Office.

The double organ concert at St. George's with Sam Batt and Scott that heralded the change in leadership in 1975 was repeated in Memphis in 1976. Kay Withrow Thomson remembers it well:

> For some reason the portable organ installed in the back of the church could not be voiced to match well with the organ in the front and Sam became so frustrated that during the final rehearsal . . . in front of all the Grace-St. Luke's choir members, he walked to the center of the aisle, jumped up and down many times, and yelled something to the effect that he was going to cut off an important part of the organ and the organ tuner if he didn't try harder to make the instruments match. During the actual concert the organ at the back behaved very well, but the front organ decided to play footloose and fancy free, cyphering at most inopportune moments. Sam was not pleased and started swearing in time to the pedal notes, but it could be readily heard from the front pews in the church! At the party following, he and Scott surprised everyone and played improv jazz until 3:00 a.m. and sang every camp and college fight song they knew, much to the amazement of some of the old ladies in the church who were present.

When Dr. Owens died of lung cancer in 1998 at the age of seventy, an entire edition of *The Journal of the Association of Anglican Musicians* was dedicated to him and to his legacy. A colleague, Dr. Victor Hill, remembered Sam Batt in that publication:

He was an active recitalist, consultant, and participant in choral and organ workshops, the designer of more than 37 pipe organs, and a founding member of the Sewanee Conference on Church Music. He served as a consultant to the Hymnal Commission of the Standing Commission on Church Music for *The Hymnal 1982*. His many compositions for organ, chorus, solo voice, handbells, and instrumental ensembles were published by various companies.

Sam Batt Owens.

One of those publishing companies, GIA Publications, has this to say about Sam Batt on its web site:

> Sam Batt Owens should have a monument erected in his honor. Any musician who has been a college professor for thirty-seven years, a parish or cathedral music director for fifty-six years, the past president of the Association of Anglican Musicians, and a Rockefeller Foundation recording recipient, and who has published 268 works deserves some recognition, if not by monument or knighthood, then certainly by some sort of public acclamation.

Sam Batt's daughter, Jody Clark, gave a somewhat different view of her father in *The Journal of the AAM*:

> "He was a man of integrity," she said, "who had the backbone and courage to stand up for what he truly believed in. One of those things was the beauty of the arts." She said that despite all Dr. Owens' enthusiasm for sacred music, he "wished he had written one country music hit that would have made him millions."

In the history of the music program, the legacy of Dr. Sam Batt Owens is priceless.

Scott Withrow took up the work that Sam Batt had begun for 1975, "continuing the previously established musical activities as efficiently as possible." Scott had substituted for Sam Batt on occasion, so Father Johnson asked him to take over as Organist-Choirmaster. He was offered a salary of $12,000—a handsome raise until one considers that he was to pay the Youth Choir Director out of that sum. Meager salary notwithstanding, St. George's once again found itself with a masterful musician at the helm of its music program.

Scott Withrow was born in Chicago. His father was a Presbyterian minister, as were seven of his uncles. After taking up the piano at age three, Scott began playing the organ at age eleven. By the age of twelve, he was playing in his father's church. He attended Oberlin Conservatory of Music, graduating in 1953 with a double degree in organ and piano performance. He then went on to the Eastman School of Music for his graduate degree. He was drafted into the Army and served as assistant to the chaplain as Organist, during which time he was asked to compose an anthem for the inauguration of President Dwight Eisenhower.

Scott S. Withrow.

After leaving the Army, Scott came to Nashville to teach at Peabody College. He also served as the Organist at Downtown Presbyterian Church for many years. Scott was much in demand as an accompanist for solo artists and traveled the country with the Artists Community Concert Series. Shortly after coming to Nashville, he became a keyboard artist with the Nashville Symphony and began conducting the Symphony Chorus in the mid-1960s—a position he retained throughout his time in Nashville. Not one to sit around,

Scott also served as the Music Director at Camp Pemi in Wentworth, New Hampshire, from 1951 until 1993.

Needless to say, anyone with that kind of energy would have big plans for an established music program such as the one at St. George's. Scott outlined some of his ideas in his Annual Report:

> The worship services at St. George's are special events, any and every day of the year. I'd like us to have more flexibility in our service music. Specifically, I'd like very soon to have copies of "Songs for Liturgy" and "More Hymns and Spiritual Songs" in the pews. At our parish dinners I'd like to have read-throughs or rehearsals of unfamiliar service music. I can promise that the various choirs will be expanding their repertoires of anthems, sometimes to unfamiliar styles, such as electronic music.

Ah, the '70s! If electronic music did make its way into the Sunday services, its appearance was mercifully rare. The two additional songbooks were not adopted, although the *Hymnal Supplement II* did make it into the pew racks in 1978. The Adult Choir did indeed expand their repertoire, however. In October 1975, the Choir presented a Festival Evensong with the premiere of a choral work entitled *The Stone*, composed by Hugh Thomas and commissioned by Mrs. Helen Robertson to commemorate St. George's twenty-fifth anniversary.

As previously mentioned, Kay Withrow Thomson took over the Youth Choirs in the fall. Scott's Annual Report for the year commented on the progress of the choirs:

> The St. Cecilia Choir started the fall with 12 children, and as of this writing has 28 on the roll.... The Youth Choir continues to be small in number but extremely loyal, courageous in what they attempt, and capable in how they do it. They are always looking for a way to do what they do better. They are a hardy group who contribute much to the church.
>
> Kay Wilkinson directs the two young choirs, as of this fall. Kay has academic training, as well as experience in working with children and young people. Further, she

supplies a continuing Anglican influence! I am delighted to have her working with these groups, and look forward to her increased impact with them as time goes on.

Kay was very well suited to take on the Youth Choirs on a number of levels. A graduate from the Royal Northern College of Music, Manchester, Kay studied with Sir David Willcocks, many of whose choral arrangements are a well-loved part of the St. George's repertoire. She credits him with teaching her a great deal about training young voices and conducting. Kay did her graduate work at the Royal Academy of Music, London. She was a soloist with the Halle Orchestra in Manchester, Liverpool Philharmonic, and a few other orchestras as well as doing a fair amount of solo recitals. After moving to the United States, Kay became a member of the San Francisco Symphony Chorus. She ultimately moved to Lexington, Kentucky, and sang as soloist with the University of Kentucky Summer Opera. She was also the middle school music teacher at Sayre School. When she moved to Nashville in 1971, she joined the Nashville Symphony Chorus where, in a happy turn of events for St. George's, she met Scott and Sam Batt.

Kay's Mary Poppins-esque presence had one immediate impact in that she quickly had the Youth Choir singing at all kinds of events and having a great deal of fun. An article in *The Dragon Watcher* in March 1976 recounts the group's winter 1975 outings:

> Our Youth Choir has made several singing appearances away from home in the past few months. In December they sang at the Fannie Battle Day Home for the annual Christmas dinner. They were invited to sing at Metro Courthouse for the Mayor's Christmas Open House, for which they received a framed memento. They appeared at Cheekwood on the final day of the "Trees of Christmas" exhibit, and in January furnished the music for the Sunday morning prayer service at Grace Church, Spring Hill, TN, after singing at the 9:00 a.m. service at St. George's. (Note: the Rector was forewarned that the entire choir would leave just before his sermon.)
>
> The group really came into its own at an ice skating party

at Municipal Auditorium, although the procession to the Altar the next day moved a little more slowly than usual!

Members of this faithful group include Giny and Lucy Adkins, Nancy Banner, Murray Clayton, Debbie and Jean Cheek, Whitney Daane, Bill and Jackson Galloway, Fran Hudson, Betsy Johnson, Cooper Lilly, Jimmy Moore, Jennifer and Julie Orth, Marc Shannon, and Grant Wilkinson.

New leadership notwithstanding, some of the old remained. Scott put it this way:

> In this year of change, perhaps the most notable non-change has been what Dr. Owens described in last year's report as "the worst organ in town." We still have it. Nuf sed fur now.

Enough may have been said about the quality of the Moller organ, and it would continue to be said in many Annual Reports over the coming years, but the organ would remain in use for another twelve years even so.

1976

The only record of the music program for the nation's bicentennial year is in the Annual Report. No copies of *The Dragon Watcher* made it into the church's archives, or they have subsequently been lost. In any event, it seems that 1976 was an unremarkable year in music at St. George's. The highlight appears to have been the creation of a new children's choir. The St. Dunstan Choir was started in the fall for third, fourth, and fifth graders. By Christmas it had grown from four members to eighteen. The St. Cecilia Choir was comprised of twenty-one kindergarten through second grade children, and the Youth Choir was for sixth through twelfth graders. Scott noted, as had other Organists before him, that "it is unusual that a choir of Junior High and High School students provides music for a service each week!"

Scott laid out his goals for the music program at the end of his first full year of service:

> 1) to enhance the regular worship of the church toward expressiveness, beauty, meaning;

A service in the mid-1970s.

2) to provide parishioners with musical talents opportunities for expression and participation in the worship of the church;
3) to encourage creative contributions to the corpus of music for the church;
4) to provide young people with instruction in music and liturgy, along with participation opportunities in worship;
5) to enhance the special celebrations of the church, such as weddings, funerals, baptisms, and confirmations.

He also looked forward to the revised version of *The Book of Common Prayer*, which was published in 1979, as meaning an "expansion of musical materials," saying that "adopting that which is worthy of St. George's Church is an immediate goal."

1977–1978

There are no Annual Reports from the music department for 1977 or 1978. However, there are several editions of *The Dragon Watcher* that give some clues as to the goings-on. In the summer of 1977, several Youth Choir members toured Europe as part of a group directed by Scott Withrow and Kay Wilkinson. Kay described their adventures in the September newsletter:

> What do organists and choir directors do during their summer vacation? Take a busman's holiday, of course! Scott Withrow was director of the Tennessee Youth Chorale—a group of young singers from around the state—giving concerts in Holland, Germany, France and England. I was an Assistant Director (they said they needed me along to translate when they reached London!). Giny Adkins, Bill Galloway, Jennifer Orth, and Grant Wilkinson from St. George's were members of the group.

Jennifer Orth remembers the trip as the first of three she took "across the pond" as a member of a St. George's Choir:

> We joined up with a group from Mississippi when we got to Holland. Their director wore the loudest leisure suits—one pumpkin and one pea green. At least he was always easy to spot in a crowd. We had a program of sacred music and a program of secular music and performed in a variety of rather odd places. I remember being in Paris on Bastille Day and watching the fireworks around the Eiffel Tower from our hotel balcony. It was a good distance away but still very exciting. The real excitement, though, was the speculation about Kay and Scott, who appeared to be quite chummy during the trip.

Indeed, Scott and Kay were married some months later.

In 1978, the focus in the music program appears to have been on integrating the music from the *Hymnal Supplement II* into the worship service, including some pieces that were called for in the proposed *Book of Common Prayer 1979*. This supplement was rendered useless by the 1982 edition of *The Hymnal*, but it introduced two "alternate" tunes that it's hard to imagine not having always had—the familiar versions of "Joy to the World" and "Joyful, Joyful We Adore Thee"

TENNESSEE / MISSISSIPPI YOUTH CHORALE

JULY 5–19, 1977

VISITING:
THE NETHERLANDS, WEST GERMANY, FRANCE
ENGLAND and BELGIUM

Director:
MR. SCOTT WITHROW
Assistant Director:
MR. MARTIN BITTICK

Flyer for the Tennessee/Mississippi Youth Chorale tour.

("Ode to Joy"). One wonders how those hymns could ever have been sung to any other music, but prior to 1978 they apparently were—at least in the Episcopal Church.

1979

The revised *Book of Common Prayer* was adopted and put into use in 1979, bringing with it new service music for the then controversial Rite II liturgy, which abandoned *thee* and *thou* for more contemporary language. The 9:00 a.m. service used Rite II, signaling an end to the use of Morning Prayer as a regular worship service, while the 11:00 a.m. service continued to use Rite I.

For Epiphany, Scott introduced a series of musical canons, or rounds, with texts based on the Propers of the Day. The origin of these rounds is unclear. Perhaps Scott composed them himself. His Annual Report says that

> we have exercised our creative spirits. The use of instruments other than the organ in worship, the Rite II music, the various hymn descants, other occasional anthems or canticles are uniquely ours and make an excitement and urgency in our worship.

In April, St. George's played host to The Scholars, an a cappella group of five singers who were choral scholars at King's College, Cambridge. They presented a program of sacred music in the Anglican tradition between services on a Sunday morning. *The Dragon Watcher* promoted the mini-concert by saying that "a child who heard The Scholars said, 'It didn't sound like singing, it sounded like music.'" In more recent years, St. George's has continued the tradition of inviting exceptional choral groups to Nashville and offering concerts to the community.

As previously noted, King's College, Cambridge, provided the model for Lessons and Carols. In 1979 it was incorporated into both morning services on the first Sunday of Advent rather than being a separate event. Readers from various groups in the church participated, as did all four of the choirs. The services also included the premiere of a choral work written by Scott Withrow and dedicated to the Youth

Choir, *The Splendor of the Lord*. The piece was sung by the Youth Choir accompanied by cellist and choir member Amy Street.

Special music was included in the Christmas Eve services as well. The 3:30 p.m. family service included a bagpipe procession, no doubt played by longtime Choir member Jackson Galloway in full Scottish regalia. The 11:00 p.m. service featured harp and recorder.

Scott Withrow looked back on 1979 with satisfaction in his Annual Report:

> Rejecting the impulse to quote statistics, we recall three areas of emphasis in our musical activities during the past year:
>
> I. It is our philosophy that music should support, not substitute for, the liturgy. As the Episcopal Church has now adopted the Prayer Book, 1979, so the people of St. George's have adopted the new music necessary to support the new liturgies. Chief item of this has been the Ordinary Music for the Rite II Eucharist, which the 9 o'clock congregation now participates in with increasing strength and confidence. On several occasions, as the members will testify, the choir's music seemed unsatisfactory and/or inconsequential until it was seen how the music emphasized or fitted into the Propers of the Day. We feel great strides have been made in adopting as our own music to support the requirement of the new Prayer Book.
>
> II. For the first time since starting the St. Dunstan's Choir in 1977, the three-choir progression is working. Anytime one needs new vigor, we invite you to attend the St. Cecilia rehearsal Wednesdays at 4:30 P.M. to see 25-30 pre-schoolers sing, squirm, and scintillate. Some have now graduated into St. Dunstan's, where they are learning to use the Hymnal and Prayer Book. Likewise, St. Dunstan's has sent its first graduates to the Youth Choir.... We look for this progression to bear even more fruit in years to come.

The third area of emphasis was the previously mentioned use of "our creative spirits" in the form of special compositions and additional instruments. The mission of music at St. George's was continuing to make good progress.

1980–1981

The emphasis for 1980 appears to have been increasing the number of congregants in the various choirs, as the Annual Report for that year is simply a listing of the rosters for the various choirs. Despite the success of St. Dunstan's Choir as reported the previous year, it isn't listed in 1980. Instead, a Boys Choir comprised of five hearty souls between the ages of seven and twelve was undertaken. The substitution was brief, as St. Dunstan's re-emerged in 1981 and the Boys Choir had disappeared.

In addition to longtime Adult Choir members Lura Kauffman, Lee Sikes, Lucille David, and Lucy Adkins, one notable member of the Adult Choir was country music star-to-be Kathy Mattea.

The Dragon Watcher included an article announcing two new music instructors to teach lessons:

The view over Scott Withrow's shoulder.

St. George's Music program has added two instructors to their staff. Both are performers with the Nashville Symphony Orchestra. Miss Terryll Arnst, cellist, will offer private string instruction and Charles Wyatt, principal flute with the symphony, will offer flute instruction.

Presumably Scott and Kay Withrow were also offering lessons in piano/organ and voice, respectively.

The 1981 Annual Report was given over to "Memoirs of Some Choir Members." They not only provided some interesting insights into the music program but also allowed Scott to enlist the help of others in his ongoing quest for a new organ. A Youth Choir member had this to say:

> During the last year, we have had a lot of neat occasions (besides our parties, that is). One was the Confirmation Service on Palm Sunday, another was the 9:00 A.M. Easter service when we sang with instruments (other than the organ, that is. By the way, the organ seems to be acting up more and more. Mr. Withrow says that some major repairs have to be done very soon). The service on St. Barnabas' Day celebrating Father [Julien] Gunn's 40th anniversary [of his ordination] was really exceptional, too, and we joined choirs again on All Saints Day for that Jacob's Ladder thing that Mr. Withrow wrote (he composed a couple other anthems for us, too).... But the best thing is to know that, each week, I'm doing something for the church and the services... as well as learning a lot of music and getting to understand why we Episcopalians do things the way we do. It makes all the hard work worthwhile.

An Adult Choir member concurred:

> We do a good variety of sacred literature, most of which is new to me, and usually we do it pretty well. We don't have a large number of singers (there is always room for more) but we have few dull moments, and I feel that my talents are being put to good use. I enjoy the music, but I also get much satisfaction from the service I perform for the church.

Finally, one of the St. Dunstan's members weighed in:

> Last year I was in St. Cecilia . . . and it's neat to look forward to "graduating" to another choir. Those bigger choir members can say what they want, but nobody has more fun in rehearsals than we do. Mrs. Withrow is so nice, and sometimes she gets down on the floor with us to sing or to help us play the rhythm instruments. She sometimes gives us treats at the end of rehearsal, too. Her husband isn't as nice—he thinks we ought to earn our treats—but he plays the organ a little better than she does!

Their choristers clearly loved Scott and Kay Withrow.

1982

> 1982 was a year of change at St. George's with regard to the music of the church. Scott Withrow, our choirmaster and organist, resigned his position and took a new job in a parish in Birmingham, Alabama. Scott left St. George's with our best wishes and our prayers for the future.
>
> —1982 Annual Report

Kay Withrow Thomson recently explained the reason for their departure, which turned out to be a familiar one:

> We decided to leave St. George's because Scott and I were offered a joint position at St. Luke's Birmingham. By the time we left St. George's it was a matter of necessity that we move to a position willing to compensate its musicians in a reasonable fashion. (Scott's total salary at St. G's at the time we left was $15,000—not a very generous compensation after almost nine years serving the church.) In moving to Birmingham we almost doubled the salary that St. George's paid. I think that Scott would have stayed at St. George's if they had been willing to meet him halfway regarding salary. After he left . . . others were paid very much higher salaries and were given much larger budgets to do the work. But that is so often the way of things.

Scott and Kay said their farewells in an open letter in the November issue of *The Dragon Watcher*:

> To the Clergy, Vestry, and People of St. George's Church:
> It is impossible for us to express what our last Sunday at St. George's meant to us; but, we want to thank you, in this inadequate way, for the reception and the gifts which we shall treasure with great fondness. We especially want to thank you for your expressions of good wishes and will, the glow of which shines brightly in our memories as we begin our work in a different place.
> You will continue to be in our thoughts and prayers. Again, our most sincere thanks.
>
> Kay and Scott Withrow

Once again, St. George's had lost its musical leadership because of salary considerations. And once again, St. George's had the great good fortune to have another exceptional musician—arguably more accomplished than any of her predecessors—in the wings to take up the baton. From the Annual Report:

> Shortly after the Withrows' departure, Wilma Jensen, a distinguished concert organist and conductor, took the position as interim choirmaster in our parish. Assisting her [are] Sue Schneller, Bettye Ann Schwede and Jeffrey McLelland. This has proven to be a fortuitous arrangement. The music at St. George's has been splendid. At present, the Rector, with the help of a small committee which he appointed, is moving toward a permanent filling of the vacancy which occurred when our former choirmaster resigned. In the meanwhile, our senior choir and junior choirs are in good hands, and our gratitude is extended both to our choir leadership and those who sing.

As had their predecessors before them, Scott and Kay continued their distinguished careers after leaving St. George's. Kay provided some highlights:

Scott served St. Luke's Birmingham as Organist and Choirmaster. During the Bach/Handel year of 1985, Birmingham was paired with Leipzig and Scott and I along with a group of musicians in the Birmingham region performed a wide variety of concerts during that time. . . . I think at one time we figured that we either performed as soloists or as a member of a chamber group every other week throughout that year. He also taught at the University of Alabama in Birmingham. We moved to Providence in 1988 when Scott was offered the position as Organist and Choirmaster at Central Congregational Church (just up the street from Rhode Island School of Design and Brown) and also served as Organist at Temple Emanuel. During that period until his death in early 1993 he taught privately, and with a colleague established the Ocean State Light Opera Company . . . a semiprofessional group that produced three operas every summer.

Kay was no less busy. At the University of Alabama at Birmingham, she was administrative coordinator and assistant to the dean for the General Clinical Research Center. In 1995, Kay went back to school and received an M.Ed. degree in organization and management from the New England Graduate School of Antioch University. She put that to good use as the vice president for development and alumni affairs at Oberlin College. Now retired, Kay is married to Haskell Thomson, former director of the Division of Keyboard Studies and chair of the Organ Department at the Oberlin Conservatory.

Kay Withrow Thomson, 1998.

3

Fulfillment

JENNIFER ORTH AND GINY BAILEY

1982

Wilma Jensen's tenure at St. George's began in a somewhat unconventional manner. As the Annual Report for the year indicates, the intention was for Wilma to serve as an Interim Organist while a search process was undertaken. However, it didn't quite work out that way, as Wilma recalled:

> Scott Withrow had just resigned and they needed an Interim Organist. And I had always wanted to learn the Episcopal service and I thought this might be a great chance for me to learn that. So I interviewed with Fr. Johnson and I started in November and he asked me to stay through Christmas. And then we kept going in January and I wondered what was going to happen and then about in February, he called me in and said, "Would you stay through Easter?" And I said, "Well, yes, I think I could do that." And he had many applications for the job on his desk—it was piling up. And people were asking me if I was going to apply for the job. And at that time I didn't know if Fr. Johnson would hire me, because I was the daughter of a Methodist minister and I was

just learning the Episcopal service. So the longer I thought about it, the more I thought, if Fr. Johnson wanted me, he would ask me eventually, and if he didn't, he wouldn't. And that would save any embarrassment. But in the meantime, everybody was noticing the music and the change, and I kept going to him for getting a few more singers and we got a few more volunteers. And then it was May or June, he called me in and said, "What are you going to do about St. George's?" And I said, "What do you mean?" He said, "Well, are you going to stay?" And I said, "Well, you haven't really asked me." He said, "Of course I want you to stay. The music is beautiful." . . . I had a chance to prove myself, and to improve during that time. And I know I wouldn't have gotten the job if I hadn't had that chance to improve.

Wilma Jensen.

It's a little difficult to believe that Wilma Jensen wouldn't have been at the top of that pile of applicants, whether or not she had "had the chance to improve." Wilma had had an extensive career as a concert organist, church musician, and teacher by the time she came to St. George's.

Wilma Jensen was born in 1929 in Illinois. She was playing the organ in her father's church by the age of twelve, earning $1.00 per week. At the time, she was the youngest organist in Methodism. Wilma earned her Bachelor and Master of Music degrees from the Eastman School of Music in Rochester, New York, where she was a student of Catharine Crozier and Harold Gleason. During that time she received the highly coveted Performer's Certificate in Organ. She had toured as a concert organist in Germany, France, England, Holland, Sweden, Norway, Denmark, Poland, and Austria. Wilma had been on the faculties of Oklahoma City University and Indiana University, where she was a tenured professor—an extremely desirable position. However, Wilma left Indiana University to join the faculty at Scarritt College. Wilma explained her decision:

> I was teaching at Indiana University and I was there for four years. I had just gotten tenure, so for me to leave was a shock to everyone but I felt that I had more to give than just the straight teaching at Indiana University.... There were three of us in the organ department—two men and me. And the two men really did not want me there. And after the first year, I suddenly had all the best students, and that did not go over well. And I just felt I couldn't take the pressure of not being wanted there.... Scarritt was a two-year master's program in either church music or Christian education and I felt that, of people who were majors in the organ world, I was a lot more interested in the church than most of them. So that was my interest and I thought I could do well and be happier.

It was certainly a happy decision for St. George's. As was Scott Withrow's before her, Wilma's priority for her first few months was carrying out the plans that her predecessor had made. It would not be long, however, before Wilma had plans of her own.

1983

Once Wilma officially took up the position of Organist-Choirmaster, she set about learning everything she could about the Episcopal service and the Anglican repertoire. One of her primary teachers was the Rev. Joseph L. Pace, who came to St. George's as Associate Rector shortly after Wilma came to the church. She said,

> After Joe Pace came, he helped me hours every week outlining the church year, the concepts of the seasons, coordinating anthem texts with the lectionary—I mean, we went through that in detail. And the first couple of years he was here, I never chose an anthem for the liturgy that he didn't approve with the text. So I had lots of fabulous training with him. And then at the same time I studied conducting with Sandra Willetts, and after she left Scarritt I studied a little bit with Angela Tipps, who was an excellent teacher. And then I studied diction with Lucille David. We had . . . weekly lessons for several years. And I completely went through the Madeline Marshall diction book—I don't mean just reading it, I mean we went through every page. I learned the International Phonetic Alphabet and what I did then was to mark the phonetic alphabet in all the anthems that we sang for choir. And then I did another book on Latin diction and so we did this in great detail and I owe so much to that—her training. And she [Lucille David] was really a mentor, both to me and the Choir.
>
> I worked a little bit with Rebecca Price also, who was a professional singer in the Choir earlier. And she's been a big voice teacher all her life. And I worked a little bit with Marcia Thom, so I tried to learn from any people who were available. And my big learning really happened the second and third years because I was working with all three at the same time: Lucille David, Father Pace, and Sandra Willetts. And

of course I'd had years and years of accompanying experience.... And also Lois Fyfe of Lois Fyfe Music—I spent a great deal of time researching repertoire. I bought so many CDs—English CDs and the best known choirs in the United States, and I really learned a vast amount about the repertoire—of course you can never learn it all—but I had a good understanding of what would be considered the basic English repertoire and we certainly were moving in an Anglican tradition.

Wilma also had the assistance of her former student at Indiana University, Janette Carrigan (now Janette Fishell) as accompanist and assistant. Janette was a masterful musician herself and went on to become a concert organist and chair of the Organ Department at the Indiana University Jacobs School of Music.

In November 1983, the Choir presented an Evensong and Choral Concert, featuring the Herbert Howells *Magnificat and Nunc Dimittis* and the *Solemn Vespers* by Mozart. Wilma expressed her approach to repertoire selection in her first Annual Report:

> In so far as possible, an attempt was made to choose texts which complimented the lectionary. Music of all periods was scheduled including Renaissance, Baroque, Romantic, and Contemporary literature in order to produce a well-rounded musical offering. The Choir's sincere interest in contributing to worship to the best of its abilities through good music has been a rewarding experience to the Choirmaster and hopefully to the participants and the congregation. The Choir and Choirmaster believe in the meaning that beautiful music done sensitively can bring to the worship service and to the individual worshiper.

While the Adult Choir was making strides under Wilma's leadership, the children's choirs were continuing as well. The Youth Choir was directed by Sue Schneller and continued to sing the 9:00 a.m. service, alternating with the Adult Choir on the first Sunday of the month when they sang at 11:00 a.m. The St. Cecilia and St. Dunstan's

Choirs were directed by Bettye Ann Schwede. There were the usual calls for more volunteers from the congregation in all choirs. However, the complaints about the Moller organ had ceased, as plans were under way for a new sanctuary, which would of course include a new instrument. It's a shame that Scott Withrow and Sam Batt Owens were never invited back to repeat their double-organ concert on the instrument they had so longed for.

1984

George Orwell may have had dire predictions for the year, but such was not the case for the music program in 1984. One significant addition was the establishment of an instrumental fund. Given by a parishioner, the fund was designed to provide instrumentalists for Christmas Eve, Easter, and other special occasions, since these were unbudgeted expenses. The interest from this fund continues to ful-

Wilma with the choir before a service, late 1980s.

fill that purpose to the present day. A gift of resonator bells was also given for the Children's Choir use.

The Youth Choir was beginning to face real challenges, primarily due to increased extracurricular offerings for girls offered by many area schools. The result was that the Choir had shrunk to a mere nine members, most of whom had come up through the Children's Choirs. An extensive recruitment effort had yielded minimal results. The St. Dunstan and St. Cecilia Choirs were faring better, with eleven and twenty members, respectively, now under the direction of Cynthia Wendel. The St. Dunstan's Choir presented *A Night for Dancing* by Hal Hopson between services on December 23, and all three of the choirs sang pre-service music at the 3:30 p.m. service on Christmas Eve.

Earlier in the year the Adult Choir presented Schubert's *Mass in G* with a string quartet on Maundy Thursday and led the opening service of the fall Diocesan Convention, which was hosted by St. George's. The pre-service concert at 10:30 p.m. on Christmas Eve featured harp, flute, chimes, and bells. Wilma was busy expanding the music library for both the Adult and the Children's Choirs to include new anthems and oratorios, turning to Lois Fyfe for guidance in many cases:

> It's really been important to many musicians in church music and especially Episcopal musicians having Lois Fyfe Music in Nashville. Lois is a walking encyclopedia. And then there was one period when I was trying to bring the copies of some good things we had in the library already up to what we needed and I called her and she said, "Oh, you must have the old edition in F. You really need to know that it originally was written for a countertenor solo." Every time I talked to her there was something new I learned. And she knew I wanted her to tell me everything I'm supposed to know.

One thing that can truly be said of Wilma Jensen is that she never stopped learning:

> I remember when I first came, Carol Battle—imagine, I remember her name!—said, "We really need to fix our vowels." And I didn't know exactly what she was talking about. There

was a tenor who was a teacher at Belmont University. And in rehearsal, he said, "Do you want a dental 't' or an American 't' in this Latin?" And I thought, "What is he talking about?" And at that point, most of the time I was ready to admit *my* failings, shortcomings. I said, "Let me think about it." And then I talked to Lucille about it and then I became a nut about it. And now it bothers me so much to hear people singing Latin with an American "t," which is very sharp. So I mean, it just shows you I did a lot of learning along the way.

1985

The year began with a progress report on the new organ, given by John Fitzgerald (as only he could) at the 1985 Annual Parish Meeting:

> I have been asked by the Rector, Wardens and Vestry to report to you, on behalf of our organ selection committee, composed of Mrs. T. Scott [Lavinia] Fillebrown, Jr., Mr. Robert H. Tosh, Jr., Ms. Wilma Jensen and myself, as to the progress of our new pipe organ to be built for the new church by the Casavant Company. As you know, this company has placed organs all over the world, but of particular interest to you might be the one at All Saints Chapel, Sewanee, and the recently constructed one at St. Paul's Church, Chattanooga.
>
> The finished instrument will be in place, assuming all goes well, sometime in May of 1986. . . . Your organ committee has labored to choose an instrument which will undergird and adorn the principal act of worship in our new building, that is, the celebration of the Eucharist.
>
> It is our hope and prayer that this instrument will celebrate with us the larger life of our parish, whether it be for quiet Lenten meditation from the soft, pensive viole de gambe of the recit, a joyful Christmas Gloria surrounded by a choir of flutes celeste in the positif, a resounding Easter affirmation of our faith in hymns accompanied by the sturdy grand orgue, or the mighty, rushing announcement of the coming of the Holy Spirit at Pentecost from the rafters of

the 61 trompettes royale to the foundation of the thirty-two foot long contre bombarde in the pedal ... may this instrument move us all to resound more and more to the glory of His Name!

On a less auspicious note, the Youth Choir had diminished to the point that members of the Adult Choir now joined them in singing the nine o'clock service—a move that was resented, according to Wilma's Annual Report. The St. Cecilia and St. Dunstan's Choirs suffered from a mid-year change in leadership when Cynthia Wendel completed her graduate studies and left Nashville. Despite efforts to recruit other leaders and singers, the children's choir programs continued to decline. Wilma lamented the loss in a recent interview:

> Little by little, I couldn't get people to do it [lead the Choirs]. And then I tried to do it and I was so sad because I just couldn't get them [girls] to come out to do it. And I don't think it was me, but it was just a certain time when it wasn't the thing to do. Because when I was young, I had a girls' choir of sixty third through sixth graders and their ensemble ... they were really good.... It's like there's a certain time when something will develop and there will be some excitement about it. And I felt that's what happened with the [Adult] Choir.

The Adult Choir was indeed flourishing. With volunteer participation on the rise, Wilma worked to get more paid singers for the Choir as well, but she changed tactics in the recruitment of those singers from her predecessors' approach:

> I wasn't too happy about the paid singers and their attitude. That was when I first came. And of course, I didn't have my confidence yet either, so it was a problem on both sides. I remember once a tenor called me and said, "I can't come to any rehearsals during end of November or December." And I said, "Well then, I don't think I can keep you because I think rehearsal is really important." So then I talked with Fr. Johnson and he said, "Do whatever you want." So I told him

> I couldn't have him as a paid singer if he couldn't come to rehearsals.
>
> And over time I moved toward more student involvement rather than an adult who might be in mid-career because I really wanted to coach with them about vowels and musicality, and the attitude of the student is usually more in line with suggestions. And so then I felt that was really working better.... Several people have told me they had more questions from me and a longer interview about a professional position here—it was longer and more involved. I wanted to know they were flexible so I would try to work with them at that time to see how they responded. And if they resented it, that was it.

Highlights of the year included a thirty-minute mini-concert before the Maundy Thursday service and the Haydn *Lord Nelson Mass* with five strings, three trumpets, and timpani after Evensong on December 1. For the first time ever, the Choir also sang three Easter morning services with brass and timpani.

In an attempt to include more parishioners in the music program, Wilma made the first of several attempts to establish a parish choir

> which might rehearse once a month and sing for services occasionally. It is the concept of the Choirmaster-Organist that all age groups have the potential for singing musically and sensitively, with appropriate phrasing. Helping the singer feel he or she is an integral part of the liturgy is an important goal.

An important goal, to be sure, but not easily achieved, apparently. Wilma remembered the turnout for the parish choir with great good humor:

> Well, the women that showed up were past middle age. I'm not going to say anything about age because as you know I'm way past middle age, but all they wanted to do was sing alto. And then we had three people who could only sing the

Wilma on her European tour, 1985.

melody down two octaves lower. Now what do you do with a choir like that?

Wilma had additional struggles during a concert tour of Germany, Austria, Belgium, Denmark, and France. Aside from dealing with a variety of organs from different periods and having truculent guards who didn't want to let her in to practice, Wilma nearly had to cancel her concert at St. Stephen's in Vienna due to electrical problems with the organ. She finally managed to communicate the problem by telling the electrician, *"Die orgel ist kaput!"* He managed to get it working, and all was well. Wilma summed up her trip in an article for the September edition of *The Dragon Watcher*:

> Continuing to learn about the organ and its development and to experience so many different acoustical environments in beautiful churches and cathedrals is exciting. But coming home was the most wonderful part of the trip. I thank the Lord for a safe return and for a continuing joy and opportunity of helping to bring music and liturgy together at St. George's. I feel truly blessed to be in this place and look forward with eager anticipation to the installation of a beautiful new, outstanding Casavant organ.

1986

The hopes, dreams, and hard work of many came to fruition in September 1986 when St. George's moved into its new sanctuary building. However, it would be almost another year before the organ was installed (note the lack of organ pipes in the following photograph). In *A St. George's Scrapbook: The First 50 Years*, Nashville architect Bruce Crabtree had this to say about his design for the new sanctuary:

> The nave was a room that was aimed at music from the beginning. It's a very hard room, which makes it difficult to hear the spoken word, but you really have to choose in a room whether it's going to be for one or the other, and then amplify whichever one you don't pick. And so the spoken word was amplified.

The occasion of the first service in the new church was significant enough to warrant an article in *The Nashville Banner* the following day:

> More than 700 people attended St. George's Church on Sunday [September 7, 1986] to usher in the opening of the new church building.
>
> ... Although most of the new building is finished, the pipe organ, to be one of the largest in Nashville, is not. The

The first service in the new sanctuary before the organ and the rose window were installed.

pipe organ, the bells, and the steeple are expected to be installed this fall and will be consecrated during the worship service November 30, church officials said.

They said the installation of the pipe organ will improve the choral music at St. George's, long known for its excellent choir.

In celebration of the new organ, a concert series was planned for the coming year, culminating in a concert by Simon Preston, Organist at Westminster Abbey. No further record of the activities of 1986 exists. Perhaps Wilma was lying low after an ill-fated Christmas Eve service featuring early music and Renaissance dancers that was not well received by the congregation and she chose not to submit an Annual Report. However the minutes from the Annual Parish Meeting indicate Fr. Johnson's support for Wilma's efforts:

The Rector briefly outlined the credentials of Wilma Jensen as an organist of international status and outstanding choirmaster and expressed how great it was for the church to have Wilma Jensen and the music she affords to St. George's.

To quote Scott Withrow, "Nuf sed."

1987

The organ and bells were finally installed and ready for use early in 1987—the organ in February and the bells in May. *The Tennessean* was positively poetic in its February 8 article about the upcoming dedication of the organ:

> In the chancel of St. George's Episcopal Church, a new organ—all majestic and massive and silent—awaits its dedication. Its four thousand nine hundred pipes—ranging from 3/16 inches to 10½ inches in diameter—glow in

Organ pipes waiting to be installed.

the mild mid-morning sunlight. Its neo-Georgian cabinetry of Adirondack oak is polished to a quiet sheen.... For well over three years, Michael Payne, regional representative for Casavant Fréres, the legendary Montreal-based organ building firm, has overseen every detail of the organ's planning, its construction, and its installation.

"Basically the job of any organ is to support the liturgy of the church," says Payne. "And closely behind that, it must accompany the choir; it must have an expressive dimension."

"This is a great organ," Payne says simply, having just put the finishing touches on the Casavant firm's Opus 3,606, which will be introduced to the general public at a concert next Sunday afternoon. "When you take into consideration all the work that's gone into it—the fact that each of its 4,900 pipes required an average of seventy-three separate hand operations—I think it's no exaggeration to say that this is the greatest organ in the state, maybe even in the South. The sound is unmatched."

The organ was put into immediate use, both in worship services and in concerts. The Adult Choir gave the aforementioned concert on February 15, followed two weeks later with an organ concert from Wilma. In April, the Choir did a Choral Evensong featuring the Vierne *Messe Solennelle* (mass with Choir and two organs) with John Semingson, Assistant Organist for the spring of 1987, playing the antiphonal organ at the back of the church.

Another fortuitous event happened in April, which was the concert given by Simon Preston of Westminster Abbey. Wilma wasn't going to miss an opportunity to strike up a relationship with this important Anglican musician:

> I picked him up at the airport. And I had cued up on my cassette player ... I think the Choir was singing the Bainton "And I Saw a New Heaven." And he said, "Oh, your Choir sounds really good." And then at the reception after

Michael Payne showing the new organ console to Dillard Adams.

FULFILLMENT 81

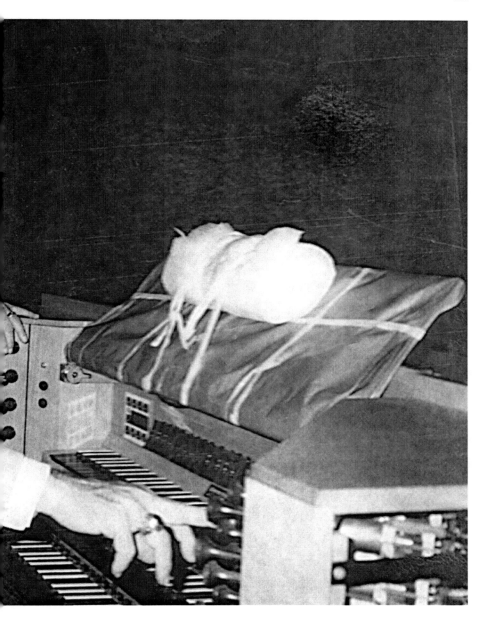

his concert, which was next door at Fr. Johnson's house, Dan Killman said to Simon Preston, "We really want to take a trip to Europe. Would there be any chance of singing at Westminster Abbey?" He said, "Oh, I think so. I heard your Choir on the tape and it sounded really good."

Thus began the planning for the Choir's first European tour, which would take place in 1989. In the meantime, the Choir was perfecting and performing repertoire that would figure into that tour. A concert in November featured the Hassler *Verbum caro factum est* and excerpts from Michael Tippett's *A Child of Our Time*, all of which would be performed throughout Europe.

Of course, the weekly services at St. George's took precedence over all else. As the Youth Choir was no more, the Adult Choir sang both services on Sundays, plus the various special services during Holy Week and Christmas. Wilma reports that a number of volunteers joined the Choir, outnumbering the paid singers at last.

Wilma's quest to expand the music library continued. The size of the Choir had outstripped the number of available copies of music. Wilma described the situation in her Annual Report:

> There are an insufficient number of copies in the library for the present choir. Gradually extra copies of all scheduled anthems are being added. With an approximate two hundred anthems sung a year, this creates an enormous expense as well as investment of time in organizing the library.... Very few copies of oratorios are in the library so that each time a chorus from *Elijah, Messiah, Brahm's Requiem*, etc. is sung, copies are borrowed from the Scarritt Graduate School library. Because of the closing of Scarritt, borrowing from the library will not be possible after May 31, 1988.

Aside from the difficulty about music, the closing of Scarritt meant that Wilma no longer had a faculty position that subsidized her salary at St. George's and provided benefits:

> I was here full-time even though I was only a part-time employee. I was so busy. And doing both choir and organ and

I was trying to find more repertoire all the time for myself for preludes and postludes and looking all the time for the best repertoire for the lectionary. I mentioned to [Fr. Johnson] once that I was here as much as the priests, but he said the Vestry wouldn't go for [a full-time position]. There were several years where it was pretty rough. I was concertizing, but the longer I was here the less I concertized because the administration finally just got so much with doing both jobs.

Wilma conducting the choir.

Not one to pull back, Wilma forged ahead with her plans for the Choir and for the organ, including recording two CDs of organ music.

1988

The planned tour of Europe made 1988 an especially busy year for the music program. In the fall, the Choir presented Duruflé's gorgeous *Requiem*. Wilma's assessment was that the performance was "perhaps the finest musical presentation to date."

The Children's Choir was growing again under the leadership of staff singers Nylea Butler-Moore and Tricia Darden. The parish choir, on the other hand, was given up for the time being due to lack of attendance.

The primary work of the year, outside of worship services, was fund-raising for the European tour. Approximately forty singers were making the trip, and an additional forty parishioners were going along as well, paying a little extra to subsidize the cost for the Choir members. A number of fund-raising events took place. The largest was a dinner at the home of Walter and Margaret Ann Robinson, longtime Choir supporters. The Robinsons underwrote the cost of the dinner, while "secular entertainment was provided by soloists and Choir with an especially good time enjoyed by all," according to Wilma. The closing number was a modified version of "Here's to You, Mrs. Robinson" by way of a thank-you from the Choir.

The Choir did a number of other gigs to raise funds, including performing as the shepherds' chorus in *Amahl and the Night Visitors* with Tennessee Opera Theatre, singing for a Choir member's wedding, and recording a jingle for a spaghetti restaurant to the tune of "Funiculi, Funicula." A tremendous amount of work and planning went into it all, however, as Wilma recalled:

> It took a long time to get permission for the Europe trip because it was going to cost money. And I finally made all sorts of financial proposals and spent a lot of hours on that—went to Fr. Johnson about it. And one time he said, "Oh, you get things so well organized I can't say no." But things like that weren't easy for me. It took me a long time in planning. . . . It was a big push—harder than anybody can know. And I wouldn't have wanted to go if the Choir wasn't going to sound brilliant.

However, Wilma must have felt that the Choir was ready. Her Annual Report for 1988 stated,

> The St. George's Choir takes a great deal of pride in its musical development of vocal sound, ensemble, and being able to bring out the expressive qualities of the music. The year of 1988 was an especially busy one in preparation for musical commitments, and 1989 will be even more so. However, the choir has worked with discipline and good spirit. I believe the choir is unique in Church music in its quality and finesse.

That assessment would be put to the test in the year ahead.

1989

The European tour was certainly a major focus of 1989, but there was other excitement as well. In February, Governor Ned McWherter

Itinerary for the European tour.

issued a proclamation naming St. George's Choir "Tennessee Ambassadors of Good Will." Wilma was invited by the Norwegian consul to the United States to be guest organist at the internationally acclaimed Bergen Festival in Norway later in the spring. In April, the Choir was invited to sing at the National Convention of the American Choral Directors Association in Louisville, Kentucky. Only eighteen choirs from across the country were invited to perform for the more than three thousand attendees. Wilma recalled it in a recent conversation:

> In order to apply for that, you have to send an audition tape and the director has to have directed the Choir I think it's more than three years. So if you inherited some wonderful Choir, you couldn't just the next year take them to ACDA.
>
> We were accepted. And I thought, being in Louisville, it wouldn't cost us anything. We wouldn't have to get plane fare for the Choir to go. We just carpooled up. And I walked out on that stage with two thousand choral conductors. You know, a lot of the choirs that come are college choirs or high school choirs and even some professional choirs, and usually the director, if it's a woman, they're out there in their sequins, you know. And I had my choir robe on just like the rest of the robes. And in the audience was Angela Tipps and somebody else was sitting next to her and he said, "Wilma Jensen is known as an organist. She's got some nerve bringing her church choir." And after we sang an all a cappella program he said, "I take that back."
>
> It was good programming. I'd even gotten some suggestions for the opening piece from Sandra Willetts because I wanted an early piece but exciting to open the program. And we ended it with the Tippett "Child of Our Time" spirituals, which have a lot of divisi—you know eight, ten parts. And at that time they wouldn't have been as well-known as they are now. And so that was a really good choice. We also sang the [Stanford] "Beati Quorum Via" and we had worked out very carefully each voice's tiny crescendos-diminuendos.... And a lot of people commented how beautiful that was. And I be-

St. George's Choir, 1989 ACDA Convention, Louisville, Kentucky.

lieve the sound of the Choir was unified. It didn't sound like, sopranos there, altos, tenors, basses.... We were a unit.

In June, that unit set out for London, the first stop on the eighteen-day tour, accompanied by Fr. Joe Pace and forty friends, family members, and parishioners. True to his word, Simon Preston had scheduled the Choir to sing Evensong at Westminster Abbey. The following day, the Choir presented a concert at the mecca of Anglicanism, Canterbury Cathedral. Tour participant Adele Smith described being in Westminster Abbey:

> How does it feel to be sitting in that hallowed place with the late afternoon sun coming through the windows, highlighting the severe marble faces of the Abbey's monuments—seeing the altar before which so much history has passed, coronations and burials, stones commemorating centuries of English and world history, listening to St. George's Choir singing their hearts out sending glorious sound up to the top of the Abbey's vaults? Humbling, inspiring.

The two great churches of the Anglican faith in their memories, the Choir left England for Belgium—but not without considerable drama. As the Choir was preparing to board two "deluxe, over-the-road motor coaches" for the trip to Dover and thence to Oostende in Belgium, one Choir member injured his hand, necessitating a trip to the emergency room. Fr. Pace was left to assist while the rest of the Choir journeyed on. Choir member Gloria Parvin gave an account of the day in *The Dragon Watcher*:

> One of the most meaningful experiences of the tour was our concert at Grimbergen, Belgium, just outside Brussels. We had had a very difficult journey that day: half of our group caught the ferry from Dover to Oostende as scheduled, but the rest of us missed the ferry and went to Calais instead. We were all very nervous about arriving in Belgium too late. As the day went on, the uncertainty of reaching our destination on time became more grating.
>
> We did arrive a few minutes late in Grimbergen, and as we drove up people were waiting for us outside the church.

Wilma confers with tour guides Gill and Keith while bus drivers Georg and Gerhard stand at the ready.

> It was very quiet as we entered the baroque church, which was already full to capacity. We quickly tip-toed through to the robing area, most of us weary and worn from a frustrating day of travel. Somehow we pulled together and did our best, giving what turned out to be one of our most energetic performances. The audience in Grimbergen was especially attentive and supportive.
>
> We were not aware until the end of the concert that we had been singing for a cancer benefit, hosted by the Assistant Prime Minister of Belgium. It was a great honor to participate in such an important event for that community and the patients and their families in the audience. Being named "Tennessee's Ambassadors of Good Will" had a very special meaning that evening.

The tour continued into Germany, with stops in Cologne and Rothenburg on the way to Nurnberg, site of the Nazi war trials. In Vienna, they performed at the Esterhazy Palace and the small parish church in Eisenstadt—a concert that was followed by an invitation to the local pub by the attendees and some impromptu singing. A highlight of this portion of the trip was singing Sunday morning mass at Schubert's church in Vienna, where the Choir trooped up a narrow spiral staircase and squeezed into the choir loft at the back of the church.

One of the truly remarkable things about the tour was that the group of non-singers traveling with the Choir attended every event, every concert—including the tour guides and the bus drivers! Longtime church member Dr. Paul Teschan had this to say in *The Dragon Watcher* following the trip:

> It was astonishing! Wilma Jensen's magic again and again transformed the "diverse" assembly of those gifted, spontaneous young singers into a single instrument: it was world class perfection, most evident in the echoing of the quieter churches that did not want the sound to die. All ninety of

The choir at Schubertkirche in Vienna.

us sounded pretty good, too, when we sang less holy tunes together in an Eisenstadt pub! It was a gem of an experience!

The next stop on the tour was Salzburg, but the Choir visited the Melk Monastery on the way and gave an impromptu concert in the chapel. Tour participant Bill Gleason served as Wilma's music stand:

> We were just there to see it—we didn't have any concert planned. But there were other travelers looking at it and so we asked the person who was in charge there if we could sing a little bit. And so in our slacks and everything we just sang for awhile because it had such incredible acoustics.

Once in Salzburg, the Choir sang at St. Peter's Church, then continued on to their final destination, Paris. The pinnacle of the tour was singing the Vierne *Messe Solennelle* for the eleven o'clock mass

Bill Gleason serves as Wilma's music stand in the chapel at Melk Monastery.

at Notre Dame. Vierne had been the Organist and Choirmaster at Notre Dame and wrote the mass specifically for the cathedral. The rehearsal the day before was a bit rocky, as Wilma recalled:

> I thought we would get to rehearse on Saturday, but the Organist for the back organ, Philippe Lefebvre, didn't show up for Saturday rehearsal, so the first time we heard it was in the mass. [His helper] was being very mean to the Choir. "Sing louder, sing louder!" What we found out on Sunday is we were miked. And then he finally had the men standing up on chairs. And then he said ... we were singing "Ubi Caritas" ... and he says, "Make it louder. Put it in a higher key." So I kept going up a half-step with each key and we were way up there. ... So I thought I would just do what I wanted on Sunday, which is what I did. ... I did go up a half-step, just to make me honest ... but only a half-step.

We sang a thirty-minute a cappella group before the mass

The organ at Notre Dame; the top of Wilma's head is barely visible above the rail.

and the Vierne *Messe Solennelle*. . . . I think singing the "Kyrie" with the back organ chords coming on the offbeat is one of the most thrilling musical experiences of my life. . . . They estimated there were five thousand people there that day. So that was a rather large . . . it was a neat deal. And then I played the afternoon organ recital. People were standing all over.

When the group returned to Nashville, Wilma expressed her thanks in *The Dragon Watcher:*

> I want to express my thanks to the members of the parish who helped make the Choir's very successful European tour this summer possible. Special thanks go to the non-singers who accompanied the Choir on the tour, serving as a wonderful support group. They attended all of the concerts, laughed with us and were moved to tears with us, worried over all our problems, and were incredibly flexible with a sometimes confused schedule.
>
> We developed such a camaraderie on the two buses that I sometimes wake up wishing I were back on the bus! We shared making music and listening to music in some of the world's most visually beautiful and acoustically excellent environments. Truly it was a rich, once-in-a-lifetime experience for us all.

In fact, the trip made such an impact on two of the non-singers who accompanied the Choir that they made generous donations to the Choir Scholarship Fund to provide voice lessons for parishioners who sang in the Choir. The fund began under Wilma's leadership and reflected the importance she placed on the volunteer members of the Choir:

> There was a period when I thought we should give as much help to the volunteers as we possibly could rather than just paying the staff singers. So I had some money that I could let everyone take voice lessons—let the volunteers that wanted to take voice lessons.... And we had some really good volunteers. I mean, I've always valued the volunteers. Many volunteers read so much better than the staff people.

One staff member who did get a much-needed raise in 1989 was Wilma herself. The notes from the Vestry workshop of that year laid out the situation under the heading of Staffing:

> Organist/Choir director—additional $15,000 needed for

organist salary (does not include money for any other part of music budget); if present organist leaves at least $45,000 will be needed to replace position ($30,000 is currently budgeted). The Rector went on record in this issue stating the parish should do everything possible to keep the current organist; a replacement of her caliber would not be available for what the parish appears to be willing to pay.

It is highly doubtful that the recommended 50% pay increase actually occurred, but it is safe to assume that some substantive changes were made to acknowledge the reality that St. George's had been underpaying its Music Staff for many, many years. Fr. Johnson, who had been so supportive of Wilma and the music program, retired in 1989. Associate Rector Fr. Edwin Coleman stepped in as interim while a search was undertaken for the first new Rector at St. George's in seventeen years.

1990

After the exciting events of the previous year, the Adult Choir experienced some turnover in 1990. Several paid singers left to pursue their careers elsewhere, which resulted in what Choir members liked to call "a kinder, gentler Choir," as several large personalities were among those who moved on. A number of exceptional parishioners also joined the Choir around this time, many of whom are still members.

In addition to regular services, there were seven concerts in 1990, including the St. Olaf Symphonic Band and an organ concert by Diane Belcher, which was sponsored by the American Guild of Organists. The Choir presented two concerts, one of which was the Fauré *Requiem* with the 1888 chamber orchestra for All Saints' Day. Four hundred people were in attendance.

The St. Dunstan's Choir was thriving under the leadership of Nylea Butler-Moore. Fifty-six children in kindergarten through fifth grade participated, singing at events such as the annual Blessing of the Pets and the Advent Fair.

Fr. Julien Gunn praised the importance of music in worship in an article in the November issue of *The Dragon Watcher*, as well as sounding an important reminder:

> Music started with creation. Are we not told so when the Lord God broke His silence and rebuked Job: Where were you..."When the morning stars sang together, And all the sons of God shouted for joy?" [Job 38:4, 7].
>
> ...Just as soon as Christianity came out of the age of persecution, special attention was devoted to music appropriate to public worship. From then on down through the ages, even in spite of the divisions within Christendom, singing and music have played an important part in worship.
>
> We as Episcopalians have inherited from our mother, the Church of England, a distinctive tradition of the finest of sacred music. St. George's Church now has as fine a choir as can be matched by any parish choir in this country. However much we may enjoy our great tradition, we must always bear in mind that organ and song are primarily being employed to the praise of God the Father, through the Son, by the Holy Spirit.

1991–1994

The congregation called the Rev. Joel T. Keys as its Rector in 1991. The next several years were a period of maintenance for the Adult Choir and experimentation for the children's music program. In 1992, a Girls Treble Choir was started with ten singers. In 1993, boys with unchanged voices were added, and the group grew to twelve members. However, the group disbanded the following year due to lack of participation. St. Dunstan's Choir, despite several changes in leadership, continued to prosper with numbers ranging from twenty to forty participants.

Although the Choir's load was lightened when it stopped singing the 7:00 a.m. service on Easter morning in 1991, the primary issue raised in the Annual Reports for this period was the demand placed on staff and volunteer singers alike by the two Sunday morning services:

A review of the time commitment for the professional singers will need to be made at the beginning of 1994. The four hour Sunday morning commitment of two preservice rehearsals and two services has become a drain both vocally and emotionally. Dividing the volunteers between two services causes difficulties musically. The volunteers are an important and integral part of the total ensemble and provide some of the very best members of the choir. St. George's is the only choir in town responsible for two major Sunday morning services. . . . A new approach will need to be found to provide music for both services.

A new approach to music on Sundays may have been desired, but a new Rector was absolutely necessary. Fr. Keys became ill fairly early on in his tenure at St. George's, so Fr. Coleman stepped in once again in 1993 while yet another search was undertaken. In 1994, the congregation called the Rev. Dr. William Robert Abstein to take the position of Rector, and a new era began.

1995

There were two musical highlights worth noting in 1995. The first occurred on a regular Sunday morning. The Choir had been working very hard on a piece by Ennio Morricone—"On Earth as It Is in Heaven"—better known as the theme from the movie *The Mission*. Wilma had arranged the work for oboe, timpani, and organ, and Nashville Symphony member Bobby Taylor was on hand to play "Gabriel's Oboe," which is both a solo piece and a theme throughout the anthem. As stunning as the anthem was on its own, it was made even more meaningful at the eleven o'clock service when Associate Rector Rick Sanders made it the focus of his sermon. It was a very moving experience for both Choir and congregation.

On May 7, the Choir sang an a cappella concert, which it repeated in July for the Regional Convention of the American Guild of Organists. After several years of rebuilding following the tour of Europe, the Choir was once again hitting its musical stride.

1996

Three additions were made to the Choir schedule in 1996. The first was the institution of an Easter Vigil service on the Saturday evening before Easter. Introduced to St. George's by Associate Rector Mark Wilson, the service continues to be an important and beautiful part of the Choir's Holy Week offerings.

The Christmas Eve services had gotten so overcrowded that an additional service was added at 6:30 p.m. A quartet and trumpet provided the music.

On a less sacred note, the third addition was a series of mini-concerts presented after the single ten o'clock service during the month of June. Choir members prepared a variety of musical styles in order to come out from behind the altar and introduce themselves to the congregation.

Other special offerings for the year included a service of Compline in April and a concert in mid-November that featured works by Marcel Dupré in honor of the twenty-fifth anniversary of his death. This concert was accompanied by Mary Catherine Race, a college student and protégée of Wilma who had accompanied the Choir on occasion from the time she was in high school.

1997

The Easter music for 1997 was of sufficient interest to warrant an advance article in *The Dragon Watcher*:

> Easter music... will include festival anthems with choir, brass quintet, timpani, orchestral chimes and organ. An opening procession will include the "Entrata Festiva" by Flor Peeters followed by the hymn "Jesus Christ is Risen Today" and a stirring "Introit for a Feast Day" by the late Larry King, formerly of Trinity Church, Wall Street, New York City. The introit features orchestral chimes, used at St. George's for the first time. The Offertory anthem by Widor, the famed organist of Saint-Sulpice, Paris, was originally written for choir and two organs. Eberhard Ramm of Nashville has arranged the score for organ and brass quintet playing the second organ

part. Wilma Jensen and Mary Race have written an English translation of this out-of-print score for St. George's Choir to sing. In addition to an interesting Baroque composition by Hammerschmidt and the Duruflé "Ubi Caritas," two sonorous a cappella works by Sergei Rachmaninoff from the *All Night Vigil*, usually referred to as *The Vespers* will be sung.

The fall of 1997 was another momentous period for music at St. George's. For the first time in many years, the Music Staff was expanded. Elizabeth Smith was hired as Assistant Organist in September. An exceptionally fine accompanist, Elizabeth received both bachelor's and master's degrees in organ performance from the University of Alabama. Her organ teachers included Warren Hutton in Alabama and Peter Hurford in Cambridge, England.

The Festival of Lessons and Carols was reinstated after a long absence with all choirs participating, but the musical highlight of the year was the recording of the first Choir CD in almost twenty-five years. *Music at St. George's* featured "beautiful but not generally known repertoire," as Wilma described it in her Annual Report, including the two pieces previously mentioned from *The Mission*. The CD was distributed by Pro Organo, a nationally known recording company. A review of the CD on Amazon.com states:

> This is easily one of the finest CD's ever produced from a US church. The choir is absolute perfection (thankfully devoid of vibrato), the organ is mighty and the acoustical environment very reverberant. The selections delicious. The icing is the use of instrumentalists throughout the disc which broadens the appeal to a wide range of listeners. All very artfully controlled by master musician Jensen.

Nashville Scene contributor Marcel Smith had this to say about the CD when it was released:

> The level of performance, though not flawless, is very high indeed. This is remarkable in a number of ways. For one thing, two out of three of the performers do it for the love of it. The choir, numbering about forty-five, has a professional

core of sixteen singers.... Christi John's voice, one of the youngest, embodies perhaps the most remarkable single feature of this choir: the rare clarity and accuracy of the sopranos. There is not a single crow in the tree. Not even Robert Shaw, in his large ensembles, completely avoids shriekery at the top. There are other Nashville vocal ensembles that sing very well—but none I know has a soprano section to equal this one.

The music ... is varied and challenging stuff.... All the music, including the two selections from *The Mission*, is appropriate for high liturgical worship. Even so, some of it contains "modern" dissonances that let the singers show how good their ears are. "Carol of the Hill" by Stephen Paulus (b. 1949), "Crux Fidelis" by Roger-Ducasse (d. 1954), and "O Salutaris" by Pierre Villette (b. 1926) show off this aspect of the full choir's disciplined musicianship.

Music at St. George's is what it is because the music director and organist, Wilma Jensen, knows what she's doing. She selects her singers carefully. She groups them so the voices blend to the best advantage. She prepares them properly. And they perform as an ensemble in the same league with the best ensembles anywhere.

1998

The music program continued to expand and improve. Angela Tipps was hired in a part-time position to reorganize and revitalize the Children's Choir program. Her efforts resulted in the restoration of St. Cecilia's Choir and the Youth Choir, which joined St. Dunstan's in singing the 8:45 service one Sunday a month. Adult Choir members Dorothy Campbell, Bryant Tanner, and Lucy Organ assisted Angela with conducting responsibilities. Approximately fifty children were involved in the three choirs.

Although the inclusion of Renaissance dancers had been a minor disaster in 1986, Wilma decided to risk using liturgical dancers for Lessons and Carols in 1998. The Epiphany dancers joined the Choir for three carols and utterly transfixed the congregation. The lovely "Still, Still, Still" by Norman Luboff, a piece that the Choir had done every Christmas for many years, took on new meaning through the dancers' interpretation of the words. The inclusion of the dancers was so popular that they continued to appear with the Choir for Lessons and Carols for the next four years.

1999

The year 1999 was punctuated by special events throughout. A listing of concerts was included in the annual music report for the year:

January 3   Roslyn Carolane organ recital—Australian organist
March 8   Ann Elise Smoot organ recital, sponsored by Nashville Chapter of the American Guild of Organists

April 11   Wilma Jensen organ recital
April 13   Corpus Christi College Choir, Cambridge, England
April 26   Vanderbilt University Symphonic Choir and Orchestra
Sept. 12   Concerto program for the 50th Anniversary of St. George's celebration—Elizabeth Smith and Wilma Jensen, organ soloists with forty-three piece orchestra. Carol Nies, conductor.
Oct. 10   Robert Munns organ recital—guest English organist
Dec. 13   Nashville Youth Symphony—Carol Nies, conductor

The Adult Choir is conspicuously absent from the list, but there was good reason. In August, the Choir was busy recording its second CD, *Christmas at St. George's*. Like the earlier CD, this recording was very well received. A review in *The American Organist* said:

> Wilma Jensen leads choir and instrumentalists at St. George's Episcopal Church, Nashville, Tenn., with accompanist Elizabeth Smith (1986 Casavant, III/85). If the Nashville scene were to lose all of its country-western potentates, a praiseworthy "scene" still would exist, and queen of same would be Wilma Jensen, who for nearly two decades has refined her choir to the highest level of quality. Rhythmically coherent, precise of pitch, and united in enunciation, ensemble and attitude, the fifty-plus volunteer and professional voices sing with clarity and conviction. Their style is non-dogmatic, non-vibrato singing that is incisive and rich as necessary, and their program is refreshingly full of delectable and unhackneyed recent repertoire, with just enough old favorites to keep things friendly. The overall emotional content emphasizes the reflective elements of the Christmas mystery. ... For refreshment and sheer beauty, this is a disc that can be enjoyed year-round.

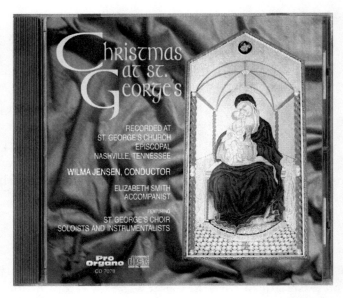

Both CDs have recently been re-released by Pro Organo and continue to enjoy air play on radio stations across the country.

2000–2001

In the spring of 2000, the church completed a large building project, which included a new wing of kindergarten classrooms, a suite of administrative offices, and most exciting for the Choir, a music suite. The Ingram Music Suite included a large Choir room with a music library space, a smaller rehearsal room, an office for Wilma, an office with adjoining storage to be shared by Elizabeth and the part-time music secretary, and robing rooms for the men and women. Just before Easter, the Choir moved in, although it would be several more months before the project was entirely complete.

As wonderful as it was to be in new and better surroundings, the turn of the century would prove to be a challenging time for the Choir. Wilma's health appeared to be failing, and no diagnosis could be made. She pressed on with her commitments at church and elsewhere, but she was clearly not well. The situation progressed to the point that longtime Choir member Tim Fudge, who had been substituting for Wilma for some time, stepped in as Interim Choirmaster while Wilma took a medical leave of absence. In a recent conversation, Tim explained how it happened that he was asked to take over:

> I moved to Nashville on March 15, 1987. It was a Sunday and I stayed with my friend Nylea Butler-Moore and she was already one of the paid altos there [at St. George's]. . . . So literally two weeks later, I was at St. George's. I went that next week—it was the first official job I had in Nashville. I loved it. Wilma was a little intimidating, but I loved it.
>
> So I sang for years and years and years. Then in the nineties . . . I can't remember a specific year . . . but I had done lots of work for Wilma because I was an actor and always looking for work. She was always really good to me. We had a conversation one day when I was over there working at the church with her. I was just telling her how much I missed conducting—that it was really what I had thought I was going to do. . . . So Wilma encouraged me. She said, "Well, I'll let you conduct a piece for the Choir some time." So I did that. I wish I could remember more specifically about what the piece was or when it was—it was probably at Communion or some inconspicuous time. And I just loved it. And she gave me some criticism, but constructive criticism. And the Choir knew me so well by then anyway that they were really receptive to it. And so over the course of those years, during the nineties, she got more comfortable with giving me more responsibility.
>
> I officially became the Interim Music Director in January of 2002. But I had been the Music Director essentially before then because Wilma was sick and she had been sick several times throughout the year of 2001 and I had to take over.

Wilma was indeed comfortable with putting the Choir in Tim's hands. She spoke about Tim recently:

> He would say in rehearsal, the tenors . . . we're having a little trouble with such and such. That didn't mean he was having trouble. He meant his sidekicks were having trouble—could

Tim Fudge.

we go over that again. And he was always very professional about it. And he was such a fine ensemble singer that, if he was gone, there was a difference in the men's ensemble somehow. I mean, he was a very good musical influence—not only vocally but rhythmically. He knew everything I was saying already and he had good training before and was innately musical.

Tim's training and experience with the Choir made him an ideal Interim Choirmaster. He was a graduate of Furman University where he earned a bachelor's degree in music with an emphasis on vocal performance. Tim had also done graduate work at Winthrop University where he was the graduate assistant in choral conducting. With Tim at the podium and Elizabeth at the organ, both with an intimate knowledge of Wilma's approach with the Choir, the transition was fairly smooth. As Tim said in the 2001 Annual Report, he and Elizabeth

> worked together to maintain the high level of musicality that Wilma Jensen has established for this choir. Thanks to her

Tim conducting the choir before a service.

wonderful planning and attention to detail, there has been little change in the quality of music for the various services presented during her absence.

As the months went by, questions lingered about when or if Wilma would be able to return to the Choir. In January 2002, after almost nineteen years of service, Wilma retired from St. George's.

2002

Wilma's retirement demanded a grand gesture from the church she had served so faithfully. Tim came up with the idea of a concert featuring Wilma's former organ students and the Choir. He talked about the process of organizing the event:

> We didn't necessarily know that many people, so the ones we knew for sure were Janette Fishell and James Melichamp, who had been visiting. They had both kept close tabs during her illness. So I approached them first and I said, "Would you all be willing to do this concert? I just think we really need to honor Wilma for years of service, not only here but

in the musical community." And Janette said, "I think that's a fantastic idea. I'm there." I mean, she didn't hesitate. And neither did James. And I said, "What I need is some names and email addresses of people that might be good people to contact." And so they were great and word of mouth sort of spread and we actually had more people who wanted to participate than we had room for, but they came anyway. I mean a lot of people came who did not perform. And what I tried to do is, with the ones who maybe weren't the big stars, was to let them accompany some things. I think Elizabeth only accompanied maybe one or two things. But it was very complicated!

We got Sandra Willetts, she was on board. . . . And I talked with local people like John Semingson and Angela Tipps, who all participated in various ways. And we just started working out the program. So various organists sent me what pieces they might want to do. . . . I wanted to focus mostly on her organ students, who were a huge part of her life, and then you know, like "Gabriel's Oboe" with Bobby Taylor from the Symphony, you know those kinds of things, and then Jeff Bailey, who she just adored. And then I knew there were some special pieces like Gloria [Parvin] singing the "Pie Jesu" from the Duruflé *Requiem*, which had meant a lot to Wilma once upon a time. I was trying to think of some of the pieces that Wilma always talked about a lot. So that's how we came up with those sorts of things; it was just whatever struck me as I could remember and talking with Elizabeth about what might be good. Elizabeth was very, very gracious. . . . She was just a great support and helped steer me if I was really headed in the wrong direction. She gently steered me back to where I needed to be.

So we got all the pieces in place and I really had this vision of doing the Randall Thompson "Ye Shall Have a Song" in the round in that space. So I asked Sandra [Willetts] to conduct that. That's how we started the concert.

As late as the week before the concert, there was concern that Wilma would not be able to attend. In addition to her other ailments, she had to have back surgery early in 2002, and her recovery was slow. However, Choir members persisted, and the concert was given on the afternoon of May 5 with Wilma in attendance. Tim gave an account of it in his Annual Report:

> Former organ students and colleagues from across the United States came to pay tribute to her [Wilma Jensen]. Nine organists played on the concert and many more were in the congregation. Former Choir members returned to sing four anthems with the current St. George's Choir. A total of seventy Choir members sang on the program including a solo by former Choir member, Gloria Parvin. Jeff Bailey, trumpeter, and Bobby Taylor, oboist, both of the Nashville Symphony, each presented a solo. Dr. Sandra Willetts, a former colleague of Wilma's at Scarritt University, conducted the Choir on two anthems, and Interim Choirmaster Tim Fudge conducted the other two anthems. One of the anthems was a piece commissioned especially for the occasion, which was written by Blair organ professor and composer Carl Smith. Interspersed throughout the concert were readings of excerpts from letters sent by friends and colleagues that were included in a "Memory Book" presented to Wilma along with a monetary gift at the end of the concert.

A CD was made of the concert, the proceeds of which went into a retirement fund for Wilma. As magnificent an event as the concert was, the most moving part of the celebration came the night before, when friends, family, and colleagues gathered at the church for a catered dinner in Wilma's honor. After Wilma thanked everyone for being there, a series of spontaneous testimonials began in which many of those present talked about their experience with Wilma and how she had impacted their lives. It was a weekend that still amazes Tim, who said,

Elizabeth Smith and Tim Fudge.

> To be perfectly honest, I don't know how we pulled it all off. I mean I think back to, how did I manage to get all of those people here? We offered nothing, basically—just the sheer joy of coming and being on the program and honoring Wilma. And everybody loved her and had such fond memories that they were willing to do that.... I know I had a lot of help, that's all I know, to pull it all off. I had a lot of help from the Choir and Elizabeth—everybody had ideas and helped pull it all together.

What was even more amazing was the impact the event had on Wilma herself. The source of her illness had finally been diagnosed, and her body was beginning to heal. It was the dinner and the concert, however, that began to heal her spirit. She stated,

Looking back, we now know exactly what it was. It was a reaction to a medication. And then I just made it so much worse by going to doctor after doctor getting high-powered drugs. And finally someone in this church [Charlie Wells, neuropsychiatrist] . . . he said, "I think your system is being poisoned. I think you need to see Dr. Petrie." I waited many months for an appointment, and then the rest is history.

What a history it has been! Since 2003, Wilma has given multiple concerts in America and Europe, including a return engagement at Notre Dame in Paris, taught numerous master classes all over the country, and produced a two-DVD teaching video that was released in 2011. Upon her retirement, Wilma was given the title of Organist-Choirmaster Emerita. When asked about her legacy at St. George's, Wilma had this to say:

I think when people heard the Choir, they were moved. The name of my teaching video for organ is "Organizing Notes in Space," and I think that's also what the conductor does. And if those notes are so well organized with the text to proclaim the text and if the sound itself is beautiful and there are subtle crescendos and diminuendos, it can be so beautiful it's moving. And I think, although we didn't have the money or the facilities to record all those services, which is my one great regret, there was something that communicated. And I think I have that ability in my playing and my teaching and in my conducting with the Choir to communicate the music. And you can build in intuitive responses to the music.

Wilma Jensen.

I think the notes aren't enough. Even the good sound isn't enough. This is that added dimension, which I feel communicates. What's most important in music happens in between the notes.

In the midst of the planning and executing of the concert, Tim, Elizabeth, and the Choir continued to prepare music for weekly services and special events. The annual Festival of Lessons and Carols featured a piece that Tim composed especially for the event. Based on the Scripture reading about Abraham and Isaac, *The Promise* was a wonderful addition to the repertoire. Tim said,

> Elizabeth and I were agonizing over that year, you know, finding pieces that worked well and that one particular scripture we just couldn't seem to find anything. . . . And I literally remember lying in my bed one night after we had been talking about it and trying to figure it out and this idea popped into my head. And the sound of it kind of popped into my head. And I immediately started working on it. And it came pretty quickly.

Along with the debut of the new piece, Lessons and Carols in 2002 featured a finale of sorts. It was the last time that the Epiphany dancers appeared with the Choir.

By this time, a search committee had been formed to find a permanent replacement for Wilma Jensen and was well under way with fulfilling its charge. The Rector and Vestry had decided to eliminate the position of Organist-Choirmaster, choosing instead to have a full-time Organist and a full-time Director of Music. Elizabeth Smith was hired as the Organist, leaving the search committee to find a Director of Music whose primary responsibilities would be planning the music and choral conducting. An additional charge to the search committee was to find someone who had the skills to institute a more comprehensive music program for the children and youth of the church.

The committee received dozens of résumés from across the country—a testament to the reputation of the music program at St. George's. After careful consideration and visiting several candidates at their home churches, the committee recommended that Dr. Murray Forbes Somerville be hired.

2003

As Dr. Somerville had previous commitments that prevented his arrival until September, Tim Fudge continued as Interim Choirmaster until the fall of 2003. In addition to planning and preparing music for Holy Week and Easter services, Tim and Elizabeth began to prepare the Choir for a previously scheduled performance of the Brahms *Requiem* that would take place in November. The concert was a joint venture with the Choir of Westminster Presbyterian Church under the direction of Dr. John Semingson, former Organ Assistant at St. George's. When Murray arrived, Tim decided not to resume his position as a staff singer in the Choir to allow Murray to establish his leadership with the Choir. Murray had this to say about Tim and the interim team in his Annual Report:

> The parish owes an immense debt of gratitude to Timothy Fudge for his superb work as interim choirmaster, as well as to Dorothy Campbell and Lucy Organ for their work in keeping St. Dunstan's Choir going; while Elizabeth Smith, with her supreme competence, diligence, and charm, is a treasure beyond price.

Tim continued his professional singing and acting career and served as Music Director for a variety of productions around Nashville before joining the staff of St. Augustine's Chapel on the Vanderbilt University campus.

Dr. Murray Forbes Somerville was born in London and raised in Rhodesia (now the Republic of Zimbabwe). His first experience in church music was as a

Dr. Murray Forbes Somerville.

seven-year-old. His mother was reportedly delighted for him to join the men and boys choir at the local parish because his constant singing around the house was "getting on her nerves." His mother was apparently not the only one who found Murray's early musical interest tedious. In the midst of one of Murray's marathon practice sessions on the piano, a visiting aunt offered him half a crown to stop playing. Later, when she heard him playing the organ on a radio program, she told him that she "rather regretted having asked him to stop practicing."

Murray trained in Munich, Germany, with Karl Richter, a renowned expert in the works of Bach. From Munich, Murray went to Oxford University in the United Kingdom, where he was Organ Scholar of New College under Sir David Lumsden. He went on to receive advanced degrees from the School of Sacred Music at Union Theological Seminary in New York City (Master of Sacred Music), where he studied under Robert Baker, and from the New England Conservatory of Music in Boston, Massachusetts (Doctor of Music Arts).

Murray served at St James's Church in West Hartford, Connecticut, and at the Cathedral of St. Luke in Orlando, Florida, where he founded the Orlando Deanery Boychoir. Murray also served as the Music Director for the Bach Festival at Rollins College in Winter Park, as Chorus-master to the Florida Symphony Orchestra, and has also worked with the Orlando Opera Company. In 1990, he was appointed the University Organist and Choirmaster at Harvard University where he was busy with the University Choir and as Curator of the University Organs. Murray did a number of recordings while at Harvard, both as an organ soloist and with the University Choir. Clearly Murray was exactly the one the search committee had been looking for.

In addition to continuing the fine music tradition represented by the Adult Choir, Murray was charged with revitalizing the lapsed music program for children and youth. Murray was more than up to the challenge. He was an Associate of Britain's Royal School of Church Music (RSCM), a program that includes teaching young singers not only singing techniques, but also the elements of the Anglican/

Episcopal services and "how to be a good choir member." Having conducted weeklong training courses for children and young people each summer in the United States, Canada, and the United Kingdom, Murray set up an RSCM program at St. George's. The St. Dunstan's Choir included third through seventh graders, and the Youth Choir was re-formed with an initial group of twelve eighth through twelfth graders. Within a year, and with the volunteer assistance of Murray's wife, Hazel, who also held a position at the Blair School of Music at Vanderbilt, these two choirs had a combined thirty-two members.

As previously mentioned, the Choir participated in a joint performance of the Brahms *Requiem* in November with the Westminster Presbyterian Church Choir and full orchestra. Murray described the other musical events of 2003 in his Annual Report:

> December began with a beautiful service of Lessons and Carols, in which the Youth Choir and St. George's Choir were joined by the Nashville Boychoir at Blair, under my wife's direction; and Christmas Eve was marked by three services. At the first, St. Dunstan's Choir sang *The Birds of Bethlehem* by Richard Shephard for the Offertory; before the midnight service, St. George's Choir was joined by baroque violinist Rebecca Tinio from the Harvard Baroque Chamber Orchestra, as well as Rebecca Cole of the Nashville Symphony and June Williams of Blair School of Music, for Charpentier's *Song of the Birth of Our Lord Jesus Christ*.

Murray added Anglican chant psalms to the Adult Choir's repertoire for the 11:10 service, a tradition that has continued. Murray also discovered a continuing issue in his first year at St. George's:

> As we look towards the future, our hope is that this growth in the program can continue. For a parish this size, the percentage of participation in the music program by both adults and children is still on the low side; here in "Music City, USA" our hope is that more and more singers and players, young and old, will be encouraged to come forward and nurture their talents to enrich our worship and to glorify the Lord in praise.

2004

Murray's first full year at St. George's was an eventful one. His connections to Karl Richter in Munich and other Bach enthusiasts enabled him to bring an unusual opportunity to the Choir. Murray was in possession of a previously lost manuscript by C. P. E. Bach, the most musical of the sons of J. S. Bach. As Murray told the story:

> I don't remember when in the [search] process I mentioned [that] I happened to have in my briefcase this music for C. P. E. Bach's 1769 St Matthew Passion and would the church be interested in doing it and I could see the eyes sort of open.

The performance, a U.S. premiere, took place on March 28, featuring the forty members of St. George's Choir, the Nashville Symphony, soloist Randall Black as the Evangelist, and Keith Moore as Jesus. Elizabeth played the organ. A generous donation by parishioner Martha Ingram made the program possible. Apart from its being a wonderful event in and of itself, the concert renewed interest in presenting a concert series at St. George's.

In May 2004, Wilma Jensen played "A Concert in the French Tradition" including pieces from Frank James, Vierne, Cochereau, Widor, Bonnet and Tournemire, and Alexander Russell, a native of Tennessee and student of Widor. The concert was masterfully performed and warmly received.

In the fall, the change of seasons brought other changes as well. Organist Elizabeth Smith left in November to take over Lois Fyfe Music. Her final performance with the Choir was the *Requiem* by Gabriel Fauré in a liturgical setting, with an orchestra funded by donations. Fr. Abstein said of Elizabeth upon her departure:

> I have enjoyed her accompanying our singers in our June mini-concerts where she calmly switches from opera to gospel and from Broadway to country.

The Choir sadly said good-bye to splendid musician and friend. Not long thereafter, the church learned that it would be saying good-bye to another good friend, Fr. Abstein, who announced his intention to retire in January 2005.

A new Organist was needed, and the church didn't have to search very far to find one. Gerry Senechal began his musical career at the age of eight when he became Organist of his father's Episcopal church. He joined the All Saints' Men and Boys Choir of Worcester, Massachusetts, and eventually was named Head Chorister. Beginning in 1994, Gerry served as Organist of Oakdale United Methodist Church in West Boston, Massachusetts. He attended the University of the South, where he received two prestigious music awards: the Judy Running Memorial Prize and Gilbert Gilchrist Memorial Music Award. Gerry had just completed a two-year music internship at West End United Methodist Church in Nashville, a mere three miles down the road from St. George's, when Murray hired him to join the Music Staff. Having been a chorister himself, Gerry was a natural fit for working with the young people in the Youth Choir.

With Lessons and Carols and three Christmas Eve services fast approaching, Gerry had to hit the ground running when he arrived at St. George's. One of his first responsibilities was to accompany the forty-second Annual Community Thanksgiving Service, for which St. George's hosted Choir members from eleven local churches, The Temple, and West End Synagogue. Lessons and Carols followed just twelve days later, which included an appearance by the Nashville Boychoir under the direction of Hazel Somerville.

The pre-service concert for the late Christmas Eve service was accompanied by a new musical group in town. Dr. George Riordan, a celebrated Baroque musician and husband of Karen Clarke, also a celebrated Baroque musician, telephoned Murray to see if he was interested in a little Baroque "jam session." Together with the creative energies of other local Baroque artists and enthusiasts, Murray founded Belle Meade Baroque (now known as Music City Baroque). St. George's was happy to play a supporting role in getting the group started

Gerry Senechal.

by providing a concert venue. If only Murray had known about the Renaissance dancers!

2005

Fr. Abstein celebrated his last service at St. George's on the final Sunday in January. Murray remembered the occasion in his Annual Report:

> We . . . bid adieu to Fr. Abstein, former boy chorister, who so enjoyed giving the new RSCM medals to St. Dunstan's choristers (especially his granddaughter!). And who could forget his air timpani on final processional hymns? His farewell service, with hand-picked anthems by Gounod and Mendelssohn, was a musical feast—and we wondered what the future would bring.

While the church waited to welcome a new Rector, the music program rolled on. The spring concert series included the Washington University Choir from St. Louis; the Boston Camerata under the direction of Joel Cohen with the Nashville Boychoir; and the Choir of New College, Oxford, under the direction of Dr. Edward Higginbottom. Murray was delighted to welcome the singers from his alma mater to St. George's. The concert was co-sponsored by the Nashville Chapter of the American Guild of Organists. In addition to these offerings, the Choir sang a Lenten Evensong, joined by the Linden Consort of Viols, featuring the U.S. premiere of the new edition of the *Magnificat and Nunc Dimittis (Second Service)* by Orlando Gibbons.

On May 1, the Choir sang at a special service to "Celebrate the New Ministry of The Reverend Robert Leigh Spruill as Rector." It was a grand occasion with trumpets and timpani. Any fears about a new Rector meaning a change in musical direction were quickly allayed. As Murray's Annual Report said:

> We have a Rector whose mother was a church musician, who taught a class on hymnody at his last parish, who knows the *Hymnal 1982* almost better than the two musicians on staff, and who sings beautifully! . . . We continue to feel supported and upheld.

The music program got some technical help with an upgrade to the church's sound system, which included the installation of microphones over the Choir and recording equipment at the back of the Nave. Murray also enlisted some help from parishioners in a new effort to involve more congregants in the music program, inviting them to come and sing with the Choir several times a year. Fondly called "Ya'll Come Sing," these occasions turned out several singers, including Fr. Spruill at one point.

Murray's efforts with the Royal School of Church Music (RSCM) program for the children began to bear fruit in the spring and summer of 2005. A first and second grade choir was under way under the direction of Hazel Somerville and staff singer Mary Fishburne. As May concluded, St. Dunstan's Choir led the 11:15 a.m. service on their own as part of Youth Sunday celebrations. During the summer, twelve of those young singers attended RSCM courses in places such as the National Cathedral in Washington, D.C.; Montreal, Canada; Wilkes-Barre, Pennsylvania; and Mobile, Alabama, conducted by well-known and experienced directors. They returned, as Murray said, "with twice the volume and twice the confidence." One of the singers, Gage Baxter, called the trip to Montreal "the best week of his life." In July, several young singers went to the Sewanee Church Music Conference along with singers from the Blair Children's Choruses to serve as the demonstration choir for Bruce Neswick of St. Philip's Cathedral in Atlanta. When the new school year arrived, Gerry took over the direction of the older singers, forming a Youth Choir, while Murray continued directing the younger ones in St. Dunstan's. Giny Bailey, who had sung in the Youth Choir herself in the 1970s and who had three children in the choir program at St. George's, had this observation about the impact it had:

> Aside from the benefits of growing up singing in a choral program like the Voice for Life Program, and especially the spiritual and service benefits of singing in our church choirs, the most important element of the program for the singers and their families was the fellowship the children enjoyed with each other on a weekly basis.... It gave a sense of purpose and belonging to those kids in the large corporate

church setting of St. George's, which had three thousand members at the time, and for that I was supremely grateful.

In August, the Adult Choir went on the first overnight Choir Retreat to Montgomery Bell State Park for some intensive rehearsal in preparation for the big events of the coming fall and winter, the first of which was a concert that Murray described in his Annual Report:

> In September . . . the choir peformed Haydn's *Harmoniemesse* (or "Wind-band mass" from the unusually extensive woodwind scoring) with the Nashville Symphony, a most rewarding work for singers and audience alike.

The program also included Haydn's *Oxford Symphony #93*.

In the life of any institution, there are members who are considered to be pillars, who underpin its life and culture and are an embodiment of its history. In September 2005, after twenty-five years as a staff singer, Lucille David retired from "active singer" status, leaving a gaping hole that has yet to be filled. Lucille sang with the Robert Shaw Chorale in her earlier years. She was pronunciation coach in many languages for the Choir, as she had been for Wilma Jensen. She could also bring down the house with her rendition of "Minnie the Moocher" at Choir parties, even at an age that was never discussed but was certainly well over seventy. An alto in her Robert Shaw days, Lucille sang tenor with St. George's Choir and never missed a rehearsal or a service except in extraordinary circumstances. She was a teacher to many in her section and an inspiration to the Choir as a whole.

Looking forward to the new year, Murray wrote a conclusion to his lengthy Annual Report:

> We are delighted to know that musical excellence emerged as one of the four most important ways St. George's is perceived in the parish self-definition exercise concluded this summer as part of its media strategic plan. Rewarding but also challenging; for as Fr. Spruill has pointed out, the danger in institutions is always for areas of success to be taken for granted and so not given the attention or the resources necessary to maintain the standard. To try and avoid falling

Lucille David.

into this trap, the Rector has called together a music long-range planning committee, under the auspices of the Vestry, with Calvin Lewis as chairman, to develop a five-year plan for the music department, to be incorporated into the parish strategic planning currently under development. This committee begins its work in January, to conclude later in the spring. [The report of that committee can be found in the Appendices.] In this way we hope to be able to enable St. George's to continue to "worship the Lord in the beauty of holiness" so that our musical teams may bring to the parish "such glimpses of that beauty that we may in God's good time behold it unveiled for ever more."

2006

The first musical event of 2006 was a Choral Evensong prepared by the St. George's Choir and presented on the last Sunday of Epiphany. As an Englishman, Murray particularly enjoyed the Hospitality Committee's afternoon tea that was served prior to Evensong, featuring cucumber sandwiches adorned with Donia Dickerson's famed homemade mayonnaise. The following week the threat of snow prevented many people from enjoying New York's Ensemble for Early Music, which presented the medieval music drama *Daniel and the Lion*. Although the attendance was light, those who came marveled at the spectacular performance.

Many of the St. Dunstan's and Youth Choir singers participated in the Diocesan Chorister Festival at Christ Church Cathedral in February. This annual event is led by invited directors who are always well known and offer a wonderful opportunity for young singers. Murray was instrumental in obtaining the services of Sarah Baldock, the Assistant Director of Music at Winchester Cathedral (and the only female in that position in any English cathedral) to be the Choral Director of the Festival in 2006. Gerry served as Organist. In addition to the activities of the St. Dunstan's and Youth Choirs, the first and second grade choir continued to rehearse under the direction of Hazel Somerville. All of the children's music programs required and received copious amounts of volunteer help from parents. Murray singled out Vicki Adkins in his Annual Report for "sterling service as coordinator of this group."

The St. George's Choir took its first tour since 1989 by attending the Spoleto Festival in Charleston, South Carolina, where it was one of the few church choirs invited to perform. The audience at the Cathedral of St. Luke and St. Paul was suitably impressed. Murray reported that some in attendance "described it as one of the best choral concerts of the festival." The lead-up to the trip naturally included fund-raising events. Members of the Choir put on a talent show, which was generously supported by the parish. Some of the acts were superb and showcased a wide range of talent. Staff singers in particular may have surprised some in the audience with the imagination and artistry of their non-Anglican selections, which included gospel, barbershop, arias, and songs penned and performed by singer-songwriters in the group.

While the Adult Choir was in South Carolina, members of the Youth Choir were off participating in more RSCM courses, enlarging their repertoire of Anglican Church music under the leadership of such nationally and internationally known directors as Paul Trepte (Ely Cathedral, England), Michael McCarthy (National Cathedral, Washington, D.C.), and Tom Whittemore (Trinity Church, Trenton, New Jersey), among others. Choir Fund money supported the young singers in attending these courses. Their experiences were put to good use in the fall when the Youth Choir sang a Choral Evensong on their own. A few male singers from the Adult Choir assisted to cover bass and tenor lines.

The tradition of Lessons and Carols continued, involving all three choirs. One highlight was the premiere of *Mary's Lullaby*, written by Mary Ready Taylor, wife of Associate Rector Fr. Tim Taylor, and arranged by Gerry. For Christmas Eve, an old tradition was revived. The Youth and St. Dunstan's Choirs took primary musical responsibility for the family service at four o'clock, with assistance from volunteer members of the St. George's Choir on the congregational hymns. The children and youth presented Mark Schweizer's *Clown of God*, featuring Youth Choir member Ben Bailey. The late service was accompanied by a new chamber organ as the Adult Choir offered Haydn's *Little Organ Mass*.

2007

The new year began with the installation of the Rev. John Crawford Bauerschmidt as the eleventh Bishop of the Diocese of Tennessee. St. George's Choir members joined members of choirs from across the diocese, forming a massive joint choir to sing for the occasion. Musical leadership was provided by Michael Velting and Marjorie Proctor of

Christ Church Cathedral, assisted by Murray and Gerry. Murray and his wife, Hazel, played a special role in the proceedings, having commissioned a choral piece from Dr. Velting entitled *Rekindle the Gift of God That Is Within You* in honor of the new episcopate of the Rt. Rev. Bauerschmidt.

The spring brought with it more notable events, including two concerts by the Belle Meade Baroque. In February, the group was joined by guest concertmaster Robert Mealy, professor of early violin at Yale University School of Music, concertmaster of the Boston Early Music Festival, and staff member at the Julliard School. In May, St. George's Choir joined the group for a concert featuring works by Purcell, Teleman, and Corelli. However, the most exciting concert of the spring was presented by the Drakensberg Boychoir from South Africa. The mix of boys and young men, black and white, had an infectious energy and a glorious ensemble sound. For the second half of the program, the group sang South African folk songs, nearly bringing the house down with their rhythms, harmonizing, and choreography. It was a memorable evening, to be sure.

The St. George's Music Series went through a transformation over the summer and emerged as *In Excelsis: Musical Evenings at St. George's* in the fall. A group was formed to support the series financially. Friends of St. George's Music went about gathering support from music enthusiasts beyond the congregation. In the flyer that advertised the series, Murray said that the vision was to

> combine liturgical music and concerts by our own and visiting musicians in a rich tapestry of offerings to our parish and the wider community.

The offerings that fall were rich indeed. Claire Hodge, Director of the Orlanda Deanery Girls Choir at the Cathedral of St. Luke in Orlando, Florida, came as guest director for a Chorister Evensong with the children and youth. The Boston Camerata, directed by Joel Cohen, performed in November, and the St. George's Choir presented a Choral Evensong, also in November. The Choir's primary focus, however, was on preparing for a pilgrimage to Winchester Cathedral in England the following summer, at the end of which it would say good-bye to Murray, who had announced his intention to retire at that time.

2008

The year 2008 began with Bach's *St. John Passion*, presented by the Choir and accompanied by Belle Meade Baroque. In March, the Aulos Ensemble, Baroque chamber players from New York, gave a concert as part of the *In Excelsis* series. In May, Murray played a last recital at St. George's, which he called *Two Hands, Two Feet, Six Keyboards*, so named because he played pieces on the chamber organ (two keyboards), the harpsichord (one keyboard), and the Casavant organ (three keyboards). It was a marvelous display of Murray's virtuosity and a fitting farewell to the church.

The impending "pilgrimage to our Anglican roots," as the England trip was described, involved a great deal of preparation. As with the other tours, fund-raising had to be done. Perhaps the most unusual activity in that realm involved selling concessions at Bridgestone Arena during hockey games. Choir members earned money for the trip by serving popcorn, hot dogs, and beverages to hungry hockey fans. As Giny Bailey remembered:

> It is memorable when a patron asks what charity you are representing, and as you get the foam just right from the beer pull you say, "St. George's Church." It's just another example of a moment when it's fun to be an Episcopalian.

Hungry parishioners were fed at a fund-raising luncheon. Staff singer and professional chef Jerry Arnold did the cooking with assistance from longtime Choir member Mareike Sattler in the role of kitchen manager. Members of the Youth Choir waited on tables while a veritable assembly line of Choir members served plate in the kitchen. Light entertainment was provided by various Choir members as the meal concluded. While revenues from the event weren't particularly high, the esprit de corps of the Choir was soaring.

In mid-July the group set out. Members of the St. George's Choir and the Youth Choir were accompanied by family members and parishioners. The clergy was well-represented in the persons of Fr. Spruill and Fr. Roger Senechal, Gerry's father and Priest Associate at St. George's.

The first stop after landing in London was Windsor Castle, where the Choir had been granted special permission to sing one piece in St. George's Chapel, burial place of King Henry VIII. The Choir was given additional permission to pose on the steps outside the chapel that are generally reserved for portraits of the royal family. It was an auspicious beginning to the trip. After a day of sightseeing in London, the Choir gathered at St. Paul's Cathedral to sing Evensong. Giny Bailey remembered the experience:

> There is no way to describe the feeling that comes over you in the hush of that place, standing in those choir stalls with history whispering all around you and singing music written for that space, rests in the music timed perfectly for the length of time it takes for the sound to reach to the back of the Nave and then echo back to us. And then the next entrance, and on to the end of the piece, and the quiet that descends as the music drifts toward heaven.

The group moved on to the city of York, singing Evensong in York Minster. Gerry was in heaven playing what he says is "arguably the finest organ in all of England." More important, it is the church where Gerry's musical hero, Edward C. Bairstow, was the Organist. Members of the Choir were equally overcome when they had the opportunity to sing in the round Chapter House during a tour of the cathedral. Choir member Amy Weeks described what happened:

> Most of the Choir passed through the cathedral itself, and found ourselves in the Chapter House, the chamber that the monks used to hold the meetings of their order. A room with a huge vaulted ceiling, designed so that each brother could sit in his alcove against the circular wall and be heard perfectly by all his brothers.
>
> You could feel it when you stepped across the threshold.

Tour participants outside St. George's Chapel, Windsor Castle.

Choir at St. Paul's Cathedral, London.

Choir in the York Chapter House after Evensong.

That expectant hush, that distant crackle at the other end of the telephone line. This is a room made for communicating. Communing. Communion.

I'm not sure any words were spoken. It was an exchange of glances, no more. And suddenly the first notes of Duruflé's "Ubi Caritas" were rising up, almost unbidden, from the Choir. And all around us the hush intensified and tightened. All conversation ceased in the crowd of tourists surrounding us, as if they too had become a part of that breathless listening. All of us, wide-eyed with wonder, in communion with each other and with God.

There is a recording of us singing the "Ubi Caritas" in the Chapter House. It happened later, when we had gathered the whole Choir, passed out music, and set up a recorder in the middle of the room. It comes as close as anything will ever get to recapturing that moment.

"Ubi caritas et amor, Deus ibi est." ["Where charity and love are, God is there."]

The Youth Choir separated from the rest of the group to sing Sunday services at St. Mark's, Harrogate, while the St. George's Choir sang at Selby Abbey, ancestral home of George Washington. The Choir felt very much at home when they entered the church and saw the American flag hung across from the English flag in acknowledgment of the Washington family. The choirs joined up again for an afternoon concert in the Yorkshire dales at Bolton Abbey.

Murray would not have allowed the Choir to miss a trip to his alma mater. New College at Oxford University was founded in 1397. Murray and Hazel hosted a lovely dinner in the cloisters of the

Murray leads the group at New College, Oxford.

college, which had also been the site of some filming for the *Harry Potter* movies. The Choir sang a service of Compline in the New College chapel.

The Choir traveled on to its final destination of Winchester to begin its role as Choir in Residence at Winchester Cathedral for the final days of the tour. While excursions to Stonehenge, Salisbury Cathedral, and Portsmouth occupied the days, the late afternoons were given over to singing. Gerry described it in the Annual Report:

> At Winchester Cathedral, we were able to enter the regular worship rhythm of a glorious English cathedral, leading Choral Evensong each day. Our tour ended with all choirs singing three magnificent services on Sunday.

A highlight of the stay in Winchester was the very elderly priest who was manning the cathedral over the summer. Age notwithstanding, he rode his bicycle to church each day, wearing his self-proclaimed "helmet of righteousness." As cantor during Evensong, he relied on a tuning fork for his pitch. When the priest had a particularly difficult time getting the right note during rehearsal, Murray offered to give him his pitch with the organ. The priest demurred, saying, "I'll just have to fork it more forcefully!" A true Englishman. Father Spruill preached at one of the Sunday morning services.

The trip concluded with a dinner honoring Murray and Hazel Somerville and their contributions to the music program at St. George's. A more fitting end to Murray's tenure would be hard to imagine. He had spent five years increasing the Choir's knowledge of and appreciation for the Anglican tradition of music. He reestablished a thriving concert series, introducing the church and the wider community to exceptional musicians, both local and international. He had rebuilt the music

Priest at Winchester Cathedral.

Hazel and Murray Somerville on the last night in Winchester.

program for the children and youth of the church using the structure of the Royal School of Church Music. He took the singers, youth and adults alike, to the heart of Anglican worship and immersed the group in it for a wonderful ten days. It was the perfect way to say farewell.

When Murray made known his intentions to retire, the parish leadership set up a search committee to find a Music Director who would continue the tradition of excellence in music and worship long established at St. George's. When the Choir returned to Nashville from England, Gerry Senechal took on the role of Interim Director of Music until a replacement for Murray could be found. Gerry took on his responsibilities with enthusiasm:

> I was so delighted to have an Episcopal church and one of this magnificent stature and reputation.... The last time I had played in an Episcopal church regularly had been when I was eight until I was twelve in my father's tiny Episcopal church in Massachusetts.... I sang in the choir at Sewanee

Gerry conducts the choir retreat, 2008.

> for four years, but I hadn't done much playing at all. I was looking forward to being a mature Anglican player in a way that I hadn't been able to before.

In addition to completing his master's thesis and directing the St. George's Choir, Gerry continued to build on his success with the Youth Choirs. One of the first things Gerry did was to officially rename the Youth Choir (singers in grades eight through twelve), calling it St. Gregory's Choir. St. Dunstan's Choir (singers in grades three through seven) was to be an independent choir. He hired Laurel Fisher (MMA from Western North Carolina University, trained in the RSCM program, and St. George's Choir staff member) to the post of Children's Choral Assistant and set up a robust schedule for these young singers. Gerry said,

> What I would consider the focus of my ministry here would be the St. Gregory's Choir.... Murray asked me if I would

begin working with this group of I think it was six choristers who were the older age. The first year or two it was pretty rough. . . . I had no idea what I was doing. . . . Then slowly they began to catch on musically, and I began to catch on to things I could improve on. I began to see their spirit that was so exemplary. . . . If you give them a goal, they will do all they can to get there. They have never ceased to reach and exceed the bar that I've placed for them. . . . It brings joy to

Gerry awards RSCM medals.

my heart when I hear one of them walking by singing one of the great anthems of the tradition. They're going to keep those their whole lives, and you can't put a value on that.... Often people learn theology best through music. That they can have these things and they will always have them—that is amazing to me. I am so proud of that.

Gerry's efforts produced amazing results. Membership in both St. Dunstan's and St. Gregory's Choirs rose, and the musical abilities and refinements made by the singers were also tremendously encouraging. St. Gregory's Choir presented a Choral Evensong in the fall, prompting Gerry to note their accomplishments in his Annual Report:

> St. Gregory's Choir became one of a mere handful of choirs in the Southeast replicating the timeless English cathedral sound with pure treble tone on top and the richness of men below. The group sings some of the finest music of the Anglican tradition. Because of the beauty and authenticity with which St. Gregory's sings, the group has accepted an invitation to serve as Choir in Residence at the Washington National Cathedral in Washington, D.C. for one week during the summer of 2009. This is a great honor for which the Choir is prepared and ready, as well as a milestone for the Music Ministry of St. George's.

One of Gerry's contributions to the worship life of the church has been the regular inclusion of the service of Compline. The men of St. George's Choir began to offer this contemplative service each third Wednesday evening. The word *Compline* comes from the word *completion* and traces its beginnings to the early centuries of Christianity in southern Europe. The men of St. George's Choir gather in the apse and sing the entire service to the congregation gathered nearby and in the Nave. It continues to provide a peaceful time of introspection and prayer at the end of the day.

Technology became an integral part of the worship at St. George's when the services began to stream live over the Internet, so outreach became even more of a reality during this year. Emails began arriving, letting the choirs know that people all over the country and the world were worshipping with us weekly. In the Annual Report that year, Gerry noted, "We have received word that our nation's troops deployed in Afghanistan and Iraq regularly worship with us via the internet." Another technological advance aided the Choir immeasurably. The installation of video monitors in the apse enabled the choirs to be more involved in worship by allowing them to see more clearly what was happening in the service. This proved to be particularly helpful for sermons, during which the Choir had been unable to see the priests' faces.

The *In Excelsis* series hosted several noted groups, including a program by the Choir from Ely Cathedral. As the word spread that St. George's was the location to hear these fine Anglican choirs, the attendance increased.

As Gerry awaited the arrival of a new Director of Music, he ex-

Gerry at the organ in Winchester Cathedral.

pressed his own relationship to the Anglican tradition and his hopes for its continuation at St. George's:

> I was ruined at an early age by being a boy soprano in a men and boys choir. Having had zero experience with any sort of truly Anglican tradition before that, I was just awash in the great beauty of the tradition. I think I was maybe eleven when I started that. I thought, "This is amazing. This is how God deserves to be worshiped." That has informed my understanding of the tradition.... [St. George's] has the infrastructure in place ... to keep this great jewel of Anglican worship going strong. Already we are doing a great deal of good Anglican worship, and I think there are more specific ways, even more beautiful ways, even more dignified and strong ways that we can add to our worship in the tradition.
>
> Our job is to further facilitate the engagement between God and man. If that's not happening, it doesn't matter what we're doing; it's not right. Hymn singing is where the rubber meets the road for worshipers, where people can connect with God in a very special, a very holy way. I think that's why God invented music.

4

Anticipation

GINY AND JEFF BAILEY WITH JENNIFER ORTH

2009

It was late spring in 2009 when Dr. Mark Ring joined St. George's as the next leader in music ministry. The difficult search had begun more than twelve months earlier with the creation of a search committee of twelve parishioners who were asked by parish leadership and the Rector to search for a new *interpreter of Anglican tradition in musical worship*. The committee's kickoff meeting was held on April 2, 2008, and in that meeting Leigh's opening remarks highlighted the importance of this position's being more aptly named Director of Music Ministries (not simply Director of Music), emphasizing the importance of taking this opportunity to move "from strength to strength" in seeking someone who had exceptional gifts and experience, who was immensely talented, who had excellent credentials and, above all else, one who viewed this role as a ministry of the church that partners with the Rector and shares in the responsibility of church leadership. St. George's reputation in the Anglican tradition of music and worship drew applicants from all over the United States and Europe. Through prayer and thoughtful process, the committee recommended Dr. Mark Ring to the Rector.

Dr. Ring studied at Union University in Jackson, Tennessee, where he earned his Bachelor of Music in Organ Performance (summa cum laude) in 1988. He went on to Yale University, earning his Master of

Dr. Mark Ring.

Music in 1990, Master of Musical Arts in 1991, and Doctor of Musical Arts in 1996 from Yale's School of Music and Institute of Sacred Music. As part of that DMA program, Dr. Ring had a collegiate music and conducting internship at Notre Dame University. He studied conducting with Marguerite Brooks, Fenno Heath, Thomas Brooks, Donald Bailey, and Kenneth Hartley, along with private study with George Guest of St. John's College, Cambridge, and coaching with Charles Bruffy, Dale Warland, and Gunther Herbig. His organ teachers include Thomas Murray, Charles Krigbaum, Daniel Roth, and Scott Bennett.

After his time at Notre Dame, Mark became Director of Music at First Presbyterian Church in Libertyville, Illinois, which had more than thirteen choirs and six staff directors. He had been there only one year when family obligations prompted a move to Minnesota. Mark accepted the position of Director of Choirs at Moorhead High School as well as that of Choirmaster-Organist at Gethsemane Episcopal Cathedral in Fargo, North Dakota, where he served for ten years prior to coming to St. George's. At Moorhead he directed more than two hundred students in five choirs, including a touring choir. His program won eight consecutive Grammy Signature Honors. In addition he was the founder and Artistic Director/Conductor of Voices of Concord, a professional vocal chamber ensemble. He was also the Artistic Director of the Fargo-Moorhead Chamber Chorale.

Mark's association with his Organist and now Associate Director of Music Ministries, Gerry Senechal, was immediately fortuitous:

> [Gerry]'s a very, very fine colleague. I've never worked with a better service player in my life. I would say without qualification that he is one of the very finest service players in any Anglican Church in the world, period. He is just a joy to work with. We get along well personally and work extremely well together professionally. That is wonderful. It's a great team.

Mark arrived in Nashville just as St. George's was about to move into its summer schedule, which meant a single choral service at ten o'clock on Sunday mornings with a Choir rehearsal immediately beforehand. Sharing a common view on the Anglican music tradition, Mark and Gerry worked together with the clergy in shaping the worship services:

> Gerry and I [would] both bleed Anglican music if we're cut. We're absolutely immersed in this and have extremely consonant views in terms of the ethos of Anglican music in worship, much of the literature and the repertoire that's done stylistically, how you approach these things. The choirs, the kids coming up, one of the wonders of the RSCM [Royal School of Church Music] program is how it educates the kids: not only [by saying] "okay, we're going to sing this

number in worship" but also why [we are singing it], [giving a] historical background. [In RSCM] you learn by doing and seeing the role of music in liturgy, specific in our tradition. The Adult Choir has through the years evolved into more and more of an Anglican literature–centered choir. Doing Anglican chant every week changes the way you approach text and how you hear each other. This is all "sung prayer," and in the Anglican tradition we are what's called the "vicar's chorale." We sing the praises and prayers of the people on their behalf when we're singing. We don't sing to the congregation. We sing to God *on behalf of* the congregation. We talk about that openly [in rehearsal], seeing that role as important. It is a continuing education effort with the choirs because we've come from a variety of backgrounds. I see that as a positive and growing thing.

Mark's approach to directing certainly made an impression early on Choir members who observed his style during the interview process. His conducting pattern was clear to read, as were his dynamic cues. The Choir displayed an eagerness to partner in interpreting the works with him. A technical observation by one of the Choir members noted his "being able to beat time with right hand, while interpreting with left hand, and talking at the same time." Mark's approach to choral conducting is straightforward:

> I come at choirs as a singer. I think you approach how you sing a line, how you form tone, the sort of repertoire that you do and how you do it, differently if you're coming at it from a more literally digital standpoint as a keyboardist than as really what's a more analog, lyrical direction coming at it as a singer.
>
> I prefer a very warm choral sound, which has to be not only with resonance but how you balance sound in a choir. To me, it's a pyramid: you're stronger on the bottom and lighter as it gets closer toward the top in terms of the voice parts, the notes that are being employed.

St. Gregory's Choir with Fr. Roger and Gerry Senechal at Washington National Cathedral.

As Mark spent the summer planning, Gerry and St. Gregory's Choir spent a week as the Choir in Residence at Washington National Cathedral in Washington, D.C. Gerry commented on the experience:

> We sang Evensong in the National Cathedral with far fewer singers than a regular-sized choir might have, certainly less than the National Cathedral choir. That room is one of the largest cathedrals in the world, and the organ is in Egypt. It is up feet and feet over your head; you have to listen so carefully for the pitch whenever you're not singing. It is a huge challenge. They were like the special forces of church music; there were so few of them. But they did magnificently.

To help expand the already successful children's music program, Mark hired Laurel Fisher and Rachel Hansbury, both staff singers with St. George's Choir and trained in the RSCM Courses. Laurel received her master's degree from Western North Carolina University in Asheville. Rachel received her master's degree from Austin Peay State University in Clarksville, Tennessee. Gerry Senechal continued to direct St. Gregory's Choir and assisted with the other Youth Choirs as needed. Mark expressed his hopes for the Youth Choirs recently:

> I want to have three or four Sundays a month where there are children participating in worship.... Sociologically one thing that we see here and in many places is that we have a smaller number of boys participating than girls in the children's groups. This year we're going to have a separate boys' choir and girls' choir. Based on everything I've seen I think that's the way to go. It will encourage the boys to be more participatory. It's something we're going to intentionally work on with families to invite specific kids to be a part of this.

The *In Excelsis* concert series continued in the fall, including a joint organ concert with Mark and Gerry. Mark commented on the success of the series:

> [The *In Excelsis* program] is a wonderful series, and I'm delighted to have inherited that. One thing that we are doing in that.... First of all, we're keeping a really strong Anglican music core to that. [It's] important to me that each year there is a world-class group performing that is specifically in the Anglican tradition.... We had St. Thomas Choir from New York, which is certainly the equal of any men and boys' choir in the empire, so to speak. Having the Tallis Scholars, you don't get any better than those guys. Just magnificent.
>
> Certainly featuring our own St. George's Choir in a variety of literature so that they can do things in a concert setting that simply don't fit as well in a liturgical setting and giving them the chance to sing with a variety of instrumental partners. [And] to combine, to collaborate, in ways that are

new, I love collaborating in ways of seeing our art in the light of how it intersects with other arts.

We are continuing to grow how we communicate these things, how we market and brand and communicate the offerings we have. We need to be capturing contact information from everyone who walks in the door to one of these things. There really has not been that mechanism in place before. I think real attention to communicating, marketing, [to] those who do come here, make sure we invite them back and have a way in which to do that.

2010

A pivotal event in the life of St. George's occurred the first weekend of May 2010, when a flood of biblical proportions hit Middle Tennessee. More than fifteen inches of rain fell over forty-eight hours, and the waters of every river, stream, creek and ditch were overwhelmed. Downtown Nashville was flooded up to Fourth Avenue. At St. George's water came into the first floor of the church through windows facing the back parking area, consumed the Kindergarten area, and flowed into the Nave during the seven o'clock service on Sunday, May 2. The entire first floor was covered with several inches of water. Two parishioners, Bill and Frankie Rutledge, were killed in the flood on the way to services that morning. The St. George's Kindergarten was closed for the remainder of the school year. Every piece of furniture that could be moved was carried to the second floor, along with every book, every file, every item that could be salvaged from the bookstore, the library, Johnson Hall, and Hampton Hall. The HVAC units were destroyed. There were no working bathrooms on the first floor for months. The water missed the Casavant organ electronics by inches. It did not miss the organ in the Weeks Chapel. Although services continued in the Nave beginning the following week, the rest of the church building was in an upheaval for months. Grieving and in shock, the congregation did as the rest of Nashville did. It came together to offer help, both at church and in the larger community, under the rallying banner, "We Are St. George's."

Having faced numerous flood threats in Minnesota, Mark commented on the situation at St. George's:

Flood waters engulf Belle Meade City Hall.

The disruption, the monumental disruption, of the flood both in terms of the physical plant of the building and in the life of this parish, I think, is larger than some people may realize. Yes, there was damage to the building, but there was still ministry going on here as well as ever. Program was not. Most of our building was gone. I think there are a lot of things that we're right now poised, because we have a better facility than we had before the flood, to do better things, better ministry, better programs. But in some ways we had a significant setback in terms of what we've been able to change and to offer programmatically because of that. We sort of hit a reset button in a variety of ways. I think we came back better both in terms of a physical plant and as a parish family than we were before. Now the facility is fully open and we're really engaging in getting some traction in moving programmatically forward in ways we haven't been able to.

The view toward the sanctuary as water covered the floor.

Despite the ongoing cleanup and restoration of the church facilities, the music program grew. In the fall, the children's program had sufficient numbers to warrant further dividing the participants by age and ability. St. Dunstan's Choir became the first and second grade group, while two new choirs, St. Alban's and St. Edmund's, were formed for the third through seventh grade singers. St. Gregory's continued as before with singers in eighth through twelfth grade. The children were participating in worship at least three times each month.

The St. George's Choir presented a Choral Evensong in November with music by Purcell, Morley, and Stephen Paulus. All of the choirs combined for the annual Festival of Lessons and Carols on December 12 in defiance of the snow and icy weather. On Christmas Eve, the entire congregation received a gift. For the first time since the flood, the hallway connecting the sanctuary to the rest of the church was open. There was still much work to be done, but the end was in sight. With all that the church had been through, it was a solemn but joyful Christmas with the promise of a happier new year.

2011

The year 2011 saw the resumption of regular programming in all aspects of life at St. George's. The St. George's Choir offered a Holocaust memorial concert in the spring, which resulted in an invitation to sing at the State Capitol for the annual Day of Remembrance ceremony on May 3.

The incomparable Tallis Scholars presented a concert in March as part of the *In Excelsis* series. Fall offerings in the series included *A Soldier's Tale,* presented by Doug Berky and his internationally acclaimed theatre troupe with accompaniment provided by local musicians under Mark's direction. The St. George's Choir sang a Tudor Evensong in October, followed by a concert in November with orchestra that featured the *Cantus Missae* for double-choir by Rheinberger, Gerald Finzi's *Lo, the Full Final Sacrifice,* and Stanford's *Te Deum.* Once again, all the choirs joined together for the Festival of Lessons and Carols and shared in the musical responsibilities for three Christmas Eve services.

In a departure from its Anglican musical heritage, the church instituted a new, more informal service at nine o'clock on Sunday morn-

Palm Sunday, 2011.

ings. *The Table* offers contemporary music and instrumentation. Aynsley Martindale joined the Music Staff to lead the musical offerings at this service.

2012 and Beyond . . .

As the church prepares for its sixtieth anniversary as a parish and the twenty-fifth anniversary of the Casavant organ in 2012, the music program is looking forward to even greater things. As the Director of Music Ministries, Mark Ring was asked to share some of his dreams for the future.

Mark is delighted with the current Choir situation, but he would like to see it integrated more into the life of the parish in order to encourage more participation:

> I have found both in all the places that I've worked and in places that I've studied, growing music across the ages of the participants almost always has to involve an evening . . . where there is a consistent turnout of a broad constituency

in the parish on a variety of things. Right now most of the time it is just choirs that are going on, on Wednesdays. It's very hard to quantitatively grow choirs in that surrounding. The places I've been before where they've really grown well, there are consistent, multigenerational offerings every single Wednesday, not just "we're going to have a class for four weeks and take three weeks off." There is a parish dinner for anyone who wishes to come every single Wednesday of the program year. You take off Christmas and Easter; otherwise people know that it's consistent, and that there are educational opportunities for children, youth, and adults, and there are music opportunities for children, youth, and adults on that evening when families tend to come. One of my prior churches where we were doing that, we had to come up with a grid of when each age would do music, when they would do Christian ed and whatnot. That required some organization, but it worked really well. I wound up in that church having to divide the children's choirs into a choir per grade because they had grown so much. It was directly attributable to great staff who worked with the kids and the fact that whole families were turning out every Wednesday night. That is one of the biggest challenges: quantitatively growing the music for children and youth in a context that is not real conducive to that.

[What I'd like to see is choir practices that are] not a stand-alone situation but simply the fabric of what this church does where we are engaging the whole person, be they [in] third grade or eighty years old, where in worship and particularly in a midweek setting where there are opportunities for education, for fellowship, for music, for worship, for all of these things that I think have to be knit together. When it's seen as part of the whole, it's more exciting and energizing than when it stands alone.

The question then became what role the staff singers play in that kind of arrangement:

I think it is absolutely ideal. You have . . . John Bertalot, who is British and was in a number of prestigious positions in Great Britain and wound up at Trinity Episcopal Church in Princeton, New Jersey. . . . I learned a lot from him personally and from his writings. He said that the only thing voluntary about a volunteer choir is the act of joining. Once you're in, you are committed to working as hard and being there as often as those who are paid to be there. It's a very dedicated group of volunteers here, with a very high level of talent. The Choir without its volunteers is markedly inferior to the Choir with volunteers. It's an outstanding group. At the same time the Choir without its professionals is markedly inferior as well. I think we have a wonderful balance of that. It's a tradition of doing extremely good music very well over many, many years. St. George's has a great reputation in the community for choral. [Professional] vocal artists want to come and sing here. That balance is absolutely essential. It's wonderful to have both. We are engaged with and a part of the parish, and at the same time our music making is elevated by those who come and join us from outside as well.

Repertoire expansion is a very important thing, and with that, making a different variety of sounds with the Choir, things that are stylistically appropriate in terms of vocal placement styles of the early music, and sounding different for different types of music. That is a musical goal. [My visions upon arriving were] broadening and deepening the choral repertoire, emphasis on Children's and Youth Choirs, involving more people in making music, particularly in worship in terms of congregational hymn singing and infusing music into as many aspects of the parish as possible. It's not just that great music is performed on Sunday morning, but that there is music infused in as many aspects of parish life as possible.

I'd love to have the chance to have both adults and youth to understand hymnody in greater depth of the traditions of what has happened and when? Why does this hymn sound and feel in a certain way because of when and where it was written, as opposed to another one? To me, you always approach it theologically first. We always look at the text as the first step of the most important song of the people, which is what hymns are, and then move to the musical aspects. I wish going forward that we will have a greater utilization of that, to have more teachable opportunities. Robust hymn singing [involves] the whole community in the song of the church.

In the fullness of time [I want] to expand the music educational opportunities of the parish, both with expanding the existing programs and adding new programs that will hopefully culminate in a stand-alone [music] academy here.

Mark's final thoughts seem to encapsulate his overall philosophy for music at St. George's, both now and for the future:

We don't have adult choirs tomorrow if we don't have great kids' choirs today. When I was teaching, I always encouraged my students that "you come in here and you make an absolutely huge mistake, good for you because you've tried to do something amazing. You blew it. Okay, we can fix that. We can grow from that. But if you come in and you're timid, you can be good but never great." These are wonderful people who are willing to do that and willing to explore and grow. By being able to do that, the sky is the limit. As long as we can inculcate that in our children, in our youth, in their families, we're dedicated to growing and nurturing and challenging all at the same time. To me, the greatest strength is the people that we get to work with.

It is a matter of engaging people in conversation and educating constituent groups so that we can continue to grow on the excellence that had been here before.

It's not a job. It's a calling. This is an extremely unusual parish. They are serious about their faith. They are serious about the value of music in the human life. We're made in the image of our Creator, and therefore we are creative. By being creative, we're living out who we're made to be. They are serious about prayer. They are serious about what they do, but they don't take themselves so seriously. It's a good community in which to live, to grow. You can come here and be vulnerable. That's the only way you can really grow, I think. I'm delighted to be a part of that.

And the history of music at St. George's continues.

5

Organs and Bells

KEVIN CARSON

The Organs of St. George's Church

Called the "King of instruments" by Mozart, the organ has long been a central force in the act of Christian worship. The introduction of church organs is traditionally attributed to Pope Vitalian in the seventeenth century. Due to its ability to provide a musical support both below and in the human vocal range and to increase brightness above the human vocal register, the organ may be the most ideally suited instrument to accompany the human voice, whether a congregation, choir, or soloist.

The first organ at St. George's Church was a small Hammond electric organ. It was used for the first service on September 11, 1949.

Then, in September 1952, James G. Stahlman, an original parish Vestryman, made a contribution to provide a new organ in memory of his wife, Effye Chumley Stahlman. The organ was to be built by M. P. Moller Co. in Hagerstown, Maryland. In order to accommodate the pipes of the new organ, an organ chamber was added to the existing church building. The organ was shipped from the factory and installed sometime in 1953.

Moller is perhaps most well known for having constructed the organ for the Cadet Chapel of the United States Military Academy at

West Point, New York, where perhaps some of the company's best building skills and practices were demonstrated. Following World War II, M. P. Moller Co. began to compete with other better-known organ builders such as Aeolian-Skinner. Two of Moller's most shining installations in religious structures still in operation are the First Congregational Church in Los Angeles and National Shrine of the Immaculate Conception in Washington, D.C. Each of these instruments has been rebuilt since original installation, which is often the case for organs surviving many years, but both remain largely as they were originally.

The specifications for St. George's Moller organ were as follows:

	Great		
8'	Diapason	4'	Nachthorn
8'	Flute Harmonic	2⅔	Nazard
8'	Gemshorn	III	Mixture
8'	Gemshorn Celeste	8'	Trumpet
4'	Principal	4'	Oboe
4'	Flute (extension of 8' Flute Harmonic)		Tremolo
			Pedal
2⅔	Twelfth	16'	Bourdon
2'	Fifteenth	16'	Rohr Bourdon
	Chimes	8'	Bourdon
	Swell	4'	Bourdon
8'	Rohrflute	16'	Tromba
8'	Viole de Gamba	8'	Trumpet
8'	Viole Celeste	4'	Clarion
4'	Octave Geigen		

It should be noted that stops indicated as 8' play the expected pitch, sometimes referred to as "absolute pitch." Those numbered 4' sound an octave higher than the key actually depressed. Stops with fractional numbers, 2⅔, 1⅗, are called "mutations," correspond with pitches in the overtone series, and are used to enrich a fundamental pitch. Stops numbered 16', therefore, sound an octave lower than expected for the key played. Stops numbered with notations II, III, or IV are called "mixtures" and sound two, three, or four pitches for every key played respectively, usually not very loudly, and are used to enrich and/or "color" a fundamental pitch.

St. George's Bells

The bells in St. George's steeple were installed in April 1987 following one full year of trans-Atlantic telephone conversations, casting, tuning, and shipping.

The bells were manufactured by the Whitechapel Bell Foundry. An entry in the *Guinness Book of Records* lists the Whitechapel Bell Foundry as Britain's oldest manufacturing company, having been established in 1570 during the reign of Queen Elizabeth I and being in continuous business since that date.

Whitechapel Bell Foundry's business has always been and still concentrates solely on the manufacture of bells and their associated fittings. The manufacture of large bells for change ringing peals in church towers, single tolling bells, carillon bells, and their complete range of accessories such as framework, wheels, clappers, and their

Blessing of the bells.

assembly in church towers accounts for approximately four-fifths of the company's output. The other fifth of the business lies in the manufacture of handbells and other small bells of many shapes and sizes.

Whitechapel's famous bells include the original Liberty Bell (1752), the Great Bell of Montreal, and probably best known of all, Big Ben at the Palace of Westminster. Cast in 1858, this is the largest bell ever cast at Whitechapel, weighing 13½ tons. To this day, a cross-section of the bell surrounds the entrance door to the foundry.

The bells supplied to St. Michael's, Charleston, South Carolina, in 1764 have possibly the most interesting story of any set of bells and may well be the most traveled bells in history. During the Revolutionary War the bells from St. Michael's were taken to England as a prize of war, but a London merchant purchased and returned them. During the Civil War, they were sent to Columbia, South Carolina, but cracked in a great fire there in 1865. The metal fragments were salvaged and sent to England to be recast in their original molds and rehung in St. Michael's, their original location. In 1964, Whitechapel was proud to provide the change ringing peal of ten bells in a radial frame for the new National Cathedral in Washington, D.C. Whitechapel has also cast the bell called "Great Peter" at York Minster and a large set of bells for Canterbury Cathedral. The masters at Whitechapel have assured that St. George's bell will not crack!

The traditions of craftsmanship and old skills working alongside modern technology today still produce bells that are renowned at the "sign of the three bells" in London's East End.

St. George's bells were the gift of Peggy Joyce and sons, Alex and Douglas Joyce, in memory of Harry Alexis Jones Joyce. The bells range in weight from 336 to 11,988 pounds. The largest, and lowest in pitch, is F, followed by G, A, B flat, D, and E. Each single bell actually produces five tones when struck. The first tone is the "strike" tone, the pitch by which the bell is identified, followed by a "hum" tone an octave lower, then a "nominal" pitch an octave above the fundamental pitch. The fourth pitch is a minor third above the fundamental, and the fifth pitch is a diminished fifth above. This combination of tones that surrounds the fundamental pitch gives the characteristic rich tone we have all come to know and love.

The bells at St. George's were rung for the first time in May 1987. The bells are usually rung by a computerized, electronic mechanism that is located in a room off the narthex. They may also be played manually using two small keyboards, one of which is mounted on a wall in the narthex, the other near the organ console in the apse.

Casavant Organ

Brothers Joseph-Claver Casavant (1855–1933) and Samuel-Marie Casavant (1859–1929) got their start in organ building in the shop of their father, Joseph Casavant, under his successor, Eusèbe Brodeur. Claver worked with Brodeur during 1874–1878, then went to France for a fourteen-month apprenticeship with the firm of John Abbey in Versailles. He and Samuel then visited many organs and workshops in Western Europe before establishing their factory on the site of their father's workshop on rue Girouard in Saint-Hyacinthe in 1879.

The sound and style of Casavant organs have varied throughout the company's history. The Casavant brothers themselves, Samuel and Claver Casavant, reflected mostly influences from contemporary France, but they traveled widely and visited many European instruments. They later brought in an Englishman, Stephen Stoot, under whose direction the tonal palette reflected additional influences from

Organ pipes.

England. Later tonal directors, Lawrence Phelps and Gerhard Brunzema, contributed styles from the German Organ Reform Movement. The most recent tonal directors, Jean-Louis Coignet and Jacquelin Rochette, are rooted in but not limited to the various French organ-building traditions.

St. George's Casavant organ was built between 1985 and 1987 and has 4,900 pipes. It was a gift from the family of the late Ralph "Peck" Owen, to the Greater Glory of God, in memory of Mr. Owen. The cabinetry is of neo-Georgian style and is built of Adirondack oak. The organ is Casavant's opus 3,306, and originally had fifty-eight stops, eighty-five ranks of pipes. On the average, it requires approximately seventy-three separate hand operations to complete the fabrication of a single pipe. The St. George's organ is designed with three manual keyboards and pedal with a separate, antiphonal division in the gallery. The main console is equipped with solid state, electro-pneumatic action. Described as "cosmopolitan," the organ is basically French in its nomenclature but much more eclectic in scope. The instrument was designed by Jean-Louis Coignet, tonal director of Casavant Freres, in consultation with the St. George's Organ Committee and Donald Corbett and Michael Payne of Casavant. Michael Payne, who was the regional representative for Casavant at that time, supervised the entire installation of the instrument, which took place between August 1986 and February 1987. The voicing was accomplished from September 1986 to January 1987, by Yves Champagne and Remi Bouchard of Casavant. St. George's Casavant organ is notable for its large-scale diapason and flute pipework and variety of reed stops. Never seen but sometimes heard, the gallery division speaks from a chamber in the ceiling above the balcony in the rear of the Nave. This part of the organ may also be played from a separate, smaller console found in the balcony.

The dedication concert series, from February 15 to April 28, 1987, featured a choral concert with organ accompaniment, a recital by Wilma Jensen, a Choral Evensong showcasing the organ's capacity to be played by two people at once by presenting the Vierne *Mass for Choir and Two Organs*, a recital by John Semingson (then the

Assistant Choirmaster-Organist), and last, a recital by Simon Preston, who was then the Organist at Westminster Abbey.

St. George's organ may be heard in several recordings. Wilma Jensen has made two professional compact disc recordings at St. George's, *Mors et Resurrectio* and *Passiontide-Easter*, on the Arkay label, and *Improvisations in the French Tradition* on the Pro Organo label. St. George's Choir has made two professional compact disc recordings on the Pro Organo label. These recordings feature Choir, soloists, some instrumentalists, and harpsichord as well as the Casavant organ.

Dr. Janette Fishell, who did her Bachelor of Music and Master of Music in Organ Performance at Indiana University with Wilma Jensen where she was teaching then, has made two compact disc recordings using St. George's Casavant organ. They are *An Eben Organ Anthology, Dances of Life, Dances of Death*, on the Pro Organo label and *Dupre, Vol. 4, Works for Organ* on the Naxos label. Dr. Fishell is considered the world authority on the organ works of Czech composer Petr Eben, having studied with him extensively.

Wilma Jensen completed a two-year project in June 2011 with the release of two DVD teaching videos made on the Casavant organ at St. George's Church. The videos, produced by longtime Choir member Jennifer Orth, include several demonstration sessions on technique and musicality as well as the participation of seven former students whom she teaches on the DVDs. These teaching videos are entitled *Organizing Notes in Space: Developing Organ Technique and Musicality* with Dr. Wilma Jensen. Dr. Jensen plans a further compact disc recording in the near future to be made using St. George's Casavant organ.

Some other significant Casavant organs in the United States include First United Methodist Church, Dallas, Texas; Broadway Baptist Church, Fort Worth, Texas; Temple complex of the Community of Christ, Independence, Missouri; Cathedral of All Souls, Biltmore Village, Asheville, North Carolina; Chapel of Lewis & Clark College, Portland, Oregon (probably the only organ in the world that was built entirely suspended from the ceiling); St. John's Lutheran Church, Conover, North Carolina; Cathedral of Saints Peter and Paul, Providence, Rhode Island; Emmanuel Church, Boston, Massachusetts; Wesley Chapel, West Virginia Wesleyan College, Buckhannon, West Virginia; Plymouth Congregation Church, Lansing, Michigan; Grace Lutheran Church, State College, Pennsylvania; The Detroit Institute of Arts Auditorium, Detroit, Michigan; Edman Chapel at Wheaton College, Wheaton, Illinois; Bethesda Episcopal Church, Saratoga Springs, New York; Organ Recital Hall, Colorado State University, Fort Collins, Colorado; University of Iowa, Iowa City, Iowa; Graceland University, Lamoni, Iowa; St. Peter's Cathedral, Scranton Pennsylvania; St. Mary's Church, Westfield, Massachusetts (the oldest Casavant organ still in use in the United States); Westminster Presbyterian Church, Dayton, Ohio; First Congregational Church, Traverse City, Michigan; and The Brick Presbyterian Church, New York, New York.

Afterword

This, then, is the history of music in St. George's Episcopal Church since its inception over sixty years ago. From small beginnings building over a period of more than thirty years to more than a quarter century of fulfillment, we are now looking ahead to a bright and rewarding future. There is something very special about our music, and it is our hope that this book reveals that to the reader. Like many histories, it is one in motion. In this book we have attempted to address not only our chronological musical history, but relate it directly to the much more ancient Anglican tradition. The first chapter has addressed that topic, and it appears over and over again in the subsequent chapters. The three central chapters—the historical narrative—cover our beginnings, our fulfillment, and our anticipation. The penultimate chapter is aptly titled "Anticipation," and its end continues as a beginning. The final chapter leaves the realm of the directly people-oriented story and details the history of our musical instruments—the organs and bells.

This Afterword is included as a bridge, not as a closure. The reader is encouraged to visit the Appendices for further information that was felt best handled elsewhere than in the main concourse of the book, but that remains quite relevant to not only our past and present, but also our future. We hope you will study the financial section, Support and Development, which sketches how our music is funded, how we manage the oversight of our music, and how extra-budgetary funding is derived and what it accomplishes. Then the transcriptions of the two interviews with our current Music Directors are presented in full. While some of this material has been quoted in the historical narrative, these transcriptions provide much keener insight into the thinking, hopes, and plans of our talented and able musical staff. Following the interviews is the seminal report of a committee that established, really for the first time, a concept of music at St. George's for the Vestry. This document is invaluable and worth reading over and over again. One might suggest that reading it should be the requirement of each Vestry as it takes shape the first of each calendar year. Four future projects—hopes for the future—are briefly explained and discussed. By reading this quartet of documents, one can get a solid glimpse into the future of music at St. George's Episcopal Church.

We have enjoyed building this book together. It is remarkable how smoothly we came together and how well we coordinated. The Acknowledgments recognize, hopefully, all who were involved in producing this history. The experience was, for each of us, a very special one, and one that intensified both the breadth and the depth of our commitment to St. George's as a friendly, interested, enthusiastic, and worshipful group of parishioners. We have been most fortunate to have been able to participate in the production of this book, and we hope all who read it will enjoy it as have we.

Finally, we hope that this book will be used as a reference tool over many years to come. When new Music Directors appear on the scene, when new Choir members arrive, when new parishioners are welcomed, it can provide a long view of our past. It also can help light the way of the future for one of our most prized gifts: our music.

Appendices

Appendix A:
Support and Development

Appendix B:
Two Interviews

Appendix C:
Long Range Music Planning Committee Report

Appendix D:
Future Projects

Appendix A
Support and Development

ALEX McLEOD

This section looks at the financing of St. George's music from three vantage points: budgetary financing, administration, and non-budgetary financing. Accordingly, it is divided into three sections, one for each of these aspects.

Paying the Piper:
Financing St. George's Music

We would have little or no music history to record at our church had that important element of our worship not been supported financially over our sixty-year history. Delving into those finances has been a fascinating venture. In the vault at the church are bound Vestry Minutes, and in those volumes are myriads of financial reports. Financial records, particularly as to music, are sparse for the first five years, beginning in 1949 until around 1953, and music financial records continue to be scant until about 1961. Thereafter the information grows visibly, year by year, decade by decade. For our last ten years those financial records are computerized and pure joy to find after facing some frustrations and seeming dead ends in the preceding maze. One of the most evident difficulties is the changing format of reporting over the years. Subcategories appear, then disappear, and sometimes reappear. In a few instances, only November financial statements are to be found. This has necessitated extrapolation to a twelve-month period. Even so, there does emerge an informing set of images of the funding of St. George's music.

First, we'll look at the big picture shown in the Total Church Expenses chart. Every year's financial report shows this figure, and it can be considered accurate *(chart 1)*.

The adjustment line in the chart reflects the figures when the annual inflation figure (CPI, or consumer price index) is factored in. It's apparent that St. George's took off on a growth spurt around 1980, and that has continued, with another such initiating about 2005.

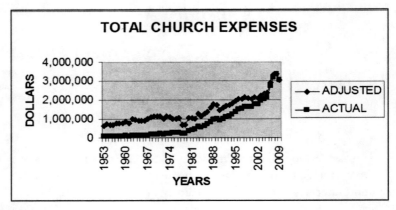

Chart 1.

It has proven difficult to come up with a comparably accurate figure for expenses on music, but we can still get a good general picture. The sub-categories that can be applied to musical expenditures include Music Staff Salaries, Choir Salaries, Choir Expenses, Concert/Instrument Expenses, and Organ Maintenance.

In the earliest years, Music Staff Salaries were non-existent because we had a volunteer Organist/Choir Director. The first paid Organist/Choir director was part-time and received $1,200 per year. We have a sequence of slowly increasing payments over the next five years, doubling to $2,400 per year. Then the recorded payments become spotty until the mid-1980s. During much of this time these salaries seem to have been included in Staff Salaries and are not recoverable from the records. Beginning in the mid-1980s we have a sequence of eight years where the Music Staff Salaries are again recorded as such, rising during that time from $26,020 to $35,393. Thereafter, the figures disappear again, concomitant with a Vestry determination to keep all clergy and music staff arrangements private.

Figures for Choir Salaries and Choir Expenses, on the other hand, are found consistently from 1962 forward *(chart 2)*.

It is interesting to look at the combination of these two expenses—Choir Salaries and Choir Expenses *(chart 3)*—as a percentage of Total Church Expenses.

The mean, or average, of the sum of all the annual values is 4.27%. In currency terms, then, for every $100 of total church expenditures during this forty-seven-year period, $4.27 was expended for Choir Salaries and miscellaneous expenses.

Organ Maintenance figures *(chart 4)* are available from 1992 through

SUPPORT AND DEVELOPMENT 165

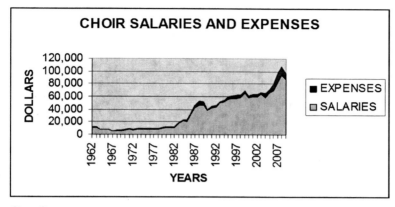

Chart 2.

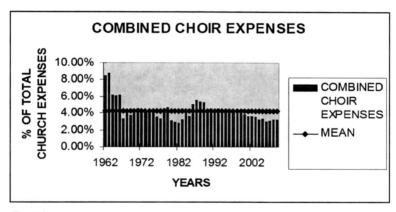

Chart 3.

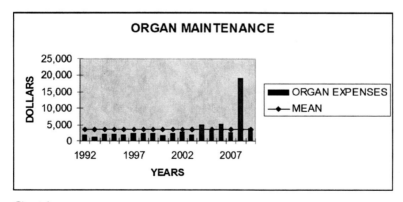

Chart 4.

2009, with a mean of $3,523. As we have learned from the report of a recent professional consultant about the organ, we have been somewhat derelict in this area. The stories of our organs over the years are covered elsewhere in this history. Both the initial main organ and the current main organ were gifted by individuals, not purchased with current church funds as such.

Concerts are an important part of St. George's musical outreach to the community. We have records of Concerts and Instrumentalists from 1989 to the present but with an unexplained three-year gap (2001–2003). In order to smooth out the curve *(chart 5)*, extrapolations have been made for those years.

Additional funding for concerts over the past four or five years has come through the Friends of St. George's Music organization, which sponsors the *In Excelsis—Musical Evenings at St. George's* concert series. The background and aims of this important fund-raising entity are further detailed later in this section.

Thus far we have looked at the following subcategories: Music Staff Salaries, Choir Expenses, Organ Maintenance, and Concerts Expenses. While admitting that the compiled figures have some inconsistencies and gaps, by combining these subcategories (with a few extrapolations) and designating them as Combined Music Expenses, we can get a ballpark idea of the percentage that Combined Music Expenses *(chart 6)* play in the Total Expenses of our church.

The mean is 4.96%.

When we consider the hugely important role that music plays in our worship, what an integral part it is with our liturgy—preludes, hymns,

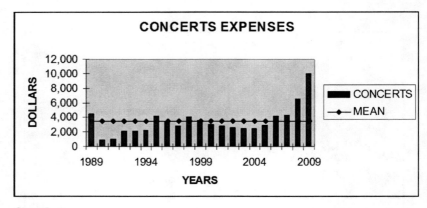

Chart 5.

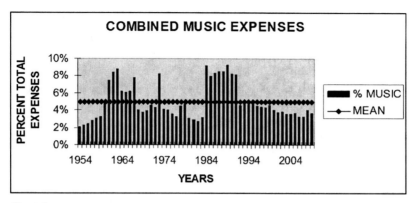

Chart 6.

canticles, chants, psalms, anthems, interludes, postludes—as well as choirs for multiple age groups, concerts, and scholarships—five cents out of every dollar is a very meager amount to pay. When we recognize the contributions made by individual parishioners for music above and beyond annual pledges, such as gifting organs, carillon, Friends of St. George's Music donations, scholarship funding, and volunteer choir members' time—the relative amount becomes even smaller.

The figures presented in this brief overview provide an objective way of looking at music's progress over St. George's sixty years of existence. It is important to see these figures not simply as a quantitative evaluation but to realize they reflect a strong qualitative evolution as well. While the percentage expenditures have, on average, remained steady for the most part, the music of our church has increasingly gained in its excellence and continues to provide a most important concomitant to our liturgy. These two elements together are cornerstones of our worship and, God willing, will continue to so serve.

Measuring the Muse: Overseeing Music at St. George's

Music at St. George's doesn't just happen. It requires planning, administration, financing, and overseeing. The planning and the administration are largely the domain of the Music Director, however called. The financing and overseeing are mainly Vestry functions. The Rector has an ear on, eye over, and hand in all of these. The following paragraphs address the overseeing.

Looking for the predecessors of the present Music Committee at St.

APPENDIX A

George's proved to be something like hunting for the proverbial needle in a haystack. A hallmark study in 2006 provided a huge leap forward, and the Music Committee of today is a direct result of that. The full report can be found in the Appendices at the back of this book.

Before 2006, the presence or absence of a Music Committee suggests a sporadic entity, more often not in evidence than being contributory. A review of Annual Reports on Music at St. George's is revealing. In the recently acquired copies of Minutes from the records at Christ Church Cathedral, the parent of St. George's, there is no information about music at St. George's for the years 1947–1951. The 1952 Vestry Minutes from St. George's mention a brief report on the Junior Choir by Mrs. Hugh (Catherine) Stanley and on the Senior Choir by John Ball. The next year, 1953, Dr. Thomas Cowan gave a brief music and choir report. In 1954 Dr. Cowan is listed for Choir, but no report is included. In 1955 his actual report is attached, and that is the first real music report. Somewhere in the records of the 1950s there is a notation of Vestryman Crom Tidwell as head of a Music Committee, though nothing further. In the 1956 Vestry Minutes a paragraph is devoted to a discussion by the Rector, Bob Shaw, concerning the hiring of Gregory Colson as Organist and Mrs. Winifred ("Winnie") Breast as Choir Director, along with some robbing of Peter to pay Paul in putting together the required $900. In the Senior Warden's report for 1957, Vernon Sharp acknowledges the work of these two and their choir members. Annual Reports for 1958 and 1959 are missing.

From 1960 through 1967 there are a regular series of Annual Reports by Gregory Colson as Organist-Choirmaster, having become full time in that capacity in 1962. These reports are well done, informative, and thorough. In September 1968 Colson submitted his resignation, effective the end of that year, and there is no Annual Report for that year. In 1969 the Annual Report is submitted by Sam Batt Owens as Organist-Choirmaster and Karen Cooper Allen as his Associate. Owens subsequently provides a regular annual series of reports through 1974. In 1975 Scott S. Withrow, who succeeded Owens, provided the Annual Report, as he did in 1976 and 1979. He probably submitted reports in the two intervening years, but records for those years are missing. Withrow's 1980 and 1981 reports depart from the customary format, the first listing members of the several choirs, the second offering three paragraphs, each written by a different member of each choir.

The 1982 Choir Report is unsigned but details Withrow's resignation and the interim position being taken by Wilma Jensen. Subsequently in the

1980s there are detailed Annual Reports by Jensen for 1983, 1984, 1985, 1987, and 1988. There are no reports in evidence for 1986 and 1989. Starting in 1990, the annual music reports take on a different format, being thorough, clearly outlined according to the several choirs and staff considerations, and almost surely continued and submitted by Jensen, although unsigned, until the 1999 report, which is signed by her, as is the 2000 report. This sequence represents a full decade of excellent reports, thorough and well detailed and complete.

The 2001 report is submitted by Tim Fudge as Interim Choirmaster, Jensen having taken an extended medical leave of absence. The 2002 report is unsigned, but utilizes the same reporting format and almost surely was submitted by Fudge. It records the retirement of Jensen in January of that year.

Murray Forbes Somerville, as Director, authors the 2003 report. Records for 2004 are missing. He reports again in 2005 and 2006. His reports are informative and indicate continued growth, both musically and administratively.

In 2007 the report is by Vestryman Calvin Lewis, as Chair of the Music Ministries Committee, which was formed in 2006 as a result of the aforementioned study. That report is so important that it is recorded in its entirety as an Appendix, minus its appendices. In brief, it addressed the broad aspect of music at St. George's at the request of the Rector, Father Spruill. Their first recommendation was to form a Music Ministries Committee. This, in itself, was a major step forward in recognizing the importance of music in the life of St. George's as well as its crucially integral presence in our worship. They made recommendations concerning the music programs for children and youth as well as adult choirs. The importance of outside groups and concert series was stressed, and recommendations were made to create what became the Friends of St. George's Music. The reader is urged to study the entire report in the Appendix because it is, unquestionably, a signal crossroads in the history of music at St. George's.

Somerville retired in 2008, and the Annual Report for that year was submitted by Gerry Senechal, as Interim Director of Music Ministry, and offers an extensive overview and updating of music at St. George's. The 2009 and 2010 reports are by Mark Ring, the current Director of Music Ministry. His reports reveal the continued growth and aspirations of St. George's for its worship through music.

It is clear to see through this overview of music administration at St.

George's that the importance and strength of the church's music have grown steadily over the years. In the early years, there seems to have been a possible Music Committee, but it is much more likely that the Rector and Vestry tended to music matters as part of their regular Vestry housekeeping measures. With the advent of its first full-time Organist-Choirmaster, Gregory Colson, the reporting of music, for the first time, becomes detailed, progressive and, in truth, exciting. His leadership was followed by a series of subsequent excellent individuals—Sam Batt Owens, Scott S. Withrow, Wilma Jensen, Murray Somerville, and Mark Ring. That it should take fifty-five years to firmly establish a Music Ministries Committee is not surprising. The pattern of solid growth through each succeeding leader of the Music Staff has led St. George's to the point where music is indeed a well-recognized and appreciated component, not just of its worship, but of its broad ministry. That a more official element of the Vestry should link itself with the music of the church is a sign not of age, but of maturity, and it is through that maturity that the music of St. George's can be led, with God's help, to even greater heights.

Supplementing and Sustaining: Major Gifts and Non-budget Funding

In the two previous sections of this Appendix we looked at budgetary funding of music at St. George's and at the overseeing of music through the Vestry. There remains another significant element in the support and development of music at St. George's: major gifts and ongoing special contributions.

Just as a building program—or a flood—requires extra financial effort for the church, an effort above and beyond its annual giving, so the "big ticket" items in music require extraordinary funds. It is easy to take for granted things such as organs and carillon, pianos and hand bells, to ignore the huge investment required by these important elements of a church music program. St. George's has been very fortunate over the years when generous special donations have made it possible for us to have not just any such instruments, but instruments of high quality to add value to both our worship and our musical programs.

The detailed stories of some of these are recorded in the section "Organs and Bells" in this history of St. George's music. Here is a summary of most of them, gleaned from *Memorials* bound volumes in the vault alongside the Vestry Minutes.

- In the 1950–1959 volume our first "real" organ, the Moller organ, given in memory of Effye Chumley Stahlman by James Geddes Stahlman.
- In the volume containing the Jane Tompkins Weeks Chapel (1967), the Chapel organ given by Sinclair Weeks in memory of his mother, Katherine.
- In the 1986 listings for the Memorials for the church building completed that year is the Casavant organ, given to the glory of God and in loving memory of Ralph Owen by Lulu Hampton Owen, Melinda Owen Bass, and Ralph Owen, Jr. When this organ was given, the Moller organ was given to St. David's, for whom St. George's had earlier been the parent church.
- In the same listing is the Steinway grand piano given "to the Glory of God and in loving memory of Marshall Tate Polk, Jr." by Sandra Murray and Marshall Tate Polk III.
- Also in the same listing are The Bells—the Carillon—given in loving memory of Harry Alexis Jones Joyce by Margaret Sinclair Henry Joyce, Alexis Jones Joyce, and Douglas Henry Joyce.
- In that same listing is The Melodean (circa 1840), the first "organ" used at Christ Episcopal Church, St. George's parent church. It belonged to the family of William Wright Crandall and was given to the Glory of God and in loving memory of Estelle Crandall Dickerson, William Buford Dickerson II, and Gordon Saint Claire Dickerson, Jr. by Donia Craig Dickerson and Gordon Saint Claire Dickerson.

In addition to these major gifts for music at St. George's, there are others:

- In 1995 a most generous bequest was made to St. George's. These funds were described as follows: "It is to be an unrestricted bequest, but the family would like to see it used to enhance the music program at St. George's."
- In 2006 and 2007 special funds were donated to St. George's by William H. Scheide, a noted Bach scholar in Princeton, New Jersey, for a scholarship that was awarded to a member of our Choir. These funds provided support for two years of study at the Jacobs School of Music at Indiana University and led to a master's degree in music. Other

funds were contributed extraneously to St. George's to repay existing outstanding student loans for the recipient.
- The Choir Room piano was purchased in 2009. The funds for the piano came from the Choir Fund, which of late had been a special beneficiary of Ruth Adkins's generosity. While her gifts were not wholly responsible for the amount needed to purchase the piano, her donations had been so numerous and generous that the piano was dedicated in her honor.
- A set of hand bells was acquired a few years ago, probably with monies from the Choir Fund.

Seven separate funds affect music at St. George's. Delving into these has been like peeling an onion—when one has uncovered one layer, there's yet another beneath it. The most obvious such entity is the Friends of St. George's Music. Above and beyond its music as part of its worship, St. George's has a long history of presenting excellent concerts. Just as with the concept of a fully functioning Music Ministries Committee, it was the Report to the Vestry in 2006 that pointed the direction for formalizing this aspect of St. George's music ministry. As a result of that, the Friends of St. George's Music was founded pursuant to the 2006 Report and has been actively raising funds for its concert series through donations since. Concomitantly, the concert series was named *In Excelsis*, and the two have gone hand in hand ever since.

The second "layer" to appear is the Choir Fund. It apparently has been in existence for many years, variably active as to input and output. It has been used to assist selected choir members in having voice lessons; in purchasing the piano for the Choir Room, as noted above; in supplementing funding for choir tours abroad; and so forth. Private donations, both spontaneous and solicited, have enriched it, as have the profits from Choir fund-raising entertainment evenings at the church before major foreign tours. The origin of the third fund, the Instrumentalists Fund, like the Choir Fund, is lost in the mists of time. It is said to have derived from a contribution from a long-time parishioner, Grace Gardner, for the specific purpose of underwriting the costs of outside instrumentalists in conjunction with St. George's Choir programs.

The Wood Bell Fund exists to help underwrite maintenance of the Carillon. There is a Robertson Music/Library Fund, initiated around 1990. It is not clear at this point just how these funds have been used, but they do appear to have been initiated as a Memorial. The Somerville Scholarship Fund is currently the residual of the funding obtained to initiate the Scholarship as described above. As will be noted below, there is hope that they may serve as the foundation and stimulus for an ongoing scholarship program.

The funds from the major bequest noted above were folded into the St. George's Episcopal Church Trust Fund, as were the Instrumentalists and Robertson Funds. These funds are invested in the Episcopal Endowment Corporation and managed by an independent Board of Trustees, which include the Rector, the Senior Warden, and several members of St. George's, most of whom have belonged to the Vestry. The other funds just detailed are currently invested with Wachovia Securities, and usage is determined by the Vestry. All of these are reported to the parish in the Annual Report at the end of each calendar year.

The following table summarizes the fully designated funds mentioned above.

FULLY DESIGNATED FUNDS

FUND	ORIGIN	MANAGED	INVESTED	VALUE 12/10
Choir	?	Vestry	Wachovia	33,660
Wood Bell	ca. 1990	Vestry	Wachovia	4,311
Robertson Music/Library	1990	Board	EEC	10,841
Instrumentalists	ca. 1992	Board	EEC	10,543
Concert Series	2007	Vestry	Wachovia	13,511
Somerville Scholarship	2007	Vestry	Wachovia	7,620
TOTAL				80,486

In order to comprehend more recent aspects of music at St. George's it was necessary to gain some clarification about the interface between the Friends of Music at St. George's and the funding of Choir concerts in the budget. Understanding this relationship is important because much of the future of Anglican music at St. George's will be impacted by their combined public performances. The term *In Excelsis* was adopted to designate special musical offerings at St. George's. These offerings include those more distinctly part of our worship, e.g., Lessons and Carols and Sung Evensong, and also the special programs offered as a concert series each year. The former are funded through the budget. The latter are funded through the Friends of Music at St. George's program. This was begun upon the recommendation of and following the 2006 Report. It is managed by a small committee, one member of which is required to be a current member of the Vestry. The committee does not function under the Music Ministries Committee but is independent. Its main function is to raise funds to underwrite the cost of these concerts. Over the years since its inception it has been supported by a cadre of interested individuals, but it has generally had a hand-to-mouth existence. The chart *(chart 7)* shows this program's financial record for its first four years in operation.

Wider support is needed, and the *In Excelsis* concept needs higher visibility. There is no question but that Anglican Church music has been and should remain the hallmark of St. George's musical worship. To not just ensure but nourish that important goal, the parish needs to be further educated in the history and musicology of Anglican Church music, and the Friends of Music at St. George's needs increased financial support from both our own parishioners and interested persons without the parish itself.

None of these represent large amounts of money, and none offer long-term security for St. George's music. They are best considered a beginning. We need to take a longer look at our funding of music, recognizing the exceptional worthiness of what we have, and supporting it financially in the strongest possible way. These funds assist the Choir and the Music Staff to do a little more than just their budgeted funds would allow. They do not represent a pot of gold, an unending source of support. Additional ongoing support for choir, for concerts, and for scholarships must be a continuing effort of our parish.

There are dreams for the future of music at St. George's that will require extra-budgetary major funds to realize. Each of these is already being

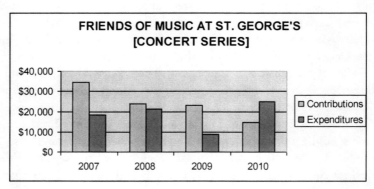

Chart 7.

studied carefully, even if it may be some years before they are accomplished. We need a new organ, one that is more attuned to Anglican Church music, with softer tones, more variable dynamics, and one that compensates for the non-stone walls of our sanctuary. We need choir stalls or moveable risers so that the Choir, instead of being hidden behind the altar, can be seen and heard to better effect. We need to continue the concept of a music scholarship by building an endowment that will permit Choristers and Music Staff to undertake further studies. Discussions are under way concerning the possibility of developing a School for the Arts that might evolve from our existing Kindergarten into an ultimately full elementary and secondary school focusing on music, to be sure, but the other arts as well. Each of these projects will require significant funding, some more than others, and all are worthy successors to the history of such giving at St. George's.

Summary

Delving into the finances of music at St. George's over its sixty years has been a fascinating, if sometimes frustrating, learning experience. That we have, more or less consistently, spent only 5% of our annual operating budget on music, which represents at least an estimated 35% of our Sunday worship experience, is significant. To be sure, that other 95% is required for infrastructure, outreach, education, and other activities. What this seems to be telling us is that we are getting a lot from our annual investment in music. The administration of music has been variable, largely in the first half century driven by the individual in the Organist/Choirmaster position. While that remains true, it is now complemented by the presence of a definitive Vestry component, the Music Ministries Committee. The challenge here will be to ensure that this committee remains involved, vital, and communicative. Finally, the non-budgetary finances, while certainly not a cohesive whole, do offer the opportunity to develop further these most important sources of funds that make excellence our standard, both in our worship and in our public concerts. As we look ahead to both structural and cultural possibilities that will require major gifts and continued extraneous giving, while at the same time steadily increasing our annual giving, we need to be certain that we constantly recognize and remind ourselves that they are not disconnected entities, but rather hugely important components of our daily worship and praise, of our strong mission, and of our future. It must be the goal of the Music Ministries Committee to keep not just the Vestry, but also the parish and the community, fully aware of St. George's music.

Appendix B
Two Interviews

This section contains transcribed interviews of Mark Ring, Director of Music Ministries, and Gerry Senechal, Assistant Director of Music Ministries. While these interviews were conducted for the use of the writers of this history, because their administration is relatively new when compared to earlier administrations, it has been considered wise to include the full interviews to make their thoughts more fully available to our parish.

Interview

Mark Ring, St. George's Episcopal Church
July 14, 2011

Q: What were your objectives when you came to St. George's?

A: Of course too many to list, but one of the most important things for me is to ensure that the primary mission of music here is in worship in a variety of settings. There are many other ways in which music is important to our parish and community through this parish. To ensure in an ongoing way that worship continues to be our focus with everything that we do and we are, toward that end, that we are engaging the broadest number of people that we can, the broadest constituency, especially with emphasis on growing music for children and youth. There were very good things already going on, but trying to expand that, to expand the type of repertoire that's done both by the Choir and in the concert series. To involve parishioners in music in a variety of ways. To infuse music into as many aspects of the parish as possible. That is an ongoing task there.

One thing I'd love to do and still is certainly ongoing is robust hymn singing, to involve the whole community in the song of the church. That is something that we still have to address and continue to work on. Also in the fullness of time to expand the music educational opportunities of the parish, both with expanding the existing programs and adding new programs that will hopefully culminate in a stand-alone academy here. That is the short list.

Q: What were your biggest challenges when you arrived?

A: I have to say the two biggest challenges that I've seen: one is, I have found both in all the places that I've worked and in places that I've studied, growing music across the ages of the participants almost always has to involve an evening, a Wednesday or a Thursday, here it's Wednesday, where there is a consistent turnout of a broad constituency in the parish on a variety of things on Wednesday evening. Right now most of the time it is just choirs that are going on, on Wednesdays. It's very hard to quantitatively grow choirs in that surrounding. The places I've been before where they've really grown well, there are consistent, multigenerational offerings every single Wednesday, not just "we're going to have a class for four weeks and take three weeks off." That there is a parish dinner for anyone who wishes to come every single Wednesday of the program year. You take off Christmas and Easter; otherwise people know that it's consistent, and that there are educational opportunities for children, youth, and adults, and there are music opportunities for children, youth, and adults on that evening when families tend to come. One of my prior churches where we were doing that, we had to come up with a grid of when each age would do music, when they would do Christian ed and whatnot. That required some organization, but it worked really well. I wound up in that church having to divide the children's choirs into a choir per grade because they had grown so much. It was directly attributable to great staff who worked with the kids and the fact that whole families were turning out every Wednesday night. That is one of the biggest challenges: quantitatively growing the music for children and youth in a context that is not real conducive to that. The second is that as the music program here has grown and evolved, some of its repertoire has changed. Some of its mission has changed. In order to do nineteenth-century and to the present day music of the Anglican tradition, we don't have an accompanimental instrument to do that successfully. That has been a real challenge. Doing the earlier music that is often unaccompanied can be done. To do the Anglican revival music, that literature, the organ was just not designed for that. It has a specific task and it fulfills that task, but it's not doing the job that the church has come to need. To do that music and to do it well and to try to provide an instrumental partner for that has been a significant challenge.

Q: What were/are your plans for a children's choir program?

A: From first grade on up, there is now a choir that meets every single week. The little guys, the first and second graders, used to meet only seasonally about a month in order to sing a song before Christmas and one time in the spring. That's now going every week on Sunday mornings following their Christian discipleship time. That can mean having more teaching opportunities, ongoing participation with them in worship and music. What I'd love to have happening here and that we started to achieve just this last year, we averaged having a youth or children's choir in worship three Sundays a month. We pretty much have the ages in place now. We have very good people working with them. I like the RSCM curriculum that they're doing wherein they learn musicianship, liturgy, there are some Christian discipleship components to it, so it's educating more of the whole child. I'd like to encourage more kids to be involved in that. I think the framework is there. There is good stuff going on, but at the same time I'd like to quantitatively grow that at this point.

Sociologically one thing that we see here and in many places is that we have a smaller number of boys participating than girls in the children's groups. This year we're going to have a separate boys' choir and girls' choir starting this fall. It will sociologically encourage the boys to be more participatory. It's something we're going to intentionally work with families to invite specific kids to be a part of this. I think the quantitative growth of that, both in terms of number of participants and to continue to grow how often they're singing in worship.

Q: What were/are your plans for the *In Excelsis* program?

A: This is a wonderful series, and I'm delighted to have inherited that. First of all, we're keeping a really strong Anglican music core to that. What would be different in a great concert series here as opposed to a great concert series in a church of another tradition that may still be excellent musically but would not necessarily have the same slant that we would have? One thing that's important to me is that each year there is a world-class group performing that is specifically in the Anglican tradition. We had for the past two years St. Thomas choir from New York, which is certainly the equal of any men and boys' choir in the empire, so to speak. This past year having the Tallis Scholars, you don't get any better than those guys. This year we're back to having an American group called Bella Voce from Chicago doing an all-Anglican program mainly of sixteenth- and seventeenth-century music. They are certainly the equal of the British groups.

Certainly featuring our own St. George's Choir in a variety of literature so that they can do things in a concert setting that simply don't fit as well in a liturgical setting and giving them the chance to sing with a variety of instrumental partners: chamber orchestra like is happening this fall. This Christmas concert is with a small wind ensemble doing the Respighi *Laud to the Nativity*, which is written for choir and winds. I love collaborating in ways of seeing our art in the light of how it intersects with other arts. The program this past year with the choir and the visual artist named Timothy Botts who did a great calligraphy work of art. The expansion of repertoire within the choir, and a lot of what we've done here is to focus on a wide variety of vocal music because it's a wonderful space for doing that and to provide our parish and the community with opportunities to hear music that they might not hear otherwise. We have the Westminster Choir, which is one of the finest collegiate choirs in the country, possibly *the* best, coming in January of next year, a very different style from the Anglican tradition but one that is equally valid and marvelously artistic. People think and feel differently about a program depending on the materials that they physically see for it, so we've been tweaking, updating the visuals for *In Excelsis*. I'm very excited about the brochure and the posters that we're going to have this year. We're working with a terrific independent graphic designer. The offerings are still very good, but this is going to look and feel differently largely because of what people have in their hand, which I think will encourage more people to check out the offerings.

Q: What are your thoughts about the choir(s) touring?

A: I love it. Depending on where they're going, I think that the choirs benefit by greater exposure; to a culture, to other artistic expressions. When you sing, for instance, Palestrina in a room where he worked, it feels different, and you never sing Palestrina the same again. You infuse your music with the ethos that spawned it. So for the Choir to have gone and sung in cathedrals and collegiate chapels in Britain was magnificent. They feel differently about music in the Anglican tradition, having done that. For St. Gregory's Choir to go and sing for a week in Washington Cathedral is magnificent. I've always toured with my choirs and I'm very much hopeful that once we get some economic recovery under our belt, we'll be able to do the same thing with St. George's Choir.

Q: Are there things that you wish by now you had seen but haven't?

A: I wish the Choir could have toured by now. There is a great deal of interest and support from the Choir. But economically, it is just not feasible to do that. I'm not sure to have it released, but I would like to have had a commercial recording at least recorded by now. Again, economic considerations forbade that. By now I wish we could have an organ contract, but again we were significantly hit in many ways by the flood. These are things we will move forward on.

Q: Name five visions that you had for the music ministry at St. George's when you came that you have seen fulfilled.

A: Some are fulfillment, and some are partial fulfillment and well on their way. I would say at the outset, one thing that's exciting to me is to see some growth in children's and youth music.

I'm extremely pleased with the continued growth of the concert series in terms of its offerings and also in terms of the growth in attendance at that. The type of groups, the repertoire, the collaboration, I'm pleased with that. I'm delighted with everything that's going on in this upcoming season.

Another one is an ongoing thing: an expansion of emphasis in the choral repertoire of doing more music from nineteenth, twentieth, twenty-first centuries that is specifically in the Anglican tradition. I come at this, yes, I'm an organist, but first I'm a conductor both in church and in secular settings, having taught secondary school, university level, and professional groups. Most of my career has been in conducting. I'm not a repertoire specialist. My specialty is being broad in the choral literature that I love and in doing each type of it stylistically where Palestrina and Brahms should never sound the same. They are totally different music, and the human voice is so wonderfully flexible in what we're able to do. I'd love to continue to expand that repertoire. We've done more things of Anglican cathedral tradition with organ. We're doing some things temporarily with the digital organ in the church in order to accompany, and expanding more music from the Continent, more music from the Americas and some recent music that is absolutely artistic, first quality in every way, some literature expansion, and doing more things with a variety of instruments as well. The first concert in our series this fall, we're doing Stravinsky, "The Soldier's Tale," and it will be staged. It's extremely rare for a church to do something that is that musically complex, that has an appropriate moral tale associated with it. This is edgy. It's almost a hundred years old, but it's extremely modern sounding. To be able to do that with the full support of the church in the concert series is wonderful.

Another one I'm pleased that happened right after I came was that we had a chance to take the Choir Room physically and warm it up. We painted that space in two different colors where it simply feels different now than it did before. Also we're delighted to have a wonderful rehearsal piano in there. Through a number of generous gifts, we were able to get a Boston grand piano that is a wonderful tonal model for the Choir. Consciously or not, choirs tend to sound like the instrument they rehearse with. The piano that was in there before had been a gift to the church. It was extremely thin and bright in its tone. It's hard to get a choir to sound warm and rich when they're accompanied thin and bright. This new piano is a wonderful tool. It's easier for them to sing beautifully with it.

I'm also pleased that we have begun the process of examining what we can do for an accompanimental organ in the church and what we've been able to accomplish thus far.

Q: How does your background inform how you adopted these visions and how you see them being fulfilled?

A: I have a degree in organ. I was Assistant University Organist at Yale. I love doing that, but I come at choirs as a singer. I think you approach how you sing a line, how you form tone, the sort of repertoire that you do and how you do it differently if you're coming at it from a more literally digital standpoint as a keyboardist than as really what's a more analog, lyrical direction coming at it as a singer. I think those things come together, having lived and worked in a variety of places, both regions of the country and two different places in Europe. So to me, it is the breadth of that, that I enjoy bringing and sharing with the Choir and with the younger folks as well.

Q: What are the five most important visions you had that have yet to be fulfilled? Speak specifically to your concept of what kind of sound needs to be heard in the sanctuary, vocally and instrumentally. What will it take to make this happen?

A: This is a great question, especially about the type of sound. A choir needs to be extremely communicative. Any other form of making music you've got something between you and your listener. The instrument, however expressive it may be, is physically between the musician and the audience, the congregation, those who are listening. There is an immediacy in using the human voice where your body is the instrument. I prefer a very warm choral sound, which has to be not only with resonance but how you balance sound in a choir. To me, it's a pyramid: you're stronger on the bottom and lighter as it gets closer toward the top in terms of the voice parts, the notes that are being employed.

Concurrent with that, it's great to have the Choir in the apse. I love having them in two rows deep and in a semicircle. That is a wonderful seating arrangement for the Choir; they can hear each other very well. However, most of their sound goes and hits the back of the altar and stops. When you move them out onto the altar steps, they sound twice as big and more immediate. It's a totally different sound, and it's not just because they are a few feet closer. I would love to have semi-permanent risers up there where when the Choir is seated, they're still not obvious but when they stand, their heads are above the level of the altar so that this wonderful sound they're making gets out into the church so much easier.

Q: What part does your passion for youth music ministry play in these visions?

A: It's huge. As the parent of two young kids, it's so important for me to see them and obviously everyone's children to have the opportunity to learn, to grow, to participate in music in a church setting. To me, it's an important part of nurturing the whole child. I think it's incumbent on us to do that for all of our children of all ages, where they have great opportunities for music, for worship, for Christian discipleship, for service. These things all work together. We don't have adult choirs tomorrow if we don't have great kids' choirs today.

Q: Why are our attendance numbers at musical events, worship and concert, not larger?

A: I'd say three things: one is obviously as is everywhere, people are simply extremely busy. Their time is very divided; there are many things pulling on them, wanting their attention. There are many worthy things that folks are not able to do. That is the cultural context that everyone has to deal with. The second one is that it will help us to collaborate where we have offerings that will appeal to more than one constituency. When we had the event this past year with the Choir and the artist-calligrapher, half the people were there because they were energized to see this artist-calligrapher. They knew of his work and wanted to come; they wouldn't have come just to a choir event and vice versa. Once someone comes and sees how wonderful it is, we hook them in with these collaborations, and then they're more likely to come back. A third one is that we are continuing to grow how we market and brand and communicate the offerings we have. We need to be capturing contact information from everyone who walks in the door to one of these things. There really has not been that mechanism in place before. Those who do come here, make sure we invite them back and have a way in which to do that. Instead of just "if you build it, they will come," to very actively market, including through social media and e-mail marketing, which has not been done very much before. And to have programs (a) that people will want to come to and (b) that they know about in ways that people tend to engage right now.

Q: What communications strategies would assist you in getting the message out as to opportunities for spiritual growth through the music ministries at St. George's?

A: Well, some of that is using electronic media. But in terms of opportunities for spiritual growth, one thing we're doing very deliberately is working through Christian discipleship, particularly with youth and children. That we're seen as not two separate entities as much as shoulder to shoulder working for the best interests of these kids together in providing opportunities for each other. It's a wonderful staff to work with here. For instance, when kids come to vacation Bible school, their parents and their siblings who may not be in VBS get specific invitations to do Kindermusik. When they come to drop off their kids at VBS, the siblings who are not in VBS can come and do a one-time class. We're scheduling things like they've never been scheduled before for youth so that kids are encouraged to do both the youth choir and the youth discipleship, which happens right after, and they have a shared fellowship time in between. We're trying to coordinate offerings so that they are seen as integrated and not something that's in a different wing of the building and where people are apart.

Q: What do you believe was the vision/direction of St. George's music prior to your arrival?

A: Some of that I would have to leave to my esteemed predecessor, Murray. I do want to take the opportunity to say how absolutely fabulously supportive he has been since I have come here. I could not ask for a better or more supportive predecessor. I am very honored to be following him and really appreciative of the support that he has shown. I think that he was, from what I have seen and experienced, along with the overall clergy leadership of the parish leading the parish into more of a specifically Anglican identity in terms of worship, in terms of music. Previously, going back and seeing the music that had been done, services, service types, it was an Episcopal church, of course, but much of the musical repertoire could have been at home in a variety of traditions, particularly the more mainline Protestant denominations. There is nothing wrong with that, but it did not have an Anglican bent in terms of the repertoire that was being done. To have Anglican chant every week is frankly the core of what's going to define us. The specific repertoire—Tudor period, Byrd, Tallis, Tye, Tavener, all those guys who helped to define the early Anglican music tradition, and then with its reinvigoration in the late nineteenth and into the twentieth century, the luminaries of English composition—Howells, Vaughan Williams, Elgar, Bairstow, Finzi, all of these wonderful composers—he was really bringing more of an emphasis on that. Also between Murray and also with Gerry, the youth choir, St. Gregory's, coming into its own under Gerry's leadership, and then the institution of the RSCM, the curriculum of church music, broadening and deepening the experience that the kids had coming up. Also under Murray's time, the formation of the concert series. Those are unique opportunities to do things that could not have been done previously.

Murray is a truly world-class expert in early music, particularly that of the Baroque. That was a real emphasis in the series. I love that music as well. It is still a significant part of what we do, but my focus is not as much on that as his was. I see a broadening of the repertoire in that series, not that it wasn't done really well before. I have nothing but praise for what was done, but a little shift in direction. I think what I am doing is to continue to grow on what he had done.

Q: Has your vision for St. George's music changed since you first began?

A: Not changed so much as refined in terms of how we try to accomplish that. To have time to listen to people, to talk to people, to see what has been done, what has not been done, what is comfortable for folks, different ways to accomplish these things. The disruption, the monumental disruption, of the flood both in terms of the physical plant of the building and in the life of this parish, I think, is larger than some people may realize. Yes, there was damage to the building, but there was still ministry going on here as well as ever. Program was not. Most of our building was gone. I think that we're right now poised, because we have a better facility than we had before the flood, to do better things, better ministry, better programs. But in some ways we had a significant setback in terms of what we've been able to change and to offer programmatically because of that. We sort of hit a reset button in a variety of ways. I think we came back better both in terms of a physical plant and as a parish family than we were before. Now the facility is fully open and we're really engaging in getting some traction in moving programmatically forward in ways we haven't been able to.

Q: What was it about the opportunity at St. George's that attracted you to apply?

A: As I said to Leigh when I came and interviewed, I didn't need a job. I had four of them at the time: one full-time, one half-time, a couple part-time doing a lot of music in a variety of ways. It's not a job. It's a calling. This is an extremely unusual parish. They are serious about their faith. They are serious about the value of music in the human life. We're made in the image of our Creator, and therefore we are creative. By being creative, we're living out who we're made to be. They are serious about prayer. They are serious about what they do, but they don't take themselves so seriously. It's a good community in which to live, to grow. You can come here and be vulnerable. That's the only way you can really grow, I think. I'm delighted to be a part of that. I think it's an outstanding team of clergy and staff here. We have a marvelous volunteer tradition in music and also some outstanding folks on stipend in music. This place values its history and its heritage, but it's not mired in it. It wants to continually grow and evolve and engage with and change the culture around it. Those things combined make a compelling place to live out a calling.

Q: What is your philosophy on having volunteer and professional singers as part of the Choir?

A: I think it is absolutely ideal. John Bertalot, who is British and was in a number of prestigious positions in Great Britain, wound up at Trinity Episcopal Church in Princeton, New Jersey. He taught on the side at Westminster Choir College for a number of years as well. He ran an amazing program there as well. I learned a lot from him personally and from his writings. He said that the only thing voluntary about a volunteer choir is the act of joining. Once you're in, you are committed to working as hard and being there as often as those who are paid to be there. It's a very dedicated group of volunteers here, with a very high level of talent. The Choir without its volunteers is markedly inferior to the Choir with volunteers. It's an outstanding group. At the same time the Choir without its professionals is markedly inferior. I think we have a wonderful balance of that. It's a tradition of doing extremely good music very well over many, many years. St. George's has a great reputation in the community for choral. Vocal artists want to come and sing here. That balance is absolutely essential. We are engaged with and a part of the parish, and at the same time our music making is elevated by those who come and join us from outside as well.

Q: If you had twice the volunteers in the Choir, would you see a need for professional singers? What do you consider the ideal mix?

A: Short answer, yes. I'd love to have more volunteer singers, of course. One thing that is important is maintaining a balance between the sections. But the professional singers, there is a level of expectation. There is more a level of accountability involved with the professional singers that is essential to doing things at the level at which they are being done. At the same time, that is not to shortchange the marvelous contributions of the volunteers. But the accountability present with the professional singers enables us to do things that we would not be able to do otherwise.

Q: Now that you have been at St. George's several years, what would you consider the music ministries' greatest strengths?

A: The greatest strengths are these wonderful people that I get to work with every week. They are very dedicated. They are very talented. I tell any choir that I work with that we all leave our egos at the door. When we walk in, we have to be vulnerable. We have to be willing to take a chance and make an absolute bloomer of a mistake. If you don't, you're not pushing the edge of how good you can be. When I was teaching, I always encouraged my students that "you come in here and you make an absolutely huge mistake, good for you because you've tried to do something amazing. You blew it. Okay, we can fix that. We can grow from that. But if you come in and you're timid, you can be good but never great." These wonderful people are willing to do that and willing to explore and grow. By being able to do that, the sky is the limit. As long as we can inculcate that in our children, in our youth, in their families, we're dedicated to growing and nurturing and challenging all at the same time.

Gerry is like a younger brother that I never had. He is a great person. Love him to death. He's a very, very fine colleague. I've never worked with a better service player in my life. I would say without qualification that he is one of the very finest service players in any Anglican church in the world, period. He is just a joy to work with. We get along well personally and work extremely well together professionally. It's a great team.

Q: How well do you think the Anglican church music tradition is understood by each of these groups? Clergy, musicians (staff and choirs), congregation, public.

A: I'd like to take these in a different order, starting with musicians. Gerry and I both bleed Anglican music if we're cut. We're absolutely immersed in this and have extremely consonant views in terms of the ethos of Anglican music in worship, much of the literature and the repertoire that's done stylistically, how you approach these things. The choirs, the kids coming up, one of the wonders of the RSCM program is how it educates the kids: not only okay, we're going to sing this number in worship but also why, historical background. You learn by doing and seeing the role of music in liturgy, which is somewhat specific in our tradition. Coming up with that for years and having been educated in that, I feel very good about the kids coming up with that. The adult choir, St. George's Choir, has through the years evolved into more and more of an Anglican literature–centered choir. Doing Anglican chant every week changes the way you approach text and how you hear each other. This is all sung prayer, and in the Anglican tradition we are what's called the vicar's chorale. We sing the praises and prayers of the people on their behalf when we're singing. We don't sing *to* the congregation. We sing to God on behalf of the congregation. We talk about that openly, seeing that role as important. It is a continuing education effort with the choirs because we've come from a variety of backgrounds. I see that as a positive and growing thing.

The congregation does, I think, have a very great appreciation for very good music. Many of them who have been here for a period of time have not experienced as much Anglican music specifically. The specific Anglican literature, how it's done, what's done, does not have a long history here. It has been a part of the mix, but it hasn't been central, except for the last few years. So I think it's not as well understood as it could be by the congregation.

By the public, probably not understood very much at all in terms of what it is and why it's different from others.

In terms of the clergy, they're all extremely supportive, and I'm very, very grateful for that. They actually come from a variety of traditions and backgrounds, so some of them have simply had more chance to experience the specific music of our tradition than others of them have.

Q: How can this understanding be increased for each of these groups by the music ministries?

A: Partly just by doing what we're doing. By living with it week in and week out, you begin to feel and understand the ethos of what's happening. Another one is by simply providing educational opportunities, explaining this as we go. If it's doing a Christian ed forum, if it's through articles in the newsletter, in the *Shield*, if it's through the bulletin on Sunday morning, through education of the young people as they come up through the program—I think it's not one silver bullet for this. Anytime you have a chance to not only do it, but to help explain and answer questions about what you're doing, to engage in dialogue about it, that's very helpful.

Q: Is the *Hymnal 1982* used adequately at St. George's as an educational tool?

A: In my opinion, no. We use it to sing four hymns on Sunday morning, but during my time here, that's unfortunately been as far as it's gone. I'd love to have the chance to have both adults and youth to understand hymnody in greater depth of the traditions of what has happened and when. Why does this hymn sound and feel in a certain way because of when and where it was written, as opposed to another one? To me, you always approach it theologically first. We always look at the text as the first step of the most important song of the people, which is what hymns are, and then move to the musical aspects. I wish going forward that we will have a greater utilization of that, to have more teachable opportunities. I'd love to have a hymnody class. Any educational opportunity like that, both inside and outside of the Sunday morning experience, would be very helpful to encourage folks that this is the music of the people. This is the song of the body of Christ.

One of the things I did in a previous church was to have all of the constituency—congregation, leadership—engage in a survey. We established thirty-six hymns that embodied the theology and the ethos of who that body of Christ was in that place. I'd love to do the same thing here. It was thirty-six so that we could do a hymn of the month, nine months of the year, during the program year, for four years. It's a reasonable number that could include things from different seasons, different aspects of the Christian faith that not only get to be memorized but learned by heart emotionally. Then hopefully to be able to record those in our church as a testament of "here's who we are theologically and musically."

Q: How can *Music as Mission*, the music history publication being prepared, best assist these efforts?

A: I think frankly by establishing a context, the breadth of what has been going on here for decades. We often experience things without necessarily thinking too deeply about them. We all live very busy lives. This is a wonderful opportunity for this Christian family and this place to think more deeply, to look and understand the many things that have gone on here for decades, to bring it into the forefront of not just experiencing it but thinking about it, what it has meant and what it can be in terms of the life of this parish and what we have done and what our mission and vision are and how we can go about achieving those things together.

Q: How aware are you of the presence of the Music Ministries Committee of the Vestry?

A: Certainly aware of it. It's not a committee that meets regularly as such, but it's a touchstone for me to be able to present visions, to get feedback, and to know that they're there for counsel and support at any time that we may need them.

Q: How could it better function in its role within the church?

A: I think that as we move forward that possibly having not only one Vestry liaison, who is of course on that committee, but to have folks on the committee to be resource people, liaisons if you will, for the different aspects of the church. Right now on that committee there are people with whom we already work in these different areas, who by the nature of that are the representative on that committee. If that person can be more actively on the team, as it were, I think that can be helpful.

Interview

Gerry Senechal, St. George's Church
Thursday, June 30, 2011

Q: What were your objectives when you came to St. George's?

A: I'm ashamed to say that when I first came, my intentions were sort of self-centered. I didn't have a tremendous vision for St. George's. I had just come from West End United Methodist Church where I was the organ intern for two years. I then moved to Plano, Texas, for two months to be, oddly enough, what I thought was a Canterbury on earth, the Mecca of Anglicanism. Instead it was a very different situation. I was brought down there to help Anglicize a music department. The truth quickly came out that was not the intention, so in a panic I wrote letters to every Episcopal church around Nashville, saying, "I'm looking for a job up there. If you all know of one, please let me know." Bless her heart, Elizabeth Smith found my letter that I mailed to her. She had already decided that she was going to move on, so she presented the letter to Murray, and that started the process of me getting here.

I was so delighted to have an Episcopal church and one of this magnificent stature and reputation that I was just thrilled to be alive. I wasn't burning with vision at that point. Of course I wanted to become a better service player. The last time I had played in an Episcopal church regularly had been when I was eight until I was twelve in my father's tiny Episcopal church in Massachusetts. There was a much different level of things back then. I sang in the choir at Sewanee for four years, but I hadn't done much playing at all. I was looking forward to being a mature Anglican player in a way that I hadn't been able to before, things like psalm accompaniment. All the demands of a service of this magnitude were what I was really focusing on at that point.

Q: How has your vision for the music ministry at St. George's changed during your time here?

A: Oh, my goodness. Everything has changed. What I would consider the focus of my ministry here would be St. Gregory's Choir. When I came, I had no real interest in children's choirs or youth ministry. Obviously I had a little bit of desire to be a youth minister of some sort, but there was no burning passion within me to get this done. Murray asked me if I would begin working with this group of I think it was six choristers who were the older age. The first year or two it was pretty rough. I had no idea what I was doing. It was just disaster. Then slowly they began to catch on musically, and I began to catch on to things I could improve on. I began to see their spirit that was so exemplary. Kids even as old as high school don't have that bar that adults do: We can't do that; that's beyond our grasp right now. If you give them a goal, they will do all they can to get there. They have never ceased to reach and exceed the bar that I've placed for them. Their sound is also wonderfully unadulterated. People sometimes have twenty minutes of vocal training, and they have all these preconceived notions and all these apprehensions about singing. These kids haven't had that; they are like a blank canvas, and you can do all these wonderful things with their voices that they are not afraid to do. They are uninhibited, and they can be so free with that.

Basically my vision for the church has changed a great deal and now encompasses not only growing youth programs of all of the youth choirs; I'm also much more comprehensive in involving the congregation in worship.

If I had a blank slate for the future, I would love to see St. George's on the same level as Grace Cathedral, the National Cathedral, and St. Thomas, not by design but because I think we could be a bastion of the Anglican tradition as far as the breadth of what we do in worship, maybe recording facilities, maybe a stunning Anglican-American instrument to keep the Anglican choir tradition alive as far as a men and boys choir and a women and girls choir. The adult choir even we could put the hammer down a little bit more with our Anglican tradition in that.

Leigh is very big on us being a resource center for the diocese because we are so blessed here, and there is no need to reinvent the wheel. Smaller parishes often come here for various things to learn how we do things to make their own lives better. I think we can be the same way even for the national church, however we want to be involved with the national church. We can be a resource parish for them musically. I think that could be in our future.

Q: What were your biggest challenges when you arrived?

A: I had to learn how to play in service the best that I possibly could. I had never accompanied a psalm before. I had sung a lot of Anglican chant, going back to being a boy soprano in the All Saints' Men and Boys Choir in Worcester, Massachusetts. I loved to chant. Playing it and singing it are very, very different. It is an art in itself because there's so much the organist can do that's not on the page to help invigorate the text, which is what all good church music does. It was a quick but pleasant learning curve, and Murray was very versatile and helped me a great deal. I'm afraid my challenges weren't lofty goals, but just personal goals for my playing.

Q: What were/are your plans for a children's choir program?

A: I have been amazed by the impact the children's choirs here has had. It's not just, "Well, the kids have to get up and sing, and the parents like it. You're supposed to have a choir for that age." The kids—I'm speaking specifically of the ones I've had experience with, which is third grade and higher—they can contribute tremendously to worship. They are a very real part and a very Anglican part, I think, of our worship. We always think, *We need to get these kids to be spiritual.* They are so much more spiritual often than we are; we just have to guide them in their spirituality. They understand worship and know what they are doing. Sometimes there are other issues of focus and attention to things that we perhaps have a better hold on than they do. Not always.

We need to have more of them. That is the ongoing challenge that we have because this type of music is not easy. Combine that with the fact that if you don't have a child singing by third grade, chances are that they never will start singing because people become very aware of their inhibitions about third grade. Singing is a very personal thing. People feel very exposed when they sing. If we don't have them that early, it's hard to retain them. I've had several students join St. Gregory's but then drop out. I've had some wonderful exceptions that have stayed—great kids that are very dedicated, very motivated. But it's hard to come in midstream. This year especially we are having a renewed push to get kids involved in first and second grade, if not third grade, to keep them going.

This is my personal greedy mission: I'd love to have a men and boys choir with perhaps a women and girls choir to complement it singing Evensong regularly, perhaps even leading one of the Sunday morning services every week. That's what I grew up doing and it was amazing. I think it has great fruits. It takes a great deal of constant work, but it would be worth every moment. So that's my grand plan, my selfish plan, for the children's program.

Q: What were/are your plans for the *In Excelsis* program?

A: This was the number one thing as interim that I had no idea what I was doing: how to form a concert series. It is multifaceted and needs a great deal of experience to do well. I relied on other people who knew a lot better than I did. Murray actually planned the entire year before he left, which was a great benefit to me. I think the questions that I raised as interim with the group were: What makes this concert series a church concert series? How does this differ from a normal concert program? The answer is not always Jesus, as it is in Sunday school. We need to really think about how this glorifies God and how to be good stewards of the considerable funds and this opportunity we have to present music to people. Mark is bringing in wild and crazy things that this program has never seen before, and he is certainly stretching my fusty old boundaries. The English cathedral choir is the pinnacle for me. Of course there are a lot of valid expressions of worship and expressions of musical praise that are coming in now. I'm slowly stretching my boundaries.

Q: Were there things you wanted to accomplish but didn't?

A: Oh, yes, there are still so many things that are unfulfilled here, but I think are still in the pipe. The children's choir program is really beginning to flourish. I say, beginning, but we have a long way to go. We don't need to have three hundred kids in the Chancel, but we do need to have a core, a strong group, where we can have three, four, five people absent and still go on well. It's not fair for those who are so faithful that they can never be out. I think we're above critical mass now, but I want this to be a vibrant, beautiful ministry that many children can take advantage of. It changed my life as a chorister. I think that is not just a product of the 1980s. That is still a valid thing today.

There is a lot to do as far as the infrastructure. We tried hard in 2008 to bridge the gap between the Choir and the congregation. We do have a lovely sanctuary. Unfortunately the layout is such, the Choir feels very, very separated. I watched the first few years I was here as the Choir seemed to become even more alienated from the worship and even from the clergy, though they were the closest to us. We were looking at the back of heads. The sound system is still not what it needs to be. The last two weeks I've hardly heard a word from the sermon. We're looking at options there.

The Choir is an integral part of worship, and they are worship leaders.

It is easy to feel as if they're the backstage musicians that are called upon to produce beautiful sounds from time to time. We had some screens put back there so they can watch the service. That makes a great deal of difference. The only qualm is when adults and children alike see that they're on the screen, they start staring at the screen instead of the conductor. "Yes, your hair looks fine. Let's keep singing. How about that?"

We are looking at trying to get some risers to bring the Choir up a bit so that they can be seen and their sound will come over the altar. It's amazing how much sound is absorbed by the altar. The Choir tends to oversing because they feel they're so far from the congregation they have to do that to be heard. But they don't. The acoustics are so live that the sound does not change very much as far as volume the farther you go back in the room. The blend becomes a little bit more luscious, which can make the spoken word be hard to understand. The consonants can drop off a bit. On the whole it tends to become more ethereal as you get further from the sound. We have to be intentional about that gap and try to fix that.

Of course the organ. We need an instrument that can beautifully and faithfully render the Anglican service. That is such a huge part of the Anglican tradition, psalm accompaniment, whether it is the congregation or the Choir. This instrument was really geared toward performance of French music. The organs in France that it was modeled after never had to accompany anybody; they were just playing this big music. It's very difficult and very cumbersome to try to do the great music of the Anglican tradition on an instrument that is sort of fighting you all the way. It has very little bass and a lot of treble. I use about the bottom third of the organ. You're hearing the best it has to offer, but it is only about a third even at its loudest. As a result, people don't feel as surrounded by sound. It's very loud, but it is sort of a spoonful of Tabasco sauce versus a steak dinner. Tabasco can really get your attention, but the sound needs to be full and warm and embracing without being loud. That is so crucial. People go down the road in their car and they bump the bass because it feels good. They can feel the music. Worship deserves every advantage like that. The only reason I'm on staff is to further facilitate the engagement between God and man. If that's not happening, it doesn't matter what we're doing; it's not right. Hymn singing is where the rubber meets the road for worshipers, where people can connect with God in a very special, a very holy way. I think that's why God invented music. I'll get more into that later when I talk about the congregational aspect of worship.

Q: Name five specific goals that you had when you began your ministry here.

A: I had three. The first was to improve psalm accompaniment. Psalm chant is a very distinctively Anglican thing, and there are no books, no DVD series. The best psalm accompanists are organists in the great cathedrals who do it every day. They do every psalm once a month, so there are ten to fifteen minutes of psalm chant every day at Evensong. Some of the greats like John Scott Whiteley, who just retired from York Minster, didn't even use a psalter. He had the pointing, everything memorized, and every moment something was happening. There was a stop coming off. The accompanist—it is incumbent upon him to make it expressive and to really express the text. There is a lot I had to pick up on there. The instrument is not as versatile as it could be to give us the colors of an Anglican chant.

I think when I came, I wanted to introduce some original music to the repertoire. I feel a great burden in that because there is so much incredible music already out there. There are a lot of people writing music because they can, and I feel a tremendous burden that if I'm going to contribute, it needs to be worthwhile. I've done a very small amount. I keep wanting to wait because I know it will be better if I do it later, but if I don't start, it will never get better. I'm trying to contribute something. I'm working on a few anthems at the moment, which I've only done once. That's one of my goals, but again more of a goal for me than for the ministry.

When I came, I wanted to improve my abilities as an organist certainly, and I think I've been able to do that. Of course I've got a great ways to go. Playing regularly here has been so helpful for bettering my skills as a worship musician.

Q: How does your understanding of the Anglican liturgy and worship tradition inform the visions that you have for St. George's now? In the next five years?

A: I was ruined at an early age by being a boy soprano in a men and boys choir. Having had zero experience with any sort of truly Anglican tradition before that, I was just awash in the great beauty of the tradition. I think I was maybe eleven when I started that. I thought, *This is amazing. This is how God deserves to be worshiped.* That has informed my understanding of the tradition. Of course it doesn't work everywhere. But if it works anywhere, it has got to be St. George's. This church has all the infrastructure in place, minus some things we want to improve, to really foster a program like that and to keep this great jewel of Anglican worship going strong. Already we are doing a great deal of good Anglican worship, and I think there are more specific ways, even more beautiful ways, even more dignified and strong ways that we can add to our worship in the tradition. A lot of those will perhaps have to do with the formation of St. George's Academy and a choir school. To really harvest the ripest fruits the tradition has to offer, for me, you've got to have the clear, clear sound of trebles. Boys and girls have very different sounds. I love the boy sound, but the girl sound is equally valid and beautiful. Then that rich, rich male sound underneath them. Our men are among the best men that I've ever heard. They rival any English cathedral. They have that wonderful dignified roar. I can thank John Fitzgerald and Don Cowan for that, for the most part. It's never out of control. It's never too wobbly or to bring attention to themselves. Instead it's this wonderfully powerful, dignified sound, and that is as much a part of the sound as the clarity of the trebles. We are already halfway there. You can train boys; it's hard to train men to do that. Boys or girls don't have this mental block yet. That's the next five years, as far as I am concerned.

Q: What part does your leadership in youth music ministries play in those visions?

A: Mark is absolutely an amazing colleague. I say colleague. I've never had a working relationship like the one I've had with him. He supports me so much in every way that he can, and because of his support and his encouragement, I'm taking an even greater role in the children's choirs this coming year. I'm going to run things, for the most part. We have some very faithful help from St. George's Choir to help us with this. I think it's important that I really am having a lot of face time with the kids and I'm dealing with them personally. I'm going to be directing three of the choirs this coming year. We're going to split what has been the third through seventh graders into boys and girls for the first time and start to play with having them sing with the men occasionally, perhaps as a foreshadowing, although Mark wants them to stand on their own often too. At first I thought we needed to have this group working well as a feeder for St. Gregory's. Then I came to realize through experience how very valuable the third through seventh graders are in their very own right, not just as the farm team for the older choir. Especially for boys, by the eighth or ninth grade, it is game over for them as trebles. I want to explore how far we can take them in that short amount of time that we have as intelligent singers for the boys before their voices change. For girls, they just keep getting better as they get older.

Q: How can the involvement of youth be increased?

A: That is the million-dollar question. It is very hard for me to find the kids that are overtly musical and say, "Hey, you need to be in the choir." I've tried and tried to think of different ways to do this. David Bennett and Sarah Kerr are absolutely amazing, and I have such great hope for what they're going to do in the youth ministry. They have been nothing but a help in every aspect that they've been involved with us. I'm going to work with them again this year to try to get ahold of which kids sing at all. They have a better chance of being the more musical ones who may enjoy choir and getting them in at a young age. I'm also writing letters to all the second-grade parents, saying, "Hey, we're starting. This is the last chance your child has to become a musician before they shut down and don't want to sing. So please let us have them and give it a shot. Here are the benefits. Here are the things that music does for your child, and they can be a vibrant part of the ministry of the church." I continue to maintain that we need to get them early. It is so hard to get them later on. We don't need to stop trying. I don't see these kids because I'm always in church or in rehearsal when they're here. I can't just drop into a Sunday school class and say, "Hey, join the Choir. Who are you?" We need to work on that.

Q: What specific examples can you give of successes and challenges in youth music programs since you came to St. George's? In adult involvement in the Choir? In new initiatives for music and worship?

A: I think the first and most pressing challenge is the organ. People say, "You've done this for all this time with what's there." I say, "Yes, but we want to go further. We want to go deeper into the tradition; we want to create more beautiful and inspiring and moving worship—music that you can feel." Especially when it comes to accompanying the choirs in the Anglican tradition, what we have now is just not able to do that. I can't begin to think of how amazing it will be when we finally have an instrument that can really accompany the tradition and produce breathtaking, glorious sounds every week. That is certainly a challenge to deal with now. We're trying lots of different ways to remedy that at least in the short term. We're getting some digital organs in there, which are not as satisfactory. We're considering a few different things. That is the number one thing that's standing in our way at the moment, and it's becoming increasingly maddening as we listen to these other samples of organs that do this so well. It makes us all the more frantic to have that here and give it to these people who come in every week and deserve to be inspired. We need to give them fire for the week ahead. They can go in their car and be able to feel and experience that. They can't do it in church. It's not fair. I think it is like our vision of heaven, sort of beautiful and lofty and glorious. Having sat in the pew a few times, it seems like what is happening at the front, the music is beautiful and glorious, but it is sort of removed, sort of distant. It's not easy to participate.

The formation of St. Gregory's, which began as the youth choir, was certainly a challenge at first. I did not enjoy it at first, and bless their hearts, they probably didn't either because their director was a hopeless wreck. Over time something amazing has evolved. I would do anything for those kids. They are so smart and such good, good people. They've brought me to tears on several occasions with the beauty of what they've contributed to worship. They're just amazing, but it didn't start that way. It was a beautiful process to turn into what it is now.

They've given rise to some of the greatest successes that we've had. Touring, they were in Washington National Cathedral in Washington, D.C., in residence for a week. That was a big deal. Every bit of that was hard, but very few choirs can say they've been in residency at the National Cathedral, and they led Evensong every day. We sang Evensong in the National Cathedral with far few singers than a regular-sized choir might have, certainly less than the National Cathedral choir. That room is one of the largest cathedrals in the world, and the organ is in Egypt. It is up feet and feet over your head; you have to listen so carefully for the pitch whenever you're not singing. It is a huge challenge. They're like the special forces of church music; there were so few of them when we went there. But they did magnificently. They sang Evensong at Champaign, Illinois, at Sewanee, and at West End Methodist. They've really been around and done a lot of really good things.

It just brings joy to my heart when I hear one of them walking by, singing one of the great anthems of the tradition. They're going to keep those their whole lives, and you can't put a value on that. I'm reading a lot of articles about people on their death beds, and even after dementia has set in and so much is gone, they still have the hymns. Music is the last thing to go. Often people learn theology best through music. That they can have these things and they will always have them—that is amazing to me. I am so proud of that.

We don't have a lot of rehearsal time. We have an hour a week. We used to have forty-five minutes. There is so little time on Wednesdays. They are all taking AP everything. They're all great kids and so involved in school and all kinds of other things. Parents say, "They've got homework." I am noticing that as the program grows and as the kids become more and more devoted to the program, there is less: "They have homework, and they can't come to rehearsal." I tried to end rehearsal early a few months ago, and there was like a riot. They wouldn't hear of it. They said, "No, we're going to sing this. Bring out this music." This is great.

St. Dunstan's and the other children's choirs sang a two-part piece in the spring of 2009. Previously St. Dunstan's had been third grade through twelfth grade, and trying to keep both those ages involved, only Jesus can do. In 2008 we split from third through seventh grade and eighth through twelfth, so St. Dunstan's, and then what was then the youth choir became St. Gregory's. I had for the first time third through seventh graders who had never sung on their own. They had always sung with the benefit of these other older kids, with the training wheels on. We started just with them, and they grew and grew because they needed to be role models. They didn't have anyone else to depend on. So often I wonder what is going to happen when so-and-so graduates. Well, the next one comes right behind and fills in those shoes. Ellie Bailey made hardly a peep before Tricia Bailey, her older sister, left. I told her, "You're the secret weapon of St. Gregory's." She said, "Oh, I don't know" [very quietly]. Sure enough, she even has a larger voice than Tricia; it's a different voice certainly. Those wee little third to seventh graders managed to sing in two parts themselves by the end of the spring in 2009. It was a great success, the culmination of so much work on everyone's part. That was a proud moment for everyone.

Successes and challenges—morning prayer certainly. Murray I think spearheaded the effort to say, "Why don't we try morning prayer?" It was a choral service really. We sang either a setting of the Te Deum or the Jubilate. It had of course the psalm and some responses. Many people remembered—I don't—when morning prayer was the standard thing, often very fondly. The decision was made that we would have the Eucharist following. I think that is what killed it. We normally ended at 11:15. It made that service even longer. The Methodists were going to Shoney's an hour before we were. We were getting out of there at one o'clock or so. That was just too much. I love Eucharist. I think morning prayer would work if we didn't have Eucharist; I think that is the only chance that morning prayer would have. Maybe if it was once a month. We might take it for granted sometimes. Maybe not having it would be better.

Evensongs are a success and a challenge because if we don't do them regularly, things don't come as easily. The more we do them, the more they become ingrained. Some of the most beautiful, stunning, gorgeous music is written for the evening service. I think Leigh likes to say that it is the greatest contribution of the Anglican tradition to Christian worship. He is quoting somebody else; I'm not sure who. Of course that is a great, great thing.

We are having a new service this fall, but I cannot be involved because it's at nine o'clock, and I'll be in the church. We're looking at bringing in some other staff who are very qualified. I'm excited to see where that goes. I have high hopes that, again, people will engage with God. That is the only important thing. Sure, the Anglican tradition is the greatest way I can think of to praise God, but there are so many other valid forms of worship as long as God and man are engaging. That is more important than taste or even a tradition. My hope is that some people that aren't already being reached will be reached with this new service.

Adult involvement in St. George's used to be a thorn in our side. We were losing singers. This is many years ago. It has stabilized a great deal. I can't remember when someone has left the Choir except for moving away. There is lots of ownership. It's not that they're coming to sing for us, but they are a valid part of leading the service. We have a great number of singers at St. George's. It's not the Mormon Tabernacle Choir, but it doesn't need to be. They can fill the church with sound. We're always looking for volunteers and more people, but we're at a good place with St. George's, and that's quite nice.

Q: Imagine that you are an outside consultant. How would you advise clergy and staff to structure interaction in order to achieve the greatest collaboration in good music ministry?

A: We have the most fantastic and supportive clergy and staff that I can possibly imagine. I am stunned by how competent and easygoing, just incredible people. The clergy are so supportive of us, and they trust us. They don't second-guess musical decisions or recommendations that we might have. It's a beautiful relationship. I would say, "Hey, use it as a model for how other musicians and clergy should interact." All organists and clergy usually do is talk about war stories, how awful it is to deal with the other one at their churches. Of course the artistic temperament maybe along with the clerical temperament don't always mix. There are times when the clergy has strong feeling about things that we may not, but they have their reasons. It is like a marriage, I imagine, with give-and-take. We couldn't have better people to work with. There is no question.

Q: Where do you see the future of the music ministry at St. George's in ten years?

A: The growth of the children's choirs is so important. The kids aren't the future of the church; they are the church. They are in the church, and they are leading worship. There is no reason to sort of pat them on the head when they have so much to offer and so much to gain. We've got to keep growing that program in any way that we can.

I think we can further Anglicize our worship as a whole. I love the classic Anglican sound of the clear trebles and the vibrant men. I don't think Mark is as wild about that sound. He loves a very full, very vibrant adult sound. St. Gregory's is already doing that. When we sing Evensong, we bring in some men from the choir, and we have that Anglican sound, which is wonderful. I'd love to have more of that.

I'd love to have Evensong every month. Parishes much less than us are having Evensong every month. English cathedrals have it every day, and nobody shows up. There is a happy medium, but I think that the Evensong service has so much to offer the worshiper. At the heart of that is the understanding that it is a choral service. The Choir is serving as the mouth of the body of Christ, just as the preacher becomes the mouth delivering the sermon. Those who are the best readers become the lecturers. Everyone has their contribution, but the Choir serves as the mouth of the whole body, so the people aren't at a concert. They are allowing the Choir to be the voice of their praise and they are very much participating, even though it is indirect. That is the heart of Evensong. It is not when you sit back with your pipe and think, *Ah, this is magnificent.* It's a very active worship as long as it's properly understood.

I love that clear treble sound, and we have some women now in St. George's that can really do that. It is so stunningly clear, and that allows the beautiful lines and the beautiful chords of so much of the repertoire to be clearly heard. When there is too much vibrato, you have no idea what's going on, especially things like Tallis and Gibbons where there is all this intricate lines, weaving all through each other. Things like Brahms—sure there needs to be some vibrancy there. It doesn't need to be as crystal clear as Tallis or Byrd. I wouldn't mind seeing us move closer to that classic Anglican sound, certainly in some repertoire more than others. Sometimes it is a case by case basis. Some of the singers are being very precise, and some are a little less so. We have a little room there to improve.

Then touring. Choir touring is a very important part of what they do. It's a perk for the choirs in order to get to take what they do here and do it in a new, different, sometimes even more glorious space, and being on a trip together solidifies the bond they have that is so important to their faithfulness and regularity, their bond to the whole group. Often it reinforces their mission when they go and give this gift to others. I think we have to be good stewards when we tour because often that is a result of a great deal of fund-raising in the church body, and we need to be doing something very worthwhile with money that we raise. Of course going to England gives us a glimpse into our roots; it serves to inspire the choirs when they come back, which is very valuable and very worthwhile. As long as we are mindful of the end result of what our touring is, we really should tour every year ideally. That is often not possible, but I think it is very important.

We've tried to tour a few times, but with the economy as it is, it has been very difficult. I'd love to tour the UK. My plans for St. Gregory's include hopefully a tour to Scotland. There is a choir school, St. Mary's in Edinburgh, that is very similar to the model that we are trying to create here with St. George's Academy. I think it would be very useful. They also have a magnificent organ, and it's a great place for a choir to go and be in residence. It would be wonderful to go there. Also the Holy Land, the Christians there have very little music because the Muslims do not allow or appreciate art or music, so the Christians there have very little to work with. They say that when choirs come there to sing, Christians come from miles and miles, spending hours traveling around, to expose themselves to this. It so happens that on their calendar, their Christmas is a week after ours. If we were to go the week after Christmas, we could sing and minister to these fellow Christians in the Holy Land in Bethlehem and Jerusalem and all these wonderful places.

As far as the adult choir, I love the UK to sing, of course. These great foundations where all of this began and continues for five centuries, even longer. Canada, as a UK province, also has a strong Anglican tradition. That for me is a great place for us to go to reenergize part of the tradition. When we go other places, we can sing and maybe not be as inspired by the Anglican tradition.

As far as ten years out, I would love to see St. George's Academy with its proprietary choir school fully involved, and that takes so much effort and so much expertise that I don't have. Again, in the body of Christ, there are people that do. If anywhere is ripe for it to happen, if any place has the resources and the laypeople and the intelligence, it is St. George's. I'm really hoping that God will see that through perhaps in ten years' time.

Recordings. Mark already has some plans to do some recordings here. I hope that in ten years we can have some serious recordings out so that we can show people what St. George's is up to. Again, national familiarity, not because we are striving for that but because of how fervently we are performing the task at hand.

Q: What is your dream for fully integrating your spiritual and professional growth during the time you have remaining at St. George's?

A: This is not a job. This is my passion, and it's my ministry. It's hard work certainly. I have the best job in the world. I'm so thankful that God has brought me here. It is so clear to me that he brought me here. I can't really separate my spiritual and professional growth. I think that is what I'm trying to say. I'm learning every day many things both spiritual and professional; they are inseparable. I care about this church so deeply; I care about the people; I care about its mission. The clergy are amazing. I'd follow Leigh Spruill to the gates of hell. I feel guilty that I get to be here and do this. When I come to "work" every day, this is where I'm coming. I get to do these things: I *have* to go and point some Anglican chant. Shucks. I *have* to go and play the organ of these great hymns that I love. I *have* to go teach exceptional young people the music that I value so dearly.

As far as my future, I know that I have to be able to say, "Yes, Lord, I will go wherever you want," but only so that he won't ask me. I know that if I say, "I will never go to darkest Africa," by golly that will be the plan. Like Abraham and Isaac, I have to be willing to put even this that I value so much on the altar. I'd like to retire from St. George's when I'm wearing Velcro shoes, and I don't even remember my own name. I would love to see the kids I have at St. Gregory's become parents and baptize their kids here, and to teach their children the same music that they learned here. John Fitzgerald says, "If you want to make God laugh, just tell him your plans." It's like manna from heaven. I can't take today's manna and hold on to it and preserve it in a glass case because tomorrow I'll have manna too. It needs to be whatever God wants.

Q: How has the vision of St. George's music changed since Mark has come on board?

A: What is so stunning is that Mark makes Jerry Garcia look like a stone hard conservative, and I'm the opposite. Despite our left and right leanings, respectively, we're great friends and colleagues, and we work so well together. I think it is perhaps a happy model for what our nation may be able to come to grips with. He really is stretching the program and me. He is bringing in drummers to the church and artists and doing very different music with the Holocaust Cantata, things I never would conceive of. I'm learning a great deal about things I knew nothing about. At the same time he appreciates the Anglican tradition, and he knows it very well. He is not going to have a CD of Stanford in his car; he is going to have Latin jazz more than likely or some Italian pop singer. He is bringing a great deal of diversity and eclecticism to the program.

Q: Can you name three things that you'd consider your proudest moments as Organist under Dr. Somerville?

A: I think I might take a liberty here and think of my three proudest moments overall. That might be a little more useful. The first was to have St. Gregory's sing in the National Cathedral. That was the result of so much work and so much vision. It was a milestone. We had never done anything like that. That was fantastic and unrivaled.

Then singing in Winchester Cathedral while we were in England on tour when Murray was here. Of course St. George's and then the youth choir, which became St. Gregory's, had sung Evensong in Winchester Cathedral, which was sort of a precursor to the National Cathedral. That was a wonderful, very special moment, and everyone involved was aware of how special it was.

Serving as interim was a proud thing for me; it certainly wasn't flawless because there was so much that went on. I was so happy to serve the church in that capacity. I was honored to be asked in the first place. The pinnacle of that would be Lessons and Carols in 2008, which might be my proudest moment yet at St. George's. We had all the choirs participating; all the choirs sang a lot. Every chorister, every singer participated in that one piece. It was some of the very best music that I can think of for Lessons and Carols. We worked very hard to prepare it all, very hard, and I think it came out very well. I saved the recording because I was so thrilled with how that turned out.

Q: What is your favorite part of your job today?

A: I would say it is twofold. Accompanying hymns is so rewarding for me because I think hymns are such an important part of worship for the worshiper. That is where the rubber meets the road. I'm ashamed to say that the best hymn singing has not been during regular services, but during the diocesan convention. You have all these delegates crammed into the church, and oh, they sing. The whole church is alive with sound because they are not used to this acoustic making it harder. When people around them are all singing, they're supported, and they can sing vibrantly. That is such a treat for me. Anytime I'm working with St. Gregory's, it's incredible. I leave rehearsal energized, even if I have been drained all day up to that point. Being with them is incredible.

Q: How well do you think the Anglican church music tradition is understood by each of these groups? Clergy, musicians (staff and choirs), congregation, and public.

A: Excellent question. I don't know that the tradition is that well understood by any of these groups. The clergy are an exceptional bunch. I am so thankful for them. We don't have a bad apple among them. To have that out of six, seven clergy, I think is unprecedented. They are like the parish in that a very few of them have a long history in the Episcopal Church. Tim Taylor has been Episcopalian since Jesus was around, I think. The rest of them have come to the denomination later, and the parish too. We don't have a lot of fusty old Episcopalians like me, which is probably a good thing. At funerals we often have requests for hymns that aren't in the hymnal, like "In the Garden," which people probably remember from their youth. That is indicative of the fact that we have a lot of people from Baptist backgrounds; some are ex-Roman Catholics. St. George's being a newer parish, we don't have this huge, huge long tradition of "when my grandmother sang 'St. Patrick's Breastplate' in 1803." There is not a great sense of what makes this tradition this tradition and how much of what we do is that tradition.

The musicians, I think, have a better understanding because we do it more. They are more actively involved. They are slowly coming to grips with what the tradition is maybe more and less about.

The congregation loves to say, "Oh, the Anglican tradition." But I think people really might assume that what we're doing is Anglican because we're doing it at St. George's, which isn't really fair, not that they're not open to understanding what it is. It's not always clear to them.

The public might give you "English cathedral choir" if you asked them, but otherwise there is little awareness beyond the cathedral tradition of a boy choir of what this might be.

Q: How can this understanding be increased for each of these groups by the music ministries?

A: I think the best way to do it is to keep doing it and to do it well. Whatever form of worship engages man with God is exactly what needs to happen. But I maintain that the Anglican tradition is of such beauty and dignity and grandeur and expression, especially in this type of liturgical setting, when people hear it, they say, "*That* is beautiful. *That* is how we need to worship. *That* is what this parish needs in the public expression of praise." When we do wonderful anthems, psalms that are accompanied well, psalms that are sung expressively, that really animate the text. A spoken psalm is so strange to me. "Let us sing to the Lord a new song." "Let us shout for joy to the Rock of our salvation." You cannot possibly have the expression that the psalm requires and that really brings voice to that prayer when it's spoken. There is no alternative sometimes; I understand. You've got to have good music. In every one of these groups—clergy, musicians, congregation, and public—we just need to do it. If we keep doing what we're doing, people will understand and say, "Oh, *that's* Anglican." They know it when they hear it: S. S. Wesley, Stanford, Bairstow, Tallis. That's the good stuff.

Q: Is *The Hymnal 1982* used adequately at St. George's as an educational tool?

A: I don't know that it's used at all as an educational tool. We refer to it every Sunday, but I don't think it gets any more press time than that. Having taken a course in hymnology two years ago when I was working on my master's at Belmont, my eyes were opened even more to what I already loved so much about these hymns. My appreciation and my role as a worship leader, I think I really got some valuable insights into them. Again, time is at a premium on Sunday and Wednesday, but we need to be intentional about making time for classes on the hymnal, on worship, on the Anglican tradition. Obviously those things all need to be done. I think if people understood the hymnal better, worship would be much more vibrant for them. Understanding where things come from, not just historically, I think their worship would be deepened.

Q: How can *Music as Mission*, the music history publication being prepared, best assist these efforts?

A: I wasn't overjoyed, not that I was against it, when I first heard about the project. I thought, *That is nice. We'll find out what the history has been.* I had no idea until I think perhaps we interviewed Greg Colson in Atlanta the amazing things that have happened here. The things I'm trying to accomplish now, like a boy choir, have already existed here. Understanding the past, realizing where we have been and what has been accomplished, is so critical to our planning and our vision for the future. I think the end result of all of this will be to improve the involvement of the congregation in worship. Worshiping needs to be in the pew. It needs to be personal; it needs to be intimate. I hope that when people see that music is not simply like playing a record back there in the apse, but is a living, vibrant thing that we want so desperately for them to be involved in, I think that an awareness would shift the amount the congregation is involved, which is the best thing that could possibly happen.

Q: You have bridged two distinct music ministries' leaderships (Murray and Mark). How would you define each of these as to approaches and results?

A: Murray had been there and done that. He grew up as an undergraduate as the organ scholar at New College, Oxford, which of course was steeped in the Anglican tradition. He was very, very familiar with the repertoire, with the order of service. I think in a way he was over it. He had to do it so much as a youngster that he knew we had to do it, but his heart was fixed on his niche, which was Baroque. The authentic accomplishing of this music—that really got his blood going. I think some of the greatest anthems and hymns in the Anglican tradition he would begrudgingly do but very seldom because perhaps he was tired of them. We're chomping at the bit, saying, "Let's sing 'Lift High the Cross,' and he'd say, 'Again?'" I think that he brought a new level of the tradition here.

Mark and I got to sort through the entire music library and get rid of a bunch of stuff that was dated and we'd never be able to use. We just wanted to see what was in there because our card filing system was kind of antiquated. It was revelatory to see what was in there. It's a good barometer for the program to see what's in the music library. What we found was music that was more of a High Methodist tradition, and a lot of the staples that I would expect to find were missing. So we've been ordering a bunch of music. I started doing that as interim. There was almost nothing for Evensong. I may be wrong, but Murray may have been the first in recent memory to do Evensong. That included the *Magnificat/Nunc Dimittis* and psalms. I don't think there was any Anglican chant before Murray. He brought in some plain chant, which does certainly have a historical place in the Anglican tradition, but for my money, Anglican chant is so much more vibrant and expressive.

Murray really brought in a lot of the greats of the tradition that weren't here before. I think he also wanted to distance himself from a reckless Anglophile like me. He loved German music; he loved Bach and still does. He has not passed away; he is still alive. Italian things too, Continental things, French Baroque, but German was a real niche for him. He premiered a C. P. E. Bach work that had never been done in the U.S., maybe not anywhere. He loved to dig up stuff that nobody had ever done before, sometimes perhaps for good reason. Often we would get just new wild German things. That was the direction he was strong in.

Mark is, gosh, so different from either Murray or myself. Mark knows the tradition very well, but he doesn't lend himself to it. The Anglican tradition does not simply mean the music of England, even though that is a great majority of it. Our hymnal is the same way; there are several American tunes; they wouldn't have that in England, of course. We also have some spirituals. There are lots of German chorales. A lot of our favorite hymns are German chorales. Hymns that we would think are Anglican greats are really German. The Anglican tradition is the same way. It takes Brahms, Bach, some French repertoire that is considered part of the Anglican tradition because it is not only English. Mark is sort of the same way; he loves the heart of the Anglican tradition, but I think what really gets him going is some crazy, out-of-the-box things. We had the Ennio Morricone "On Earth as It Is in Heaven" on Easter Day this year, which had bongos with it and drums of some sort. That is not exactly what you'd expect on Easter morning at St. George's. I think John Fitzgerald calls it "Bongos on the Boulevard." Marvelous. Mark is stretching us a little bit in that way and bringing his own flair to what we're doing. It's working well.

Q: What are two major positive things you individually have learned from each of these persons?

A: Murray, in his endless pursuit to more faithfully render Baroque music even to the point of a contest to prove who had read the latest article on scholarship. "So-and-so has just said that these triplets probably should be dotted. But is that just the Venetian school?" Yes, fine. You get *Early Music Weekly*. People love to go way too far with authentic early performance practice, but I knew way too little at the beginning. I've really appreciated what Murray taught me about how to bring Baroque music to life. Having forty cellos playing recordings in the fifties doing Bach all slow and ponderous and woooh instead of being sprightly and alive as it was supposed to be. I have a better appreciation for that music, and it has really informed how I play that sort of thing, for which I am really thankful. Murray knows psalm playing well, and I was able to learn a great deal from him about the correct way and things I was doing wrong, actually impeding the choir, when they were trying to chant psalms. So I was grateful for that.

Mark Ring is an encyclopedia of organ knowledge. I have never met a person who knows more about organs and their workings and the different stops than him. Through the process of us looking at new instruments, I have learned a tremendous amount about things I had no idea about, but I need to know about the organ. It is a delight when I get to hear more about that because it is so interesting. I don't know how he ever learned it all.

Mark has taught me to delegate. As interim, I had no one to delegate to. I had taken on much too much personally, and it was hard to get anything accomplished because there was such a huge amount that needed to be done. Mark doesn't pass off everything to me, but he is good about sharing the tasks among the three of us so no one is overworked. That is very valuable for our sanity.

Q: What are the two major negative things you individually have learned from each of these persons?

A: A bit sticky but I trust this will be taken in the spirit that it should be. Maybe I won't say who corresponds to what. I have learned that the people have to come first. If you don't have people to be in your program, you've got nothing. You have to be aware of people's feelings, not overly so; you don't have to be governed by every whim. But the people are not to be underestimated; they have a lot to offer. Some people obviously will have more to offer than others or think they do. You have to be very aware of the morale of a group and whether they support you. If you are leading and it's a one-man parade, you have to stop and think, *What is going on? Why am I not being followed?* The people have to support you, and the way to do that is to be doing what needs to be done, which is difficult sometimes if your agenda, which you want so much, is not the agenda that the place wants or that the people are really hungry for. That's complicated.

I think it is very important to be aware of the effectiveness of your ministry and how what we do in the apse affects the person in the pew because nothing else is important except for, are they engaging with God? There are so many factors in the church ministry that can get totally in the way of worship. We all have to evaluate. Especially as an organist, if I'm going to lay on the horns in the back every Sunday, people are going to quit coming to church because they'll be tired of having their eardrums blown off. We have a priestly duty to bring the people before God and to facilitate that engagement. That is a very, very serious duty that we have to be so aware of what we're doing.

You have to love the people that you minister to; you *have* to. If we could just figure out in government and church, how to do it without people, it would be great. People ruin everything, but we can't do that. Not yet, still researching. People are not always easy to get along with or to minister with. I think Murray said, "You have to be a Christian to work with the Christians." But you do have to give them the benefit of the doubt. If you don't genuinely care about the people you are ministering to, you won't be effective. I'm not saying you need to produce false caring. You've got to care about them because you're a minister; you're a shepherd. If you don't care about the sheep, you're not going to be a good shepherd.

The ends don't justify the means. As good and as holy and as wonderful as the goal you may have, the means still have to be honoring to God. You can't cut corners there to get somewhere good. I think an element of that is to trust God. If here is the vision and here is what we want to accomplish, we have to trust that God will get us there. Abraham continually tried to shortcut his way to God's promise of giving him countless descendants. His wife, Sarah, gave her slave girl to him to bear a child, and that didn't work out that great. He thought he would be killed more than once because of his wife, so he lied and said, "This is my sister. Sure, take her into your harem, O king." That happened twice. Come on, Abraham. What he should have done and eventually did do was to place his trust in God, even on the altar with his only son, his promised heir, that God still would make a way. I think that is the important lesson that if there is a quick way to do it, perhaps that might cause you to question the ends and the means, you need to take the high road. That is the way that things will work with God's plan.

Q: What have been your major roles with each of these persons?

A: Murray came from New College, Oxford, the cathedral tradition in which the Organists are paid nothing, which has nothing to do with this. But there are several things that are true about how that all works. Organists are taken for granted in England, and the assistants are even lower than the Organists. It wasn't slavery by any means, but my title was Organist because I think Murray didn't want to do a lot of the playing. It was not assistant or associate; I was very much the Organist, although I was sort of his assistant when it was time to do the nuts and bolts sorts of things. I never conducted the Choir unless he was going to be gone.

Mark and Murray are night and day. Mark—I am absolutely his colleague. I have never felt more supported in my professional life. He asks my opinion and really wants to hear it. He doesn't just want to hear, "Oh, yes." I was stunned to find that out when Mark came. "Really? I'm your colleague?" I am still Organist because I still do most of the playing, but I am also enjoying the role of Associate Director. I welcome the responsibility that comes with that and just happy that I can use my gifts more in ministry and be of more service to the church.

Q: You served as Interim Music Director between Murray and Mark. Describe how you functioned as Interim Music Director.

A: I had a very interesting position at that point because I had been in a church for many years, and I was able to observe from an outside perspective what worked very well and what needed some attention. When I started as interim, I had a hit list of things that I thought we could improve. I was a man on a mission. I love this place, and I saw some things that needed to be running better. The organ is one of them.

What is amazing is that when Mark came, in the first week he was here, we sat down at the organ, and he outlined the same changes that had taken me five years to come up with. It was spooky how similar that was. I did suggest initially some modest changes to the organ that would not disturb the waters too much. That was before I really understood the gravity of the issues we were facing with the organ. That was one of the things that I was intent on.

St. Gregory's had been called the youth choir up until then. I think that was an effort to connect it to the youth program more where there had been and still is some alienation for all kinds of geopolitical reasons. I really had come to know and love these kids and wanted to make this program blossom. We changed the name from what I thought was a very "Dear Occupant" name for a youth choir to St. Gregory's to give them their own identity and give them their own space. I started doing activities with them. We do lots of activities. We have been rock climbing. We have been to choir camp. A high ropes course. Paintball. Ice skating. Laser tag. We have done it all. They began to become what they are now.

I wanted to focus on the adult choir. It was getting a bit spread; I won't say sloppy, but the sound was just not very refined. It was very loud, but it wasn't controlled. There was never a soft dynamic; it was very rare. It was loud and less loud. We started to explore the range of expression and emotion that they were able to come up with. I'll get a bit closer to that in my ridiculously idyllic goal of that cathedral sound. A lot of people like me get accused of trying to make women sound like boys. I'm not interested in that. A woman can have a very full but a very pure sound if she is supporting it with enough air and some other techniques. That is part of what I was looking at. I was determined to bridge the gap between the Choir and the congregation. That was probably the most important thing I wanted to address because they were so alienated up there. We made great strides. We got monitors; we got a better sound system for the back. We appointed a clergy chaplain to come and liaise with the Choir and be a shepherd for them. Before that, they didn't have much clergy contact. We started the blessing, which I've never seen before. After the announcements, at the beginning of the offertory, I think it is the subdeacon who comes and blesses the Choir before they sing the anthem. The reason for that is that I wanted the Choir to be really aware that what they were about to do was *their* preaching. The preacher gets blessed before ascending into the pulpit. We were doing the same type of thing. It had the atmosphere before of just being background music for the money changing, which is a shadow of what it can be. I think that when we get blessed before we sing the offertory, we sing better. I want them to see that what they do is a sacrament, not just "Hit play until they're done. Then we'll stop and do something different." We looked very hard at getting choir stalls back there to raise the Choir and give them a sense of belonging. They have chairs now that look temporary. They don't have the same weight as where the clergy sit. I don't want the Choir to feel like second-class citizens. If they had a place to put their music and have better lighting, that would help. We've made some progress on that. It is still a ways from fruition.

The Choir's spiritual life wasn't magnificent. They weren't getting fed on a regular basis because they couldn't hear what was happening in church. There was this attitude that wasn't quite as ministry oriented, and I think that came from the top. We started to talk a bit more about the incredible texts that we sing, and I think it made a difference. I think people started to see themselves as having a priestly role in the worship, not just as "us" and "them," which it so easily can become with musicians and clergy and congregation, especially if they are so far separated in the back. The Choir used to walk in and out all the time during the sermon. If I occasionally went out during a sermon, I would see six choir members sitting around. I finally said, "No." We cleaned up a lot of things about that.

The other huge thing that I wanted to address was congregational participation because that is the whole point of corporate worship: to inspire the congregation for the week ahead, to edify them, and to praise God. It breaks my heart still to look out on the live stream and see people in the midst of our beautiful hymns with their arms crossed. I used to get mad at them and think, *Why aren't they singing?* I realized there was nothing wrong with these people. They were no less prone to singing than the Methodists down the street who blow the roof off every Sunday. The acoustic and the organ were really being a detriment to congregational singing. It is not their fault, but it still breaks my heart. They need, they deserve, to have that. We go to the mountain. I'm looking forward to this year. I've been once. I'm looking forward to going this year. When six hundred men are singing together, it is beautiful. It's amazing. How would our lives be different if we had that every week? Not just because "this is singing and everyone needs to be singing." No, this is for the benefit of the congregation. Worship is the absolute foundation of the entire life of the church. If we can improve our worship life by having greater participation, that will affect every last tendril of the ministry of the church. It all depends on worship. If we can enrich that, that's an ongoing goal.

Q: In retrospect what would you do differently?

A: I took too much on myself. I loved it, but I was too disorganized at first. I learned to organize quickly, which was a blessing. I learned by necessity. Oh, boy, I slept on the couch in my office some nights because there was so much to do and so little time to get it all done. I didn't want to cut corners, and I think that is the right thing to do, not doing it halfway just to get it done. I think I should have tried harder to find someone else to help me, like an assistant type. But there aren't a lot of people who can play the organ out there that aren't already doing it. The people that aren't doing it anywhere—it's hard to find a good person that's looking for that, especially as a part-time assistant.

I was so bent on really reinforcing the greats of the Anglican tradition. I did all the great Anglican anthems in the fall. It was a gangbuster fall; we were getting two to three of the best anthems of the tradition every Sunday. I got to about February, and I thought, *Well, I've done a lot of the really, really good stuff.* February, March, and April weren't quite as good as the fall was because I didn't spread it out like I should have. It was a learning process.

Otherwise I think things went pretty well. Obviously I learned a lot about things I could do better as a director and a leader. That comes with experience.

Q: What were the most pleasant aspects of that time for you personally?

A: The whole thing. It was what I was born to do. Since I was a young child, I knew that what I wanted to do and what I felt God's plan for me was to lead worship at a large liturgical Episcopal church. The feeling of being able to make all of this happen was just unbelievable, such an at-ease feeling: this is God's plan for me. I wouldn't trade that for anything. I was actually doing sort of two and a half jobs. I wasn't getting a lot of administrative support, and there was a whole lot going on. I got to try my hand for the first time at being a leader. I was able to pour myself fully into this, without anybody saying, "Wait now. Don't do that. Don't do this." I had been waiting to burst out of the gate for years, and it was a delight.

Q: You now serve as Associate Director of Music Ministries and Organist. What are your current responsibilities?

A: My biggest responsibility is to play the organ. I play almost all of the time. Mark plays if one of my choirs is going to sing. I direct them, and he'll play. If I'm going to be away, he certainly plays. He plays at weddings and funerals. It's mostly organ playing. Directing St. Gregory's is second in line. I devote myself to that a great deal, thinking about how to grow that program, trying to support them, how to make their time more profitable. Then as Associate Director, I am Mark's friend and colleague. We just sit and talk a lot about what's happening here, what we want to see happen here. It is a constant stream-of-consciousness: "What are we going to do about this? How are we going to make this better?" It's unlike any working relationship

I've ever had. There is planning coordination. We meet with the clergy every Monday and with the staff every other Wednesday. There are lots of little details, lots of e-mails and phone calls and dealing with other things.

Q: What would you change in your present job description to better utilize your interests and capabilities?

A: One of the greatest things about Mark being here is that I was able to go home now and then, which is great, but he allowed me to keep so many of the things that I so love, that I'm called to do and I've got to do or I'll go crazy. I still point the Anglican chants, and I teach the Choir every week the chant. St. Gregory's is still mine. I get to play, which I love. My job description is very close to what I have to offer. Obviously I would love to see a men and boys choir, a men and girls choir, come to fruition. I would just pour myself into that so fully. I think it's coming. The time is not right yet. Evensong—I would love to see monthly Evensong, which I could be a large part of. Just the traditional Anglican choral service, I could do even more of that. Other than that my job description is quite accurate.

Q: How aware are you of the presence of the Music Ministries Committee of the Vestry?

A: Not tremendously. I believe John was the Chair at least last year, perhaps still. I think I became most aware of them when they were trying to drum up support for the organ. I think I remember being with them as interim. I think we met, and I was using them as a sounding board to see what they were wanting. It does impact my work. I do remember that what I heard from them was very helpful as an interim. They were a way to get to the pulse of the congregation, how they responded to changes, how they were feeling about things. That was very helpful for me.

Q: How could it better function in its role within the church?

A: My end goal would be to improve congregational participation. We've got to fix that. I think that if we were able to meet more often—the music staff, Mark and I—to meet with them and be able to figure out what is making them tick, what might be impeding them from a fuller worship life because I want to tackle this head-on and figure out why this is happening and see if we can solve it. It may be difficult, but I think we need to do it. Also if there is any grumbling among the pews, let us know so we can fix it.

Appendix C

Long Range Music Planning Committee Report to the Vestry [2006]

This section contains the final report of an ad hoc committee formed to effect an in-depth review of music at St. George's. It is felt to be such a seminally important document that it is included to provide a ready reference tool for reflections over time as to our progress and directions in our music.

Vestry Report
August 2006

Committee Charge: The Long Range Music Planning Committee was established by the Reverend R. Leigh Spruill to study the St. George's parish music ministries under the chairmanship of Calvin Lewis. Father Spruill charged the Committee "to explore ways that we might strengthen our already-robust choral tradition, deepen and broaden participation in all the various music ministries of the parish, as well as explore possible new initiatives for our common life and worship moving forward."

Committee Members: The members of the Long Range Music Planning Committee included individuals representing various demographic groups within the parish and persons with extensive experiences in music ministries as well as other parish activities. The members appointed by Father Spruill were Giny Bailey, Kevin Carson, Mary Dale Fitzgerald, Kim King, Claudia Lyday, Brent Neal, Treasurer, Dyer Rodes, Junior Warden, Steve Taylor, and Amy Weeks, with Dr. Murray Forbes Somerville, Director of Music, Gerry Senechal, Organist, and Father Spruill as ex officio members.

Committee Vision: The Committee and Director of Music, Dr. Murray Forbes Somerville, and Father Spruill initially explored a vision for the St. George's Music Ministries noting that both within and without the parish, musical excellence is one of the main ways this parish is perceived and that our music and choral programs are an integral aspect of our vision of "inspired worship." We believe that St. George's should remain "steadfast" to the Anglican musical tradition by glorifying God through a rich setting of choral and instrumental music as it expresses and interprets faith. Such music raises our collective and corporate vision and elicits our best. St. George's is in a relatively rare position of having the resources to offer a traditionally approached, classically-based repertoire. The parish has unusually robust resources and leadership, and it serves an educated and sophisticated constituency for whom this literature provides a truly Spirit-filled worship experience. The danger of losing this rich heritage is of concern not only to all who were nourished and raised on this foundation, but to a future generation who would be impoverished by its absence (See Appendix A *Singing the Lord's song in a pleasant pasture: the music program at St. George's look to the future*, January 2006, Director of Music, Murray F. Somerville).

Committee Process: Following its initial meetings on January 9 and 23, 2006 to explore the current status of the music ministries at St. George's and to generally discuss the vision and long-term goals for the music ministries, the committee divided into three subcommittees to research areas defined as major areas for new initiatives "to strengthen our already-robust choral tradition and deepen and broaden participation in all the various music ministries of the parish." (See Appendix B for minutes of all Committee Meetings). Each of the three subcommittees, Children and Youth, Outside Groups and Concert series, and Adult Choir and Infrastructure, met during the spring to develop recommendations for the Committee to consider in its deliberations. (See Appendix C for the reports of the three subcommittees). The Long Range Music Planning Committee met on February 27, March 12, and March 30 to hear reports from the subcommittees and discuss committee recommendations. The committee approved the following recommendations to be presented to the Rector, Wardens and Vestry as a part of the strategic planning process for the parish on [May], 2006:

Recommendations:
1. Create a parish Music Ministries Committee to coordinate various aspects of the St. George's instrumental and choral music program and to support the Director of Music and the Music Ministries. This Music Ministries Committee would include lay representatives from the parish at large, representatives of the various music ministries, a Vestry liaison, and representatives of the music leadership in the parish as well as appropriate ex officio staff and parish leaders.

2. Children and Youth Music Ministries Recommendations (Subcommittee Members: Giny Bailey, Kim King, Calvin Lewis, Dyer Rodes, Gerry Senechal, Murray Somerville) Appendix C

A. Increase awareness and familiarity of the parish youth and children's ministries by publicizing the choir programs in the Church School and Youth areas through a Young Singers' Parents Committee. This goal would include highlighting the Royal School of Church Music "Voice for Life" program to teach musical literacy, technique, knowledge of a broad range of worship music and how it is involved in worship through hymns, anthems, and service music. This goal is based on our belief that children are the church of today and tomorrow and those children who sing begin their ministry in the church. This goal would include capitalizing on every opportunity to show the example of children singing in choirs by bringing them into church and putting them in as visible a location as possible.

B. Current membership in St. Dunstan's Choir is approximately 30; current membership in the Youth Choir is approximately 15. Our goal is to double membership numbers for both choirs.

C. Strengthen the connection between the Music Department and the Church School Department by working together to teach the Catechesis songs, the pageant songs, and hymns so that children are comfortable and well-prepared to sing as a group in church as often as is feasible.

D. Increase the hours or hire an additional music administrator to improve organization among the various choirs and to oversee a team of guitarists who would go to the Church School classes through the 5th grade level to assist with the music program.

E. Hire one intern or trainer to help with practices and training on Wednesdays and to lead practices for the 1st and 2nd grade children so that these practices can be more consistent. Develop more volunteers and parent helpers for training as well as using older children and youth to train the younger children.

F. Establish a team of guitarists to lead music for the lower grades. These guitarists would be of varying skill levels and should be given direction and practice time to prepare. Candidates would be sought from the Adult Choir, Youth, and adult members of the congregation who have guitar skills. St. Dunstan's and Youth

Choir members should assist in providing singing leadership because of their treble voices.

G. Increase the visibility of the St. George's Director of Music and the Organist in the Youth area to encourage familiarity among the youth and encourage reluctant youth to sing in the Youth Choir. The Director of Music would have input on the musical selections for Youth Sunday and would assist in developing repertoire with the Jam Session participants.

3. Outside Groups and Concert Series Subcommittee Recommendations: (Subcommittee Members: Steve Taylor, chair, Kevin Carson, Mary Dale Fitzgerald, Calvin Lewis, and Dr. Murray Somerville) Appendix C

A. Invite and coordinate performances by outside groups during the regular worship services through the newly created Music Ministry Committee with the guidance of the Director of Music. These invited groups would foster goals of diversity and exposure of the parish to musical expressions of worship that are different from our Anglican tradition, yet sacred in their own right.

B. Nurture and continue the already successful Concert Series centered on traditional sacred choral and organ music presented at the highest level of excellence with program series throughout the season to showcase this special music and to utilize the Concert Series as a form of outreach, education and recruiting for St. George's.

C. Create an ongoing "Friends of St. George's Music" with the approval of the Vestry. The "Friends of St. George's Music" fund would be modeled on other arts-related nonprofit organizations and church-related choir sustainer groups with various levels of giving and benefits in order to support the Concert Series and the music programs at St. George's and to supplement the funding received through the annual parish budget.

4. Adult Choir and Infrastructure Subcommittee Recommendations: (Subcommittee Members: Amy Weeks, chair, Kevin Carson, Claudia Lyday, Brent Neal, Gerry Senechal, and Dr. Murray Somerville) Appendix C

A. Make the musical offerings at the Sunday morning 8:45 and 11:15 worship services distinct.

(i) The 8:45 service would have music that is warm and invit-

ing in varied musical styles led by an intergenerational choir. This music would be somewhat simpler and more accessible although still in the Anglican musical tradition to allow more youth involvement in leadership in worship as well as making this service the "entry point" to the choir for adult parishioners who wish to become involved in the music program.
  (ii) The 11:15 service music would reflect the best of the Anglican tradition, with a chamber choir of professional singers and highly sophisticated volunteers who would "stretch" musically attempting more complex music, perhaps suitable for a smaller ensemble, and thus avoid singing the same music twice in one morning.
B. Improve recruitment of new choir members through increasing the visibility of the choir through enhanced physical visibility during the worship services and visibility at parish events and in written publications. In addition a recruitment strategy would include guaranteed child care during Wednesday evening rehearsals through the annual church choir budget. Our hope is to double volunteer membership numbers from 20 to 40.
C. Make infrastructure changes to enhance the visibility of the choirs and provide acoustics and instruments suitable for a wide variety of excellent music.
  (i) 2006-2007 Short-term infrastructure improvements would include softening and modulating the organ in the Nave (See Appendix for specific details on this proposal).
  (ii) Mid-term improvements would include installing choir stalls with kneelers, lighting and slots for music placed on rolling platforms in the chancel.
  (iii) Long-term improvements would include renovating the chapel to improve the acoustics and make the space more conducive to a range of music for contemporary Eucharists, Evensongs, and Compline as well as other services. Specifics of this renovation could include:
    a) remove carpet to make chapel more "live" acoustically
    b) replace some of existing pews with chairs so reconfiguration of space for specific events is possible
    c) rework and/or replace organ
    d) investigate family stipulations RE altering space
D. Increase visibility of the Adult Choir in a wider context, and thus

serve the evangelical part of the Choir's and St. George's mission, by continuing the tradition of choir tours, following the precedent of the European tour in 1989 and the recent appearance of the Adult Choir at the Piccolo Spoleto Festival in Charleston. There is a proposal to make our next tour one of exploring our roots in the Anglican musical tradition by making our next tour to England. It is hoped that we can utilize Dr. Somerville's contacts there to substitute as a cathedral choir-in-residence. As has been the case for both previous choir tours, members of the congregation would be encouraged to accompany the choir.

The intent of the Long Range Music Planning Committee has been to create permanent support and structure for a vitally important ministry in the life of St. George's Church. This should be an ongoing process that helps our music program flourish now as well as for generations to come.

Respectfully submitted,
Calvin Lewis,
Chair for the Long Range Music Planning Committee

Appendix D
Future Projects

This section contains summary information about four future projects concerning music at St. George's. These might have been called needs, hopes, or goals. The first concerns the need for choir stalls and/or risers. The second explains a Music Scholarship that has been awarded and the hopes for continuing the concept for others. The third describes the rationale for a new organ. The fourth presents the initial proposal for a secondary School for the Arts—St. George's Academy. Together they provide a glimpse into a remarkable future.

Choir Stalls and/or Risers
MARK RING

I have proposed the construction and installation of semi-permanent risers for the Choir in the apse. In the current configuration much of the Choir's sound is being stopped by the altar, which is directly in front of the singers' mouths. It is analogous to singing directly into a concrete wall. The drop-off in sound (in volume, tone color, and intelligibility) is very substantial. The congregation simply cannot hear what the Choir is really doing—they receive only a shadow of the Choir's actual singing. The rationale for the risers is to get the Choir raised just enough to where their voices will carry over the altar. This is strictly an auditory, rather than visual, goal and purpose. This would also help improve the balance with the organ, as more of the Choir's sound could be heard in the church. In addition, from a performance standpoint, it would improve sightlines between choir and conductor. When they are seated, they would still be largely "invisible" to the congregation. This is a project that has been desired for many years here; in years past, the Director would have the Choir stand on their chairs sometimes, just to be heard better over the altar.

The St. George's Choir is truly magnificent—one of the finest choirs in any Episcopal church in the country—yet much of their sound is stopped before being heard by worshipers in the church. When the Choir sings

Evensong or concerts, they stand on the altar steps. The difference in sound in the church is immediate and extreme. It simply sounds like a different choir.

Some Anglican churches use permanent stalls rather than risers. Stalls incorporate both risers and a permanent music stand/rack in front of the singers that also includes a place for storing music folders and prayer books when not in use. This is an option for St. George's, but I have not yet included that in my proposal because of the additional costs involved. It would probably double the cost of the project. While convenient and ideal, stalls are not aurally necessary; risers are. The risers, however, could be built so as to incorporate stalls at a future date.

After comparing proposals from three builders, I have recommended a local craftsman for this project, using all wood construction and stained to match exactly the existing woodwork in the Chancel. The total cost for the risers would be just under $10,000, with a lead time of six to eight weeks. This is less than half the cost of his competitors, with absolutely no loss of quality.

It would be wonderful if these risers are in place in time for the national exposure St. George's will receive at the 2012 National Convention of the American Guild of Organists, to be held in Nashville in July. Of course as always our primary purpose is to lead the worship of God in our parish on a weekly basis, and it is for this that we desire the best tools to enable us in our calling. One such important tool would be risers.

Music Scholarship
DON A. SHRIVER

Establishment of a Scholarship at St. George's for Advanced Studies in Sacred Music

In May of 2008, the Rector, R. Leigh Spruill, the Wardens, Don A. Shriver and Calvin P Lewis, and the Vestry approved a scholarship fund. This fund was named for Murray Forbes Somerville, Director of Music at St. George's from September 1, 2003, until September 1, 2008.

The idea for a music scholarship came from Dr. Alexander C. McLeod. He and Clay Jackson presented the idea to the Rector and Wardens in

March 2008, because there was in the choir a gifted countertenor whose name was Andrew Rader in pursuit of a career in ancient music and in need of the funds to seek advanced academic training. These church leaders hoped that the discovery of financial aid for Andy Rader could set an important precedent at St. George's to promote excellence and attract future talented choristers and musicians.

Concurrently and catalytic to the establishment of this scholarship fund, a benefactor, who was a friend of Alex McLeod, offered "seed" funding. The amount offered was substantial and led to others interested in sacred music at St. George's to participate in creating a fund to enable Andy Rader to receive a full scholarship and stipend to complete a master's degree at the University of Indiana in Bloomington, Indiana.

The approval was granted by a purpose document executed by the Rector and Wardens, and that action serves as the foundation for a sustaining scholarship process. In summary, "the purpose of this fund shall be to advance excellence of performance, interpretation and understanding by choir members, in order to glorify God through sacred choral music at St. George's." That document is part of the permanent record of St. George's and is in the office of the Rector. It is attached hereto.

St. George's Murray Forbes Somerville Scholarship Fund Purpose

Because of the generosity of William H. and Judith Scheide and the devotion of both the Scheides and Alexander C. McLeod to promoting greater understanding and appreciation of early sacred music, this fund was established. The purpose of this fund shall be to advance excellence of performance, interpretation and understanding by choir members, in order to glorify God through sacred choral music at St. George's.

The fund will provide financial aid to members of the choirs of St. George's Episcopal Church, Nashville, Tennessee, who seek to further their education and development in the profession of music. The principal and accrued interest shall be paid to assist choir members with the costs of tuition, books, and other materials, room and board, related transportation expenses, conferences, seminars, and such other costs as may be pertinent to advancing musical education.

Although it is the intent of this scholarship fund to benefit individuals who are current members of a choir at St. George's, other funding purposes that may enhance the ministries of choral music at St. George's may be considered. In order that there shall be consistency over time in the use and management of the funds, all decisions concerning expenditures shall be made at the discretion of the Rector and consistent with the Canons and Bylaws of St. George's. In the absence of the Rector, such decisions shall be made in adherence to the aforementioned Canons and Bylaws by the Wardens.

Agreed to and accepted by,
R. Leigh Spruill, Rector
Don A. Shriver, Sr. Warden
Calvin P. Lewis, Jr. Warden

New Organ

Recommendation to the Vestry
Ad Hoc Organ Committee
September 20, 2010

Our ad hoc committee was asked to consider the current condition and status of the Casavant Organ and to make a recommendation to the rector, executive committee and vestry on its possible replacement. Our first meeting was held on July 8, 2010, and three other meetings have been held, during which we developed a better understanding of the strengths and limitations of the Casavant instrument, the current needs of our music program in terms of instrument use and support, and the parish's long range plans for developing more fully a classical, traditional Anglican music ministry to enhance our liturgical offerings and worship.

In the course of our work, we have received and reviewed the work of an independent organ expert/consultant, Mr. Jack Bethards, President of the Schoenstein & Co., Organ Builders, who was retained to provide an objective review and opinion of the Casavant instrument and its role in classical/traditional Anglican music programs. In addition, we have talked with experts in the field and others knowledgeable in this area, including music directors from other parishes and our own music director and organist. We also reviewed proposals from four highly regarded Organ Builders concerning the substantial refurbishment or replacement of the Casavant organ so that we could develop a good understanding of what costs could be contemplated or expected, depending on what strategy we adopted.

Our committee recognizes the severe damage our Church has sustained during the recent floods in May of this year. We also recognize and wholly agree that the main priority of the Parish is and should be the rebuilding efforts that must be funded by the congregation through a capital campaign.

The committee recommends that the Vestry pursue the replacement of the existing organ with a new instrument, rather than spending substantial sums in attempting to upgrade the current organ. This recommendation is not made lightly and is based on much discussion and consideration. The following is a brief explanation.

We have concluded that the church does not "need" a new organ in the sense that there are structural, workmanship or quality defects in the current instrument. Properly maintained, the Casavant organ should last as long as the building. However, we have also concluded that the current organ should be replaced because, as our expert's report stated, "if you are serious about developing a first class Anglican-style music program you must start with a fresh organ" because "it is not a good match to your present requirements and your building." The organ's design emphasizes treble tones and minimizes bass tones, which is a very poor match for the acoustical limitations of our building, which deadens bass tones and enhances treble tones, the exact opposite of what is needed. The tonal qualities, loudness controls, and dynamic range of the current organ also limit the organ's use for accompaniment. The Casavant organ was designed as a particular style of a solo repertoire organ and not for Anglican-style choral accompaniment. In short, it is better to replace the organ than to attempt fixing its current limitations.

We are extremely sensitive to the current competing needs and priorities of the parish and its long range plan. Notwithstanding the immediate needs caused by the flood's destruction, however, we understand that excellence in worship is the first focus of our long range strategic plan and a robust and world class Anglican style music program is a key component of such a liturgical offering. To fulfill that component of our strategic plan, we have concluded that the organ should be replaced at some point in time but the question remains: is this the right time?

We recommend that a quiet campaign for possible funding of the Organ should be conducted simultaneously, and in a parallel manner, with the overall current Capital Campaign of the Church to determine the level of funding interest for this part of our Music Ministry. If such an interest is identified and it does not detract from our overall capital campaign funding, the vestry should pursue the evaluation, review, selection and purchase of a new instrument to support and enhance a classical Anglican music program at St. George's. If such funding is not identified in the near term, the vestry should include the replacement of the organ in its continued long range planning and determine a strategy for future funding of a new instrument.

>Ad Hoc Organ Committee
>John Fitzgerald, Chair
>Clay Jackson
>Calvin Lewis
>Steve Taylor
>Jim Ramsey
>Amy Norton

Please note that Schoenstein & Co. is not one of the firms from whom proposals were obtained. Mr. Bethards was hired on a fee basis to provide an opinion without being considered as a source for providing a new instrument. Summaries of the four proposals reviewed by the Committee are as follows:

1. Ruffatti: Keep much of the current Casavant, and try to revoice pipes where possible and replace others as possible. Proposal costs $787,100.

2. John-Paul Buzard: 4-manual, 96-rank organ for $1,491,865 plus building preparation (approximately an additional 20%). Mr. Buzard has offered to extend his warranty to a period of 20 years.

3. Charles Kegg: 4-manual, 78-rank organ for $1,694,000 plus building preparation (20%, as above). Mr. Kegg has offered to extend his warranty to a period of 10 years.

4. Casavant Freres: 4-manual, 87-rank organ for $1,890,320 plus building preparation (20%, as above). We have no information regarding a warranty from Casavant.

ORGAN BUILDERS

CUSTOM BUILDERS OF DISTINGUISHED INSTRUMENTS FOR FIVE GENERATIONS

July 27, 2010

Mr. John D. Fitzgerald, Jr. Esq
Tune, Entrekin & White, P.C.
Regions Center, Suite 1700
315 Deaderick Street
Nashville, TN 37238-1700

Subject: Pipe Organ Survey

Dear John,

On July 7th and 8th I conducted a survey of the organ including: (1) inspecting the main organ, remote divisions, blower, and console; (2) testing every action and playing every note from the console; (3) reviewing the maintenance history; (4) observing the acoustical properties of the church; and (5) becoming familiar with the music program of the Parish. I also surveyed the Chapel organ briefly.

My objective was to determine the condition of the instrument and evaluate its suitability *vis-à-vis* the current and projected musical program of the Parish and the acoustics of the church. The following is a summary and amplification of the report presented verbally on July 8th.

I wish to make it absolutely clear that any negative comments about the organ are not made to place blame. When an organ comes under scrutiny, I usually find that the reason is a change in circumstances that brings into question decisions and actions that were not only well-intentioned, but logical at the time they were taken. Re-evaluating an organ, even one as new as this one, is not unusual. A lot can change in the musical life of a Parish over 25 years.

HISTORIC SAN FRANCISCO
FACTORY & ARCHIVE

CORPORATE OFFICE AND MAIN PLANT
4001 INDUSTRIAL WAY. BENICIA. CALIFORNIA 94510 (707)747-5858 WWW.SCHOENSTEIN.COM

Mr John D. Fitzgerald, Jr Esq
July 27, 2010
Page 2 of 17

SUMMARY

1. The present organ has a **replacement value of $2,100,000**.

2. The builder, Casavant, has an exceptionally high reputation for quality of engineering and construction. **I found no systemic or hidden mechanical faults. The organ is relatively new; its mechanism should perform well.**

3. **The current malfunctions as well as tonal regulation and tuning problems are the result of deferred maintenance.** Over the last 10 years the maintenance budget has been only one-third of normal.

4. **With proper maintenance the organ can be a good example of its tonal style, but its style is totally wrong for your present music program and for the acoustic profile of the building.**

5. The three elements absolutely required for proper Anglican-style choral accompaniment are: variety of tone color, wide dynamic range, and precise control. **It would be hard to find an organ more ill-suited to Anglican choral accompaniment.**

   - **Despite having 58 voices, there is hardly any tonal variety.** It is as though you had a symphony orchestra of just strings and brass without the beauty and delicacy of wood winds and horns.

   - **The variation in loudness is limited.** Most of the pipes are voiced at approximately the same loudness and the expression shades do not have very effective control over the enclosed divisions.

   - **The console is not provided with the full range of couplers and other accessories** to give the organist flexible control of such a large instrument.

6. **Your building absorbs bass tone and emphasizes high treble tone.** Unfortunately the organ, following the neo-classic ideal, minimizes bass tone and strongly emphasizes treble tone. **The organ's tonal balance does not complement the building's acoustic.** To be successful in this acoustical environment, an organ must be designed with exceptionally full bass and a very carefully proportioned treble. Although it may be possible to make some improvement in the building's acoustical response, **it is extremely doubtful that enough acoustical improvement could be made in the structure of the building to make up for the shortcomings in the organ's tonal balance.**

Mr. John D. Fitzgerald, Jr. Esq
July 27, 2010
Page 3 of 17

7. **The organ is not a bad one – it is just not a good match to your present requirements and to your building.**

8. **The present organ could be improved to some extent, but attempts to reverse completely its tonal character will be a very costly and fruitless venture.**

9. **If you are serious about developing a first class Anglican-style music program you must start fresh with a new organ.** It would be smaller than the present organ because space must be used for larger bass pipes and better expression boxes. It would, however, have vastly more variety of tone and expression and would be fully able to meet all of the requirements of your program. Your organists, who are thorough professionals, are able to cope with the present organ and with clever musical tricks make it sound presentable, but think what they could do if provided with a truly proper instrument!

10. **Whether or not you keep this organ you should get it properly maintained and consider acoustical and HVAC improvements.**

Those not interested in technical details may go to the Recommendations section on page 15, which includes cost estimates for the various alternatives.

Mr. John D. Fitzgerald, Jr. Esq
July 27, 2010
Page 4 of 17

DESCRIPTION & VALUE

This is a three-manual and pedal electric-pneumatic action pipe organ of 58 voices, 85 ranks, 4,900 pipes plus Chimes and Cymbelstern. The main divisions are located on an east end apse balcony platform. The Antiphonal divisions are located in a chamber above the west end balcony with expressive tone openings both down to the balcony and out to the nave. A chamade Trompette-de-fête is located on the west end balcony rail. The Antiphonal division has a separate one-manual console. Other special features include a high pressure, hooded Trompette Royale in the Positiv, and a half-length 32' Contre Bombarde in the Pedal. The organ was built by Casavant in 1985/1986 as Opus 3606. The firm has made some subsequent modifications including some re-voicing and reduction of wind pressures and mechanical repairs. Others have added a digital tone generator to replace one of the 32'stops. The present day cost to replace this instrument is estimated at $2,100,000 excluding any state or local taxes, freight, hoisting, preparation of the building to house the organ, electrical hook-up, and the travel and living expenses of on-site installation personnel.

It would be prudent to have the organ insured for at least this amount. Using this asset value as a benchmark helps clarify decisions on maintenance and improvements.

Mr. John D. Fitzgerald, Jr. Esq
July 27, 2010
Page 5 of 17

MECHANICAL CONDITION

Casavant organs are noted for their quality of engineering and construction. An organ just 25 years old is still considered new and I could find no reason why this one should be an exception. Most of the problems I noted were the result of deferred maintenance and can be corrected easily. The few problems that are not maintenance related are also relatively minor. **The organ does not appear to have any systemic failure or hidden defects.**

I found 21 individual malfunctions and was able to correct all but 10 during my investigation. A technician with the proper tools should be able to fix the rest on a maintenance visit. Other work needed to bring the organ up to par is covered in the following paragraphs.

I must caution, however, that it is impossible for anyone to discover all of the peculiarities and quirks of a large and complex instrument on a survey visit. Pipe organs are affected by seasonal humidity and temperature changes and the person who understands the organ best is the one who takes care of it regularly. I had a lengthy discussion with Dwayne Short, the local technician, who verified my findings based on his experience with the instrument. He should be looked to for advice on service issues.

WIND SYSTEM

The wind system consists of blowers, regulators, concussion bellows, tremulants, and conductors that produce, control, and transmit wind to operate the organ. The system is judged by its capacity, steadiness, and silence. **The system appears to be in good condition and is operating properly with one exception.** The high pressure blower for the Trompette Royale stop was not functioning on my visit. I understand that the motor is "burned out", but this is quite unusual and the problem may be something else. The blower should be checked out by an electric motor expert. If there is a motor problem, you must contact the manufacturer before attempting any kind of repair. In the worst case, a new blower may be required and the cost including installation should be around $5,000. If it is determined that the motor was stressed by heat build-up, it would be wise to provide a recycling bleed from the blower output to help cool the motor.

Mr John D. Fitzgerald, Jr Esq
July 27, 2010
Page 6 of 17

ELECTRICAL SYSTEM AND CONSOLE

The primary equipment is by Solid State Logic, a very well respected company. The console is typical of Casavant organs of the period. **It is in normal condition** for its age. One toe lever had a sluggish return and the veneer is chipping off the toe stud rails. The Antiphonal expression shoe cut-out switch is not operating. A malfunctioning stop in the Swell may be a console contact or open connection. All of these are maintenance items. The digital tone generator is not operating, but should be repairable. It was made by Peterson – a very reputable company.

WIND CHESTS AND ACTIONS

There are a few malfunctions in the wind chests but, with the possible exception of the Great, these should be normal maintenance issues. The Great wind chest being located directly below the apse window has been exposed to greater than normal variations in temperature. I also understand that the old HVAC system did not control humidity as well as the present system does. There is a very small crack in the table of the front Great chest. It is possible that one of the current chest malfunctions can be
traced to this; however, this cannot be determined without disassembly. This problem should be repairable and if humidity is kept within a reasonable range, the cracking should not increase and the chest should operate properly.

PIPES AND RACKING

The large, grey-painted pipes are made of zinc. During the period when this organ was built, all organ companies suffered from supplies of zinc that were not as strong and fit as the zinc they had previously been using. If not very thoroughly supported, this material has a tendency to bend of its own weight. This problem did not show up until several years after organs were completed. It can be counteracted by proper racking that holds pipes firmly in place or by replacing the zinc pipes with the new type of zinc that has been formulated for greater strength. I understand that some work has been done over the years to alleviate this problem; however, **I noted some zinc deformation, but nothing so serious as to require replacement**. Instead, I recommend straightening any pipes that need it and making some additional racks. Also, the Casavant racking system provides for adjustment to keep the pipes in tension. Your technician should go through the organ, making adjustments as necessary and inspecting all of the racks for integrity. I found one rack that had come loose from its support and had by its own weight bent several pipes! I was able to fix the pipes and the rack. Obviously, this is another point requiring fairly regular inspection.

Mr. John D. Fitzgerald, Jr Esq
July 27, 2010
Page 7 of 17

EXPRESSION SYSTEM

The relationship between expression pedal motion and shade motion is not in parallel. With this type of system it will never be perfect, but I believe that some careful adjustment will result in a smoother action. **The expression motors and shades all appear to be in good condition, but the musical effect is seriously limited because closing the shades does bring the volume down to a true** *pianissimo*. This is because the expression boxes do not seal tightly. Many very small gaps remain when the shades are closed. This is due to the extraordinarily large number of shade, each of which has hairline gaps, and an open space where the two sections of shades in each division join one another. This problem will be addressed more fully in the musical section below. I don't believe, however, that there is a practical solution to it without major re-engineering and replacement of the system and boxes.

INSTALLATION QUALITY/MAINTENANCE ACCESS

The installation looks to have been hurried. Usually Casavant installations are well finished and detailed. This one was placed on an unfinished plywood floor with gaps in it. The wiring is haphazardly strung around with large excess coils. Some of this mess is due to audio and other communication wires strung through the organ area. It is difficult to get around some parts of the organ for lack of adequate handles, steps, ladders, etc. Some of the wind lines are not protected with covers and have been damaged as a result. Water damage has caused peeling paint to fall into the organ on the right hand Pedal division. In the Antiphonal, the chamber door strike plate is misplaced so the door will not remain closed, which ruins the effect of the air conditioning and heating equipment in the Antiphonal expression box. Finally, the lighting for service work is inadequate. Some lighting should be provided in the under sections of the organ to make access for repair easier and more efficient.

All of these points are rather minor irritants, but when put together they spell an organ that is hard to take care of. **One way to encourage excellent care of an instrument is to provide your technician with good lighting, a clean environment, and the funds necessary to get the installation cleaned up and made more accessible.**

Mr. John D. Fitzgerald, Jr. Esq
July 27, 2010
Page 8 of 17

TONAL CONDITION

GENERAL

On my visit the organ was badly out of tune and regulation to the extent that many stops were unusable. This type of organ needs a good deal of careful attention to both tuning and regulation on a regular basis.

REGULATION

In a well regulated instrument, all the pipes speak properly and clearly. Volume and tone color are even from note to note. Stops and choruses and divisions balance with one another. Every time the organ is tuned it should be checked for regulation inconsistencies, particularly in the reed stops. Many of the flue stops, especially some of those constructed of zinc, need remedial attention from time to time. What you face with this organ is years of inattention to this work. The organ is certainly ready for a solid session of remedial regulation.

No amount of regulation would change the tonal style of the instrument; however, by correcting the problems, particularly uneven pipe speech in the flues and inconsistent tone and loudness in the reeds will make the organ a much better example of its style.

Mr. John D Fitzgerald, Jr Esq
July 27, 2010
Page 9 of 17

ACOUSTICS

Your building has a pleasant reverberation, and good sound distribution, but a frequency response curve that is exactly opposite of what is ideal for church music. Your building emphasizes high treble tones and de-emphasizes low bass tones. The reasons for this are a lot of smooth non-porous surfaces that reflect the short high frequency waves and flexible wall and ceiling surfaces that absorb the large bass waves. The ideal church building is made of solid stone. Bass tones can't move the stone so they are reflected out to the listener. High treble tones are slightly dampened by the lightly porous surface. To replicate this in a modern building, wall surfaces are made thicker by adding layers of drywall and providing more closely and randomly placed support studs. The extremely bright treble can be attenuated slightly with various materials and shapes. It's very important, however, not to go too far with dampening high frequencies as that can result in a dull and lifeless sound.

I understand you've had extensive acoustical consultation by first class experts in the field. **It would be a great benefit to your congregation, your choir and any organ you may have to improve the frequency response of the building.** I caution, however, that no matter how much work you do and how much money you spend, you will not achieve the effect of a stone building. Therefore, **all of your musical forces, particularly the organ, will have to meet the building half way by making up for any inconsistencies that remain** by emphasizing the frequencies that the building absorbs and de-emphasizing those that it over-amplifies.

ENVIRONMENT

Temperature and humidity control are important to an organ's performance and longevity. The simple rules are that the temperature should be the same when the organ is played as when it is tuned and humidity should not vary more than 30 percentage points throughout the year. A detailed explanation of these requirements will be found in the attached temperature and humidity guidelines. I understand that your new system provides excellent control. Even though it may add a bit to your heating and cooling cost, in the long run **it will save the Parish a good deal of money in organ repair to provide a reasonable environment.**

There is some unpleasant noise in the HVAC system. A qualified Air Balancer should be engaged to adjust the system for quieter operation. Reduced background noise enhances every aspect of both music and the spoken word.

Mr. John D. Fitzgerald, Jr. Esq
July 27, 2010
Page 10 of 17

TONAL STYLE

Left to last is the most important element that you asked me to evaluate — the organ's tonal style. Normally I am asked to determine whether an instrument is a good example of its tonal style. In this case I was asked also to determine whether this organ could be re-built into a different style. Before evaluating the organ, I will outline my understanding of the two styles under consideration.

THE NEO-CLASSIC STYLE

The present organ is what I would term an eclectic neo-classic organ with a Germanic tonal accent and an architecture (distribution of pitches and tonal families within its divisions) designed to cover a broad range of organ solo repertoire. The French nomenclature, although not indicative of the organ's tone color, is appropriate to the degree that the architecture provides resources minimally necessary for much French repertoire. The three characteristics of this style are:

1. **Light weight bass, "transparent" mid-range and bold treble.** The treble is dominated by what voicers call "fluty" tone. This character adds dramatically to the unyielding, hard-edged quality of the high pitches making them irritating rather than sparkling.

2. **Minimal variation in tonal color.** This represents a kind of "neutral" approach to organ tone: diapasons (or principals) at the center with flutes adding a touch of fullness and strings adding a touch of lightness counterposed with reeds that add grit and clatter. Your organ, for example has so much duplication of tone color that it delivers variety of an organ only half its size.

3. **Limited dynamic range.** The majority of stops are voiced in the middle range of loudness and the expression box produces shading rather than dramatic contrast.

4. **A Spartan approach to coupling and borrowing.** The console is equipped with only the bare minimum of couplers and hardly any borrowing so that the flexibility of resources is further limited.

Mr. John D. Fitzgerald, Jr. Esq
July 27, 2010
Page 11 of 17

The neo-classic style reflects a kind of scientific approach to music similar to that found in modernist art and architecture, which is summed up best as a reaction to the so called excesses of romanticism. It de-emphasizes sentiment and emotion and invites an intellectual, analytical approach. With this in mind, it's easy to see why an organ would be considered a neutral element in presenting the composer's ideas — an instrument that does not inject its own personality in to the proceedings.

THE ANGLICAN STYLE

The Anglican choral service demands an instrument designed specifically and primarily to accompany the choir and congregation. Solo repertoire is a secondary consideration. The great British builders developed a style of instrument that rivaled the symphony orchestra in the ability to provide any tone color at any dynamic level so as to suit the demands of the great Anglican composers and choir masters. The characteristics of these instruments are:

1. **Solid, profound deep bass and a full singing mid-range with high treble employed for color rather than power.** Solid bass is required to maintain rhythm and congregational singing. Full tone in the mid-range which is the range of the human voice is required for good accompaniment.

2. **As great a variety of tonal colors as possible.** The proper accompaniment of Anglican chant and the great anthems is one of the most demanding of musical tasks. Without a full palette of colors, the musical artist cannot create the emotional impact required to illustrate the texts being sung.

3. **Broad dynamic range from *ppp* to *fff*.** One of the most important effects in choir accompaniment is being able to bring a large ensemble of pipes down to a whisper and to gracefully and quickly make crescendos and dimuendos in melodies, counter melodies and obbligato lines.

4. **Flexible control.** The Anglican service demands the most of an organist's talent. He must be able to make people sing hymns with authority, provide intricate accompaniments for the choir, improvise, and play solo voluntaries. His music provides a "score" for the drama of the liturgy. He should have available the resources to make full use of the organ's tonal qualities. This means a good array of couplers and other playing aids. Without these facilities, an organist faces discouraging limits.

Mr. John D. Fitzgerald, Jr. Esq
July 27, 2010
Page 12 of 17

STYLES COMPARED

There are many styles in the world of organ building, but **I cannot think of two more diametrically opposed than the neo-classic and Anglican styles.** This is true for each of the characteristics mentioned above. Each style has its adherents, but I believe that even the most convinced neo-classic enthusiasts would agree that an Anglican organ would do a better job in a Lutheran Parish than a neo-classic organ would in an Episcopal Parish. In other words, the Anglican style organ can do a far better job of playing the general organ repertoire than a neo-classic organ can do in choir accompaniment.

STYLE EVALUATION OF THE PRESENT ORGAN

Your instrument is a large and comprehensive example of the neo-classic style. It has the appropriate architecture. I believe that with a thorough and meticulous tonal regulation, this instrument would become a good example of its style.

I understand, however, that your Parish has been developing a traditional Anglican-style music program and that you intend to intensify this and aim for a program that distinguishes this Parish as an outstanding proponent of this musical genre. If that is the case, **the present instrument could not be more inappropriate.**

The question then becomes, could this instrument be changed to the Anglican style? The answer is clearly and unequivocally no, at least for a budget any less than it would take to buy a new organ perfectly suited to the purpose. Your instrument, with such a strong musical personality, can be made a better example of what it is but cannot be transformed into a style that is its direct opposite. It would be like trying to make a Richard Neutra modernist house into an H.H. Richardson Victorian. **If your aim is a thorough-going Anglican music program, you must start over.** With first class tonal regulation, the tone could be made smoother and more pleasing but would still be strictly within the neo-classic style. If you changed a large number of stops, you could aim the organ more in the Anglican direction. I identified 28 stops that should be either fully replaced or completely re-voiced. This includes all of the reeds, much of the upperwork and some of the flutes. These would make a difference; further changes would make only a slight difference and diminishing returns would soon set in. **Even changing the majority of stops would not create a true Anglican style instrument for the following reasons:**

Mr. John D. Fitzgerald, Jr. Esq
July 27, 2010
Page 13 of 17

- The Swell boxes do not provide adequate expression.

- The wind system is not adequate for English-style reeds that require higher pressure.

- The console lacks the range of couplers required.

- Of the greatest importance, **the layout provides no room for the large scale Pedal pipes** necessary to produce solid bass. This is a requirement not only to serve the music, but to fit the building's acoustic.

By the time all of these points were changed, you would have spent enough to buy a new organ.

I must re-emphasize that this is not a bad organ, it is just not the right organ for your present music program.

ACOUSTICAL EVALUATION OF PRESENT ORGAN

Your instrument has an acoustical profile exactly opposite of what the acoustic profile of the building requires. Both organ and building are weak on bass and strong on treble. Since the building profile can be improved only slightly, the organ should make up the difference with powerful bass and more restrained treble.

It must be pointed out that the acoustical imbalance may be due in great part to the building not living up to acoustical expectations. Often builders are promised a certain acoustic based on plans and computer models. The organ is built to that plan, but the building is not constructed as planned often due to "value engineering." In such cases, the builder can hardly be blamed for such a mismatch.

Mr John D Fitzgerald, Jr Esq
July 27, 2010
Page 14 of 17

RECOMMENDATIONS

1. **If you want a first class result to serve properly your music program, you should sell this organ and start fresh.** A new organ will have to be smaller since it will require much of the existing space for the large bass pipes and good expression boxes. I suggest approximately 38 stops (as opposed to the 58 you now have). This would cost approximately $1,500,000 not including decorative casework and display pipes which can only be priced on specific designs. Other extra costs include: state and local taxes, freight, hoisting, building preparation, electrical hook-up, and the travel and living expenses of on-site personnel, which could add 20%.

   I do not recommend re-using any parts of the existing organ in a new one with the possible exception of the chamade Trompette. Its installation is, in a way, part of the building fabric and its pipes can be re-voiced for a softer tone. Nothing else would add much to a new organ and the financial saving would be miniscule. It is better to keep the organ together as a unit so that it may sell at the highest possible price.

   The Antiphonal organ and its console should be sold with the main organ. An Antiphonal organ of this type and size is certainly not needed in your building. I recommend preparing the console of a new organ for a possible Antiphonal stop or two and add them if it is found necessary to have additional support for congregational singing. An 8' Diapason and perhaps an additional 16' Violone to highlight the bass line would be quite adequate and, unless an ethereal stop such as a flute celeste is desired, would not require expression shades.

   I believe that you could net between $60,000 and $120,000 for this instrument as a unit.

2. **If you wish to keep the present organ, I suggest spending no more than $650,000**, which would include replacement or radical re-voicing of 28 stops plus additional tonal regulation and would do as much as is practical to edge it slightly in the Anglican direction. This estimate is based on local work and does not include all of the normal extras such as shipping, crew travel, and work by other contractors. As stated above, this will **not** create a proper Anglican-style organ.

Mr. John D. Fitzgerald, Jr. Esq
July 27, 2010
Page 15 of 17

3. **It is urgent to get a good program of maintenance established** whether or not you decide to keep the present organ. Your musicians deserve an instrument that at least works well and plays in tune and if you are interested in selling the organ, it must be in the best possible condition to get the best price.

   A well proven formula for perpetual maintenance of a pipe organ is to dedicate one percent of its current replacement value to maintenance each year. Approximately one half of that fund ($10,500) should be put away for the eventual replacement of perishable parts, which usually happens around the 50 year mark. The other half ($10,500) should be used for yearly tuning, regulation, adjustment and minor repairs. In reviewing maintenance records over the last ten years, approximately one third of this amount has been spent and most of that has been on mechanical work. **The organ has received nowhere near the amount of regular tuning and regulation that it should have.** This accounts for its poor condition today. Here is a recommended program:

   - Make it clear to your technician that he is responsible for keeping the organ in good shape. Give him "ownership" of the responsibility. Up to now, there has been, as far as I can tell, no regular maintenance program for various quite valid reasons including continuing warranty work by the manufacturer. Several people have worked on the organ and no one has assumed charge of it.

   - Working with your local technician, develop a budget for bringing the organ up to par. This includes improving access, cleaning, fixing the mechanical malfunctions including the auxiliary high pressure blower, improving racking as needed, and tuning and regulating the instrument. My rough estimate for this is $28,000; however, your local technician is the one who should guide you on this. You should engage an electrician to improve lighting at the direction of your technician.

   - Establish a yearly budget for continuing maintenance.

   - If you decide to keep this organ, add to the yearly budget an equal amount to be put into a fund for future major repairs.

Mr John D Fitzgerald, Jr Esq
July 27, 2010
Page 16 of 17

4. Whether or not you use the organ you should:

- Follow the acoustical improvement recommendations of your acoustical consultant to the extent practical.

- Engage an Air Balancer to reduce the noise of your HVAC system and follow the attached guidelines.

Mr. John D Fitzgerald, Jr Esq
July 27, 2010
Page 17 of 17

CHAPEL ORGAN

The chapel instrument is a two manual and pedal, 2-1/2 voice, 2-1/2 rank electric-pneumatic unit action organ. It was built by Möller in 1967 as their Opus 10520. It is a stock model studio organ without expression shades. The pipes are located on a shelf over the chapel entrance with the console to the right of the entrance and facing the altar. Its replacement value is $90,000.

I could not operate the organ since it was disconnected after the flood, but I inspected it thoroughly and believe that there was no significant damage caused by the flood. This organ should be able to work properly with the minimum of service attention.

Like the church organ, this instrument is in the neo-classic style and is not well suited to an intimate Episcopal chapel. It lacks the appropriate expression and tonal color. This would make a nice practice organ for a home or school. Trying to alter it would be ineffective. **If you keep it, it should be left as is. Otherwise you should sell it and start fresh with a new instrument.** Because it is so small and easy to move and re-install, it should be easily saleable and should bring between $5,000 and $10,000.

There are many alternative new approaches ranging from a simple mechanical action chamber organ to a small electric-pneumatic English-style chapel organ with full expression. A mechanical action organ would have to be placed on the chapel floor. An electric-pneumatic chapel organ of three to four voices could be placed in the location of the present instrument. A budget of $110,000 to $150,000 should be adequate. The first decision that must be made is whether or not you can give up any seating space for an organ case on the chapel floor.

* * * * *

In the course of my survey I developed quite a bit of detailed information that cannot be included in a summary report of this type. Please call me with any questions you may have and I'll be glad to provide whatever other help I can.

Yours sincerely,

SCHOENSTEIN & CO.

Jack M. Bethards
President and Tonal Director

JMB:ab
37238dic.72010
Enclosure: V-3

School for the Arts
St. George's Academy Proposal

MARK RING

I have been asked to share some thoughts regarding the formation of a Fine Arts Academy at St. George's. I am happy to do so, as part of a strategic vision for music and arts at our parish.

First, as part of the overall rationale, I would like to stress that I see St. George's as a flagship congregation among the Episcopal denomination. As demographic shifts have taken place in America over the past decades, the cultural centers of the country have shifted southward. Yes, New York and Boston are still outstanding; however, they are not the only places with deeply substantial cultural and ecclesiastical resources. As our parish takes an ever-increasing role in examining the intersection of Christianity and culture, it seems only fitting that we take our place among those who form the future by creating it among our young people.

Few places could realistically contemplate founding a Fine Arts Academy in a cultural, spiritual, and intellectual tradition as rich as the Anglican one we have inherited and nurtured at St. George's. We are fortuitously located in a city that deeply values music and other arts, is a center for publication, and has a significant history of supporting faith-based educational endeavors.

Such endeavors are naturally a long-term process. I envisage a multi-step development, with each step effectively being a new incarnation in the organic growth of the academy. Each step can and will stand on its own, all the while being a gradation or component of that which is to come. Let us "begin with the end in mind."

I dream of a final stage in which there is a full-day, fully accredited private K-12 school with a complete across-the-board curriculum. This may be located at St. George's current site, or it may be elsewhere. Two unique aspects set this school apart: (1) every student has a "major" in one of the fine arts, while being exposed to, and participating in, the other arts being taught; and (2) this school has a distinctly open-minded Anglican Christian emphasis throughout. In this school, the various arts will live together, ideas will cross-pollinate between fields, interdisciplinary projects will spontaneously coalesce, and students will be able to fluently articulate the place of artistic expression within their lives of faith. Exhibits, workshops, and performances will all enhance each other's artistic potency, all borne out in a context of living out our callings as creative children of the Creator. Concurrently, a rigorous academic program will ensure the intellectual growth of the students in non-arts fields, while at the same time giving them the opportunity to learn about and communicate these fields in artistic ways.

Toward that end, I see several intermediate stages, each viable on its own.

One stage would be the formation of a multi-arts educational center, perhaps beginning with two or three disciplines (music, theatre, and visual arts, perhaps.) Instruction could take place in these disciplines either after school and/or on Saturdays, with an RSCM-based Choir School as a vital constituent from the outset. Such instruction could become a "for-credit" activity if we can partner with one or more accredited educational institutions. Additional artistic disciplines would be offered as personnel and facilities become available. The initial organizational structure and facility requirements, while substantial, would not be anywhere near the level needed for a full-day private school. I would see this going for a couple of years before moving on to the next stage.

A second stage would be the expansion into an elementary-level accredited Fine Arts Academy, building on (but not limited to) the base of St. George's Kindergarten clientele. This would of course require considerable additional space, personnel, and funding. I would see this going for five years or so before opening the next stage.

A third stage would be expansion first into the middle school grades, then the high school grades, perhaps tracking the first entering class so that an entering kindergarten student in the first year could graduate high school from the same institution thirteen years later. Each expansion of the student base, and therefore the activity schedule, would require considerable additional space, personnel, and funding.

Along the way, I feel it is essential for this to also be a place where others interested in teaching these disciplines in such a thoughtful Christian context can come and learn how to do so. We should offer continuing-education workshops for artists and artist-teachers who wish to learn more about (1) examining their own creative work through the lens of a thoughtful Christian perspective and (2) teaching their students and/or colleagues how to do this for themselves. By enabling and teaching teachers from other places, we will multiply our mission in the world—to share the abundant riches of our Creator.

Acknowledgments

If ever a book was written by a group of people (as was the King James Version of the Holy Bible!), it is *Music as Mission: A History of Music in St. George's Episcopal Church*. It should be noted that it was written by a group, not by a committee. We came together more or less spontaneously and worked both independently and together over a period of more than two years. Of the twelve St. George's parishioners involved in our project, seven are longtime Choir members. The total number of combined years of Choir service by those writers (named in the paragraphs below) comes to over a century and a half—more than 150 years. That is impressive, and that they would, in addition, give so freely of their time to see this project through speaks both loudly and clearly to their devotion to St. George's and its music.

Ann Orth served as editor and carefully nurtured her writers and diplomatically corrected their writings, all with remarkable patience and expertise. Ann Wells as consulting editor contributed second opinions on Ann Orth's edited sections and offered suggestions to the project in many other ways. Between them they parsed our sentences and perfected our words, corralled our thoughts and ensured that our potholes would be filled. Bertie Shriver was our research coordinator and with her concomitant position as archivist for St. George's was invaluable in digging through the vault to blow the dust off old Vestry Minutes and other records.

The writers about people—organists, choirmasters, choristers—divided their subjects chronologically. All are long-term Choir members and thus know the story firsthand and as frontline soldiers. Jennifer Orth did the yeoman's chore, covering from the very beginnings through Wilma Jensen, as well as ensuring a seamless connection to the contributions of others that followed, accomplishing much of this while continuing her profession and concomitantly earning a master's degree. Giny Bailey, with the assistance of Carol Armes, interviewed Murray Somerville. Giny wrote about the tenure of Murray Somerville, and her husband, Jeff, the more current roles of Gerry Senechal and Mark Ring. John Fitzgerald contributed to the broad scope of this section by traveling to Atlanta to interview Greg Colson and noting his personal remembrances up through and including the current music administrations. These writers are responsible for the main body of the book.

Sensing that, while all of us parishioners at St. George's have a deep appreciation of the Anglican Church music tradition, most of us do not have a great deal of knowledge about just what that is, we decided that the subject needed to be included, standing on its own, and Gerry Senechal agreed to write an essay in lay language to help us. Kevin Carson, also a Choir member, and a knowledgeable organist himself, wrote about Organs and Bells, the stories about and details of our major instrumental history.

Alex McLeod wrote about the nuts and bolts—funding and oversight—in Support and Development, and Claudia Padfield did some research in the early stages of this section. Those of the group who were writing about former Music Staff submitted questions for interviews with Mark Ring and Gerry Senechal. These interviews were conducted and recorded by Alex McLeod, who also contributed the Introduction, Afterword, and these Acknowledgments. Abridged transcriptions of each interview are included. The work of and Report to the Vestry by the Long-Range Music Planning Committee in 2006, chaired by Calvin Lewis, was considered such a seminal document in the history of our music that it is included. Don Shriver wrote about our Music Scholarship. Mark Ring provided information about the need for choir stalls and/or risers. John Fitzgerald selected information about the need for a new organ and the hopes for a School for the Arts.

A number of people were helpful in building our information about our past. Several helped us "discover" Thomas Cowan, our first paid Organist and Choirmaster: Victor Felts, Charlene Harb, Shirley Watts, Ruby Jean McLeod, Richard Cowan, Harriet Mabry, and Anne Glass. Greg Colson, Wilma Jensen, Tim Fudge, Murray Somerville, Gerry Senechal, and Mark Ring were interviewed about their years at St. George's, while Kay Withrow Thomson spoke for herself and for late husband Scott Withrow. Jodie Owens Clark and Susan Markley helped bring Sam Batt Owens's years of involvement to life for us. Father Bob Abstein was another great resource. As previously noted, John Fitzgerald interviewed Greg Colson in Atlanta and contributed to the material about Gerry Senechal and Mark Ring. Lois and Peter Fyfe were helpful in making suggestions where we might go to find missing information about early Organists. Steve Taylor clarified the origins and operations of the Friends of Music at St. George's.

Several people were instrumental in helping to bring the printed book to fruition. The expertise and patience of Dimples Kellogg as copyeditor and

Gary Gore as book designer were paramount. Dennis Carney restored several old and decrepit but key newspaper photographs. Ron Watson helped us find an appropriate printer. The early generosity of Bob Hilton in his willingness to underwrite the cost of producing and printing the book relieved much anxiety for us and, at the same time, gives us the pleasure of remembering his parents, both stalwart members of St. George's. His father, Robert Clark Hilton, was on the Vestry from 1968 to 1971 and was Senior Warden his last year. His mother, Cecelia Candee Hilton, was on the Vestry from 1970 to 1973.

Throughout the course of these months of preparation, Father Spruill was always supportive, always interested, and always available.

Index of Personal Names

Abstein, William Robert, 96, 114–16, 251
Adams, Dillard, 80
Adkins, Giny, 53, 55
Adkins, Lucy, 53, 59
Adkins, Ruth, 172
Adkins, Vicki, 120
Allen, Karen Cooper, 38–40, 168
Armes, Carol, 250
Arnold, Jerry, 123
Arnst, Terryll, 60

Bailey, Ben, 121
Bailey, Donald, 136
Bailey, Ellie, 202
Bailey, Giny, xii, 65, 117, 123–24, 135, 219, 221, 250
Bailey, Jeff, xii, 106–7, 135, 250
Bailey, Tricia, 202
Baker, Robert, 112
Baldock, Sarah, 120
Ball, John, 168
Banner, Nancy, 53
Bass, Melinda Owen, 171
Battle, Carol, 71
Bauerschmidt, John Crawford, 121–22
Baxter, Gage, 117
Belcher, Diane, 94
Bennett, David, 200
Bennett, Scott, 136
Benson, Maxwell, 12
Berky, Doug, 144
Berndt, Douglas J., 25
Berry, Chris, 35
Bertalot, John, 147, 188
Bethards, Jack, 228, 230–47
Black, Randall, 114
Bouchard, Remi, 156
Breast, Winifred ("Winnie"), 18, 20–21, 23, 168
Brooks, Marguerite, 136

Brooks, Thomas, 136
Brown, Betty, 42
Bruffy, Charles, 136
Butler-Moore, Nylea, 83, 94, 103
Buzard, John-Paul, 230

Campbell, Dorothy, 100, 111
Carney, Dennis, 252
Carolane, Roslyn, 100
Carrigan, Janette (see also Fishell, Janette), 69
Carson, Kevin, xii, 151, 219, 222, 251
Casavant organ, 72–73, 76–81, 123, 141, 145, 155–57, 171, 228–29, 230–47
Champagne, Yves, 156
Cheek, Debbie, 53
Cheek, Jean, 53
Clark, Jody Owens, 49, 251
Clarke, Karen, 115
Clayton, Murray, 53
Cohen, Joel, 116, 122
Coignet, Jean-Louis, 156
Cole, Rebecca, 113
Coleman, Edwin, 94, 96
Colson, Betty Nohe, 20, 38
Colson Chorale, 37
Colson, Gregory, 19–23, 25–33, 35–38, 40–41, 168, 170, 250, 251
Corbett, Donald, 156
Cotton, Dick, 27
Cotton, Edina, 27
Cotton, Larry, 27
Cotton, Margie, 27
Cowan, Donald, 12, 199
Cowan, Mildred, 12–13
Cowan, Richard, 16, 18, 251
Cowan, Thomas Wynn, 14–19, 168, 251
Cowan, Tom, 16,
Crabtree, Bruce, 76
Crandall, William Wright, 171
Crozier, Catharine, 67

INDEX

Daane, Whitney, 53
Dandridge, E. P., 13
Darden, Tricia, 83
David, Lucille, 59, 68, 72, 118–19
De Moss, Suzanne, 35
Dickerson, Donia Craig, 120
Dickerson, Estelle Crandall, 171
Dickerson, Gordon Saint Claire, 171
Dickerson, Gordon Saint Claire, Jr., 171
Dickerson, William Buford, II, 171
Duke, R. S., 24

Edwards, James Lloyd, 45
Edwards, Judy, 45
Erickson, Ralph, 19

Felts, Victor, 251
Fillebrown, Lavinia, 72
Fippinger, Arthur, 22
Fippinger, Carol, 35
Fishburne, Mary, 117
Fishell, Janette, 69, 105–6, 157
Fisher, Laurel, 130, 140
Fitzgerald, John, 26–27, 33–34, 37, 72, 199, 206, 211, 218, 230–31, 250–51
Fitzgerald, Mary Dale, 219, 222
Fudge, Tim, 102–8, 110–11, 169, 251
Fulton, Charles, 39
Fyfe, Lois, 69, 71, 114, 251
Fyfe, Peter, 251

Galloway, Bill, 53, 55
Galloway, Jackson, 53, 58
Gardner, Grace, 172
Glass, Anne, 251
Gleason, Bill, 90–91
Gleason, Harold, 67
Gore, Gary, 252
Guest, George, 136
Gunn, Julien, 60, 94

Hammond organ, 12, 17, 151
Hansbury, Rachel, 140
Harb, Charlene, 251
Hartley, Kenneth, 136
Heath, Fenno, 136
Henkel, F. Arthur, 13–14, 17
Herbig, Gunther, 136
Higginbottom, Edward, 116

Hill, Ann, 34
Hill, Victor, 48
Hilton, Cecelia Candee, x, 252
Hilton, Robert Candee, x, 252
Hilton, Robert Clark, x, 252
Hodge, Claire, 122
Holeman, Eugene, 17–18
Hudson, Fran, 53
Hurford, Peter, 98
Hutton, Warren, 98

Ingram, Martha, 114

Jackson, Clay, 226, 230
Jacobs, Bill, 18
Jacobs, Nita, 18
Jensen, Wilma, 62, 65–78, 82–86, 88–94, 96–110, 114, 118, 156–57, 168–70, 250–51
John, Christi, 98
Johnson, Betsy, 53
Johnson, James L., 42, 65–66, 73, 77, 82–84, 94
Johnson, Leslie, 42
Joy, Mildred (see also Cowan, Mildred), 12
Joyce, Alexis Jones, 154, 171
Joyce, Douglas Henry, 154, 171
Joyce, Harry Alexis Jones, 154, 171
Joyce, Margaret Sinclair Henry, 154, 171

Kauffman, Lura, 59
Kegg, Charles, 230
Kellogg, Dimples, 251
Kerr, Sarah, 200
Keys, Joel T., 95–96
Killman, Dan, 82
King, Kim, 219, 221
Krigbaum, Charles, 136

Latimer, Bob, 27
Lefebvre, Philippe, 91
Lewis, Calvin, 119, 169, 219, 221, 224, 226, 228, 230, 251
Lilly, Cooper, 53, 222
Lloyd, Ladelle, 26
Lumsden, David, 112
Lyday, Claudia, 219, 222

INDEX

Mabry, Harriet, 251
Markley, Susan, 251
Martindale, Aynsley, 145
Mattea, Kathy, 59
McCarthy, Michael, 121
McLelland, Jeffrey, 62
McLeod, Alexander C., 226–27, 251
McLeod, Ruby Jean, 251
McWherter, Ned, 84,
Mealy, Robert, 122
Melichamp, James, 105–6
Mitchell, Jonathan N., 13
Moller organ, 17, 27, 53, 70, 151–52, 171
Moore, Jimmy, 53
Moore, Keith, 114
Munns, Robert, 101
Murray, Thomas, 136

Neal, Brent, 219, 222
Neswick, Bruce, 117
Nies, Carol, 101
Norton, Amy, 230

Organ, Lucy, 100, 111
Orth, Ann, 250
Orth, Jennifer, xii, 11, 39, 53, 55, 65, 135, 157, 250
Orth, Julie, 53
Owen, Lulu Hampton, 171
Owen, Ralph "Peck," 156, 171
Owen, Ralph, Jr., 171
Owens, Jeanne, 41
Owens, Sam Batt, 38–41, 43–50, 52–53, 70, 168, 170, 251

Pace, Joseph L., 68, 87–88
Padfield, Claudia, 251
Parvin, Gloria, 88, 106–7
Patrick, Frances, 12–13
Payne, Michael, 79–81, 156
Polk, Frances, 42
Polk, Marshall Tate, III, 171
Polk, Marshall Tate, Jr., 27, 171
Polk, Sandra Murray, 171
Preston, Simon, 157
Price, Rebecca, 68
Proctor, Marjorie, 121

Race, Mary Catherine, 97–98

Rader, Andrew, 227
Ramm, Eberhard, 97
Ramsey, Jim, 230
Reuther, Laura, 38
Richter, Karl, 112, 114
Ring, Mark, xii, 135–42, 145–48, 169–70, 179–92, 196, 199, 207, 210–12, 214, 217–18, 225, 248, 250–51
Riordan, George, 115
Rivers, Richards, 30
Roberts, Thomas A., 37, 41
Robertson, Helen, 42, 51
Robinson, Margaret Ann, 38, 83–84
Robinson, Walter, 84
Rodes, Dyer, 219, 221
Roth, Daniel, 136
Ruffatti, 230
Rumbaugh, Dottie, 27, 34–35
Rutledge, Bill, 141
Rutledge, Frankie, 141

Sanders, Rick, 96
Sattler, Mareike, 123
Scheide, Judith, 227
Scheide, William H., 171, 227
Schneller, Sue, 62, 69
Schoenstein & Co., Organ Builders, 228, 230–31
Schwede, Bettye Ann, 62, 70
Semingson, John, 79, 106, 111, 156
Senechal, Gerry, xi, xii, 1, 115, 117, 120–24, 128–33, 137, 139–40, 169, 187, 189, 193–222, 250–51
Senechal, Roger, 124, 139
Shannon, Louise, 38, 42
Shannon, Marc, 53
Sharp, James R., 13
Sharp, Vernon, 168
Shaw, Robert (choral conductor), 36, 99, 118
Shaw, Robert (reverend), 18, 22, 168
Sherry, Denver, 43
Shriver, Bertie, 250
Shriver, Don, 226, 228, 251
Sikes, Lee, 59
Smith, Adele, 87
Smith, Carl, 107
Smith, Elizabeth, 98, 101–2, 104, 106, 108, 110–11, 114, 193

INDEX

Smith, Marcel, 98
Smoot, Ann Elise, 100
Somerville, Hazel, 113, 115, 117, 120, 122, 127–29
Somerville, Murray Forbes, 111–23, 127–30, 169–70, 187, 193–94, 196, 202, 207, 210–14, 219, 221–22, 224, 226–27, 250–51
Spruill, Leigh, x, 116–18, 124, 128, 135, 169, 187, 194, 203, 206, 219, 226, 228, 252
St. Alban's Choir, 144
St. Ambrose Choir, 24, 29
St. Cecilia's Choir, 45–46, 51, 53, 61, 69, 71, 73, 100
St. Dunstan's Choir, 24, 53, 58–59, 69, 71, 73, 94–95, 100–11, 113, 116–17, 120–21, 130, 132, 144, 202, 221–22
St. Edmund's Choir, 144
St. George's Choir, 46–47, 61, 84–87, 90–91, 96, 98, 101, 107, 113–14, 118–20, 122–27, 130, 140, 144, 157, 172, 181, 190, 199, 203–4, 207, 225
St. Gregory's Choir, 24, 42, 130, 132, 139, 140, 144, 181, 194–95, 199, 201–2, 205–8, 214–15, 217–18
St. George's Chorale, 35–37
Stahlman, Effye Chumley, 151, 171
Stahlman, James Geddes, 34, 151, 171
Stanley, Catherine, 168
Stewart, Sherry, 35
Stifler, Julia, 38
Street, Amy, 58

Tanner, Bryant, 100
Taylor, Bobby, 96, 106–7
Taylor, Mary Ready, 121
Taylor, Steve, 219, 222, 230, 251
Taylor, Tim, 121

Terry, Madeline, 15
Teschan, Paul, 89
Thom, Marcia, 68
Thomson, Kay Withrow, 47–48, 51, 61, 63, 251
Tidwell, Crom, 168
Tinio, Rebecca, 113
Tipps, Angela, 68, 86, 100, 106
Tosh, Robert H., Jr., 72
Trepte, Paul, 121

Velting, Michael, 121–22

Warland, Dale, 136
Watson, Ron, 252
Watts, Elizabeth, 38
Watts, Shirley, 251
Weeks, Amy, 124, 219, 222
Weeks, Jane Tompkins, 171
Weeks, Katherine, 171
Weeks, Sinclair, 171
Wells, Ann, 250
Wells, Charlie, 109
Wendel, Cynthia, 71, 73
Whittemore, Tom, 121
Wilkinson, Grant, 53, 55
Wilkinson, Kay, 45, 46, 51–52, 55
Willcocks, David, 52
Willetts, Sandra, 68, 86, 106–7
Williams, June, 113
Wilson, Mark, 97
Withrow, Kay (see also Kay Wilkinson and Kay Withrow Thomson), 55, 60–62
Withrow, Scott S., 46–48, 50–53, 55–63, 65, 67, 70, 78, 168, 170, 251
Wyatt, Charles, 60

Zepernick, Werner, 36

This book is set in Jenson types, the work of master printer Nicolas Jenson of Venice, whose mark is shown above. His roman type was first used in *Eusebius' De Praparatio Evangelia* in 1470. It has survived to this day and is known for its Venetian letterforms. The version used here is by Adobe, which maintains much of the character of the original. The book design is by Gary Gore.

CPSIA information can be obtained at www.ICGtesting.com
Printed in the USA
LVOW061123130312

272860LV00002B/1/P